Reading a Relational Situation: The Contending Lenses

Reading a Relational Situation: The Contending Lenses

John Dixon
Rhys Dogan
and
Alan Sanderson

Nova Science Publishers, Inc.
New York

For permission to use material from this book please contact us:
Telephone 631-231-7269; Fax 631-231-8175
Web Site: http://www.novapublishers.com

LIBRARY OF CONGRESS CATALOGING-IN-PUBLICATION DATA

Dixon, John E., 1946 May 9-
Reading a relational situation : the contending lenses / John Dixon, Rhys Dogan, and Alan Sanderson.
p. cm.
Includes bibliographical references and index.
ISBN 978-1-60741-547-3 (softcover)
1. Social interaction. 2. Social action. 3. Interpersonal relations. I. Dogan, Rhys. II. Sanderson, Alan. III. Title.
HM1111.D588 2009
302.3--dc22 2009010494

Published by Nova Science Publishers, Inc. ✦ New York

To the late Professor Dame Mary Douglas

For Tina, Piers and Aliki,
Emily, Joseph and Samual.
and
Helen, Richard and Jennie

Contents

Preface		**ix**
Chapter 1	Introduction	**1**
Chapter 2	Relational Situations in the World of Persons	**11**
Chapter 3	The Relational Individual	**17**
Chapter 4	Making Sense of a Social Arena	**23**
Chapter 5	Epistemology and Truth	**33**
Chapter 6	The Epistemological Dichotomy: Naturalism and Hermeneutics	**39**
Chapter 7	Ontology and Reality	**79**
Chapter 8	The Ontological Dichotomy: Structure and Agency	**83**
Chapter 9	The Contending Social-reality Dispositions	**107**
Chapter 10	Conclusion	**113**
Bibliography		**115**
About the Authors		**199**
Index		**201**

PREFACE

This book has explicated and critically reviewed the competing ways that a social arena can best be coherently described, explained and understood and that social actions within it can best be ascribed It has identified, from the epistemological and ontological dichotomies drawn in the philosophy of social sciences, a set of four mutually exclusive and mutually incompatible social-reality dispositions: naturalist structuralism, naturalist agency, hermeneutic structuralism and hermeneutic agency. These constitute the contending lens through which a cognitively consistent person can choose to frame a social arena. This, it must be emphasized, is not to suggest that such a person would necessarily have the same epistemological or ontological preferences in all social arenas. Indeed, the very point is that he or she can choose the lens through which a particular arena is to be observed and interrogated. Once a social-reality disposition has been adopted for a particular social arena, then there are a set of core values, attitudes and opinions that flow from it, which become the salient constituents of that person's cognitive system when he or she is in that arena. This brings to the fore how a person chooses his or her preferred lens.

Chapter 1

INTRODUCTION

Before embarking on a social action[1] (Marks 1986), an action-taker must have drawn two conclusions about envisaged social action.[2] The first is that it is

1 Social actions are physical actions that are directed towards carrying out "any intention, aim, plan, purpose, and so on which encompasses another self," who is taken to be "a perceiving, thinking, Moral, intentional, and behaving person," and that follow the garnering of "the intentional or rational meaning of the other's field of expression," which, in turn, generates "expectations about the other's acts and actions; and manifests an intention to invoke in another self certain experiences and intentions" (Rummel 1976: 9.2). They constitute a subset of human actions (conscious, purposeful and meaningful physical actions), which, in turn, constitute a subset human behaviors (physical actions that are carried out consciously or unconsciously, and voluntarily or involuntarily). Social actions develop into social interactions (sequences of social actions and reactions between individuals). These social interactions can be focused ("when individuals directly attend to what others say and do" (Giddens 2001: 92)—Goffman's (1959, 1963) encounters—or unfocused "whenever individuals exhibit mutual awareness of one another's presence" (Giddens 2001: 91)). Social interactions build social relations (relationships between individuals), which, in turn, build up groups (collections of individuals who have some common attribute or purpose, or who are connected by means of relatively stable patterns of social interactions) and social networks—Simmel's ([1922] 1955: 126–27) "web of group affiliations"—which make up the world of people or the social world (the totality of human relationships). A social action is, thus, the fundamental building block of a social phenomenon (Durkheim [1895] 1982: 50–59), see also Weber ([1924] 1947), which Markey (1925–26): 733) "considered as including all behavior which influences or is influenced by organisms sufficiently alive to respond to one another," although Johnson (2000) prefers to include under this rubric "identity (individual and collective), culture, symbols, ideas, norms, principles, narratives, and collectively held beliefs," which should be should be treated as potential subjects of a person's actions (Znaniecki [1940] 1968).

2 Weber ([1921] 1968) initiated the search for causal laws to explain social actions by reference to value and perceptual variables (Social Action Theory). On the relationship between ideas and action, he ([1915] 1948: 280) reflected: "Not ideas, but material and ideal interests, directly govern men's [sic] conduct. Yet very frequently, the 'world images' that have been created by 'ideas' have, like switchmen, determined the tracks along which action has been pushed by the dynamics of the interest." The Weberian approach "is seen as standing in a tradition of

possible course of action, which requires the action taker to hold firm beliefs about the actuality—true essence or fundamental qualities—of the relational situation or social arena[3] in which the social action is to take place. How he or she chooses to comprehend that social arena is contingent upon his or her points of view on how it can best be known and on to what the envisaged social actions of others[4] in it can best be attributed. The second conclusion is that the envisaged social action in that arena is likely to have desirable consequences for the action taker in terms of his or her hopes, aspirations and goals. Thus, whether or how he or she wishes to engage with others in that arena is contingent upon the personally desirable consequences that he or she anticipates flowing from that engagement.

historico-cultural, qualitative analysis of the realm of the spirit and ideas" (Donaldson 1985: 107). Philosophy and psychology also have long-standing contending perspectives on what causes or motivates the taking of social actions (see, for example, Audi 1993, Brand and Walton 1976, Campbell 1996, Collins and Kusch 1998, Frese and Sabini 1985, Melden 1961, Mele 1997).

3 Present in this arena are, contentiously, material objects and phenomena (which exist as objective facts, apart from the human mind, inclusive of social objects (material objects that have been assigned a function or role by a group of individuals who share a common intention and who have agreed to act accordingly because the experiencing individual behaves as if they exist (Searle 1995)), and of evocative objects (material objects that are "companions to our emotional lives and provocations to thought" (Turkle 2007: 3, but definitely see Proust [1913] 2002)); socially constructed propositions about determinate and indeterminate phenomena (which exist, as collectively agreed interpretative propositions, because a group of individuals agree to behave as if they exist (Berger and Luckmann 1966)); and individually constructed propositions about phenomena (which exist, as idiosyncratic interpretative propositions generated by transcendental acts by a perceiving mind, because the perceiving person behaves as if they exist (Husserl [1928] 1931, [1928] 1964)). Its environment is the broader economic, sociocultural and linguistic *milieu* of the host society. These are all integral to a person's lifeworld (a phenomenological concept that emphasizes the meaning a person derives from his or her environmental interactions in a spatio-temporal world). Husserl's ([1931] 1960) lifeworld is the taken-for-granted everyday world as lived in, which gives rise to the beliefs and meaning that justify attitudes to self, others and the objective world. Schutz and Luckmann's (1973, 1989) life-world is the familiar physical world that is functionally meaningful. Habermas's ([1981] 1985) lifeworld is the lived world of informal, culturally-grounded understandings and mutual accommodations, which constitute the shared values, and which develop through face-to-face contact with others over time.

4 Other people can be classified by their degree of importance to self: from significant others—those who are of great importance to a person's life or well-being and who have a strong influence on his or her self-evaluation, self-identification and social status and role (Anderson and Cole 1990, McGuire and McGuire 1982)—to insignificant others—who tend to be categorized (by grouping them according to individually established common category attributes), stereotyped (by grouping them according to socially constructed common category attributes), subtyped (by separating out those who do not fit a stereotype), prototyped (by representing them abstractly in accordance with exemplar category attributes), and labeled (by branding them) (Fisk and Taylor 1991).

The purpose of this book is to provide the reader with heuristic[5] insights[6] that make social interactions more predictable by better understanding how and why people come to the conclusion that a particular social action is both possible and desirable in a particular social arena.[7] These insights are acquired from what people do and say—their social interactions—in that arena. This it does by demarcating and exploring the implications of a set of situational logics[8] that are grounded in how a person can coherently choose not only to comprehend the actuality of a relational situation, but also to understand why social actions are carried out the way they are in that situation. A person when confronting a social arena has to decide whether or how best to engage in social interactions with those present. This means that he or she must read that situation in order to discover its logic for him or her, which provides the directional guidance that he or she needs about whether or how best to interact with others in that situation. This book's fundamental contentions are seven-fold.

The first is that a social action can be ascribed to, and thus can be predicted by, reference to how the action-taker discerns the logic of the situation in which that action is to take place, premised on all the actors involved thinking and acting

---

5 Derived from the same classical Greek root as *Eureka!* meaning "to find".

6 These heuristic insights give rise to heuristics—decision rules-of-thumb—that form part of a heuristic process that facilitates the making of judgments (Kahneman *et al.* 1982).

7 The possible relationship between situation and action is explored in a variety of disciplines. In psychology, situationalism holds that the *cause* of behaviour can be found in the nature of the particular situation in which the individual finds him or herself, which makes personality an epiphenomenon without any explanatory power (Harré 1980, Mischel 1968, 1973). This study does not seek to contribute to that causation debate. It argues that situational factors at the very least guide social action by interconnecting meaning, purpose and action, and that personality impacts on a person's adaptive capacity in different situations. In sociology, social situationalism holds that the *reasons* for social actions are to be found in the *social* situation in which they occur, because social context gives them meaning. This makes the action-taker an observer of, rather than an actor in, that social situation (Campbell 1996: 153): under social situationalism "human actors typically possess neither mind nor body ... the individual human being, who as a living, thinking actor was once at the very centre of the sociological stage, has been completely dissolved away, stripped of both mind and body, now no more than a ghost in the social machine" (p. 151); and that "micro-events determine the macro-social sphere and that the latter has no independence from the former" (methodological situationalism) (Sibeon 2004: 124, see also Knorr-Cetina 1981). This study acknowledges social situationalism as one coherent perspective on social actions, and does not seek to explain anything in the macro-social sphere. In economics, where situation has been given time connotations, "situationalism [is] the view that people isolate *decisions* and overweight immediate aspects of the situation relative to longer term concerns" (Ross and Nisbett 1991: 1, emphasis in original). This study does not explicitly engage with the issue of short-term/long-term decision-making.

8 Popper's ([1957] 2004: 136–40, [1974] 1992: 117) use of the term "situational logic," drawing upon Menger ([1883] 1963), focused only one form of rationality, namely, instrumental (means-ends) rationality (see also Jarvie 1998).

as if they are cognitively consistent. Cognitive consistency theorists (Festinger 1957, Heider 1946, [1958] 1982, Osgood and Tannenbaum 1955) argue that a person strives to have thoughts, beliefs, expectations, attitudes and perceptions that fit together without contradiction beyond a tolerable level of cognitive tension.

The second contention is that there is a limited set of competing lens through which a social arena can be read—these are mutually exclusive configurations of assumptions about what can be known in that arena, and what has explanatory power in it—that a cognitively consistent person can choose from, so as not only to comprehend the quintessence of its actuality in the best way (whether that be either an objective reading as a observer (perceiver) of only its material or objectively factual qualities, or a subjective reading of its material and immaterial qualities, which produces first-person mental discernments that are product of transcendental acts of a perceiving human mind[9]); but also to understand to what the social actions of others in it can best be ascribed (whether that be either to the internal factors present within the action-taker, grounded in his or her self-determined and authentic hopes, aspirations and goals, or to the factors external to the action taker that have shaped those intentions, grounded in the social, cultural, economic and linguistic situational influences). A cognitively consistent person can choose the best way to read a social arena by choosing to use one of four lenses, each of which enables him or her to comprehend that arena in a particular way:

- As a domain that is material in form with objectively factual qualities, which can be described, explained and predicted by reference to objective data, the truth-value of which can be established by generally agreed enquiry procedures involving deductive logic and/or and inductive inference; and that is one in which those engaged have no real capacity to control how they conduct their social interactions, because the group rules or codes of conduct that define their social roles, and the roles of

9 "The operation of the mind ... is not so much an aspect of our lives, but in a sense, it is our life" (Searle 2004: 6). To Berkeley ([1710] 1962: 38) the mind is "wherein ideas exist … whereby they are perceived." Substance dualists believe that the mind exists in a nonmaterial realm (Eccles 1994, Popper and Eccles 1977). Metaphysical realists assert that "the existence of the mind is a contingent fact" (Stroll 2006: 12). Physicalists believe that the mind supervenes on the brain (Firth 2007, Pylyshyn 2007). Eliminativists believe that the mind does not exist (Feyeraband 1963, Rorty 1971). Somewhat facetiously, McCloskey (1998: 27) remarks:

It is a postulate of modernism, largely unspoken and therefore unargued, that minds do not exist. The puzzle is that the modernist who examines his [sic] mind when getting dressed in the morning and assumes the existence of other minds when driving to work, claims to deny both as soon as he flicks on the lights at his laboratory.

others, which justifies how they conduct their social actions and social relationships, have been defined, sanctioned and propagated exclusively by important others.

- As a domain that is subjectively experienced by individuals, the meaning of which is socially constructed (on the basis of a shared perspectives) by a process of discourse amongst those engaged, the truth-value of which can be established by reference to a consensus emerging from discourse, perhaps grounded in testimony; and that is one in which they have the capacity to influence how they conduct their social interactions, because the group rules or codes of conduct that define their social roles, and the roles of others, which justifies how they conduct their social actions and social relationships, are defined, sanctioned and propagated by discourse processes in which they can engage.
- As a domain that is subjectively experienced by individuals, the meaning of which is individually constructed on the basis of their personal experience, the truth-value of which can be established by reference to the beneficiality of that experience; and that is one in which they have the potential capacity to determine how they conduct their social interactions, because they can choose to draw upon their power of will, although the struggle of will to achieve authenticity may proved to be too much, so generating an inclination toward self-referentiality in the conduct of their social actions and social relationships.
- As a domain that is material in form with objectively factual qualities, which can be described, explained and predicted by reference to objective data, the truth-value of which can be established by generally agreed enquiry procedures involving deductive logic and/or inductive inference; and that is one in which those engaged have the capacity to determine how they conduct their social actions and social relationships, because they consider that such conduct can shaped in accordance with their hopes, aspirations and goals.

The third contention is that the lens through which a person chooses to read a social arena is established by how he or she wishes to engage with others in that arena for the purpose of mutual transactions. Prior to any social engagement, that person must decide the limits that he or she is prepared to accept on his or her individual autonomy, in terms of his or her individual decision sovereignty and self-determination of his or her social actions. This will determine his or her choice of relationship-arranging principle, and thus the status and role relationships that he or she wants with others. A cognitively consistent person who reads a social arena using what he or she considers to be the best lens, can, correspondingly, draw one of four conclusion about his or her best level of group incorporation in that arena:

- A person who reads a social arena as an objectively knowable material domain in which the group rules that govern the conduct of his or her social actions and social relationships have been defined, sanctioned and propagated exclusively by important others, accepts that his or her position in that arena is established by them, which means he or she would seek a very high level of group incorporation. Thus, he or she accepts the idea of constraints, in the interest of the group, being imposed by important others on both his or her individual decision sovereignty and the determination of his or her social actions.
- A person who reads a social arena as a subjectively experienced domain, the meaning of which he or she socially constructs with others, in which he or she can, through discourse, influence the group rules that govern the conduct of his or her social actions and social relationships, presumes that his or her position in that arena is established by discussion, which means he or she would seek a relatively high level of group incorporation. Thus, he or she accepts the idea of constraints being consensually imposed by like-minded others on his or her individual decision sovereignty, but rejects the idea of any constraints being imposed on the determination of his or her social actions.
- A person who reads a social arena as a subjectively experienced domain, the meaning of which he or she individually constructs, in which he or she has the potential capacity to shape the conduct of his or her social actions and social relationships, by drawing upon his or her power of will, although the struggle of will to achieve authenticity may proved to be too much, so generating an inclination toward self-referentiality, which means he or she accepts that that his or her position in that arena is self-constrained, which, in turn, means he or she would seek a relatively low level of group incorporation. Thus, he or she rejects the idea of any constraints being imposed by others on his or her individual decision sovereignty, but willingly self-imposes the constraints on his or her social actions that his or her past experience suggests others expect of him or her.
- A person who reads a social arena as an objectively knowable material domain, in which he or she can shape the conduct of his or her social actions and social relationships in accordance with his or her hopes,

aspirations and goals, presumes that his or her position in that arena is self-determined, which means he or she would seek a very low level of group incorporation. Thus, he or she rejects the idea of any constraints being imposed by others on either his or her individual decision sovereignty or the determination of his or her social actions.

The fourth contention is that a cognitively consistent person who has decided that it is best to read a social arena using a particular lens, and who has, correspondingly, decided what the best level of group incorporation to strive for in that arena, can, correspondingly, draw one of the four following conclusion about the best mode of social engagement to be adopted in that arena:

- hierarchical, which guides him or her to believe that he or she must be loyal and duty-bound to important others, making his or her social actions and social relationships in that arena the product of a sense of duty and obligation;
- egalitarian, which guides him or her to believe that he or she must make and express common commitments to like-minded others, making his or her social actions and social relationships in that arena the product of a sense of commendable collegiality;
- egocentric, which guides him or her to believe that he or she must approach social engagements wearily and reluctantly, mindful of what other people expect, making his or her social actions and social relationships in that arena the product of past experience and happenstance; or
- individualistic, which guides him or her to believe that he or she must author his or her own life in his or her own self-interest, making his or her social actions and social relationships in that arena the product of self-interest calculations.

The fifth contention is that in deciding what is the best relationship-arranging to adopt in a social arena, a cognitively consistent person has decided that it is best to be guided in that arena by the corresponding situational logic. This provides that person with a distinctive way of perceiving, feeling, thinking and acting—characteristic ways of acquiring, validating and using information; characteristic emotional patterns; and characteristic social behaviors—that constitute the basis of a stable orientation for social actions, and that together, produce the consistent set of social impressions that he or she must sustain, whether sincerely held or not, in order to build meanings and understandings that are compatible with those held by those with whom he or she wishes to engage. These contending situational logics constitute worldviews that enable a cognitively consistent person to be typified as:

- *Homo hierarchus*: those who see a social arena as an objectively knowable material domain, in which those engaged are considered to have no real capacity to shape how they conducts their social actions and social relationships, which means that their position in that arena is established by important others in the interest of the group. Their preference is for a very high level of group incorporation, which means they accept the idea of important others imposing indispensable constraints both on their individual decision sovereignty and on the determination of their social actions. This perspective guides them to believe that they must be loyal and duty-bound to important others—*I must do what they say I must do.*
- *Homo sociologicus*: those who see a social arena as a subjective domain, the meaning of which is socially constructed, in which those engaged are considered to have the capacity to influence how they conduct their social interactions, which means that their position in that arena is established by discussion. Their preference is for a relatively high level of group incorporation, which means they accept the idea of their individual decision sovereignty being constrained—by mutual agreement—by like-minded others, but they reject the idea of any constraints being imposed on the determination of their social actions. This perspective guides them to believe that he or she must make and express common commitments to like-minded others—*I shall do what we say I should do.*
- *Homo existentialis*: those who see a social arena as a subjective domain, the meaning of which is individually constructed, in which those engaged are considered to have the potential capacity to determine how they conducts their social interactions, which means that that their position in that arena is self-constrained. Their preference is for a relatively low level of group incorporation, which means they reject the idea of others imposing any constraints on their individual decision sovereignty, but they willingly self-imposes the constraints on their social actions that their past experience suggests others expect of them. This perspective guides him or her to believe that he or she must approach social engagements wearily and reluctantly—*I must do whatever I think necessary to meet life's challenges and tragedies allotted by luck and destiny.*

– *Homo economicus*: those who see a social arena as an objectively knowable material domain, in which those engaged are considered to have the capacity to determine how they conducts their social interactions, which means that their position in that arena is self-determined. Their preference is for a very low level of group incorporation, which means they reject the idea of any constraints being imposed by others on either their individual decision sovereignty and on the determination of their social actions. This perspective guides them to believe that they must author their own life in their own self-interest—*I must do what is my best interest.*

The sixth contention is that for a cognitively consistent person to change the lens through which a social arena is read—thereby be guided by a different situational logic—is a fraught process, necessitating him or her to choose a different relationship-arranging principle, and thus adopt a different set of status and role relationships with others in that arena. The process begins when a surprise brings into question that person's set of assumptions about a social arena, and the social interactions that take place in it. With this comes an awareness that his or her chosen situational logic is increasingly less able to explain, interpret and predict what he or she is experiencing in that arena—because of fundamentally distorting flaws in these lens, all of which decry either the nonmaterial or the material dimensions of a social arena, and devalue either the internal (intra-personal) or the external (extra-personal) reasons for social actions. Thus, the desire grows to reformulate the chosen set of assumptions, so as to minimize the divergence of beliefs and certainties. Such a person would be willing to adopt a new lens through which to read, and garner directional guidance from, that social arena only if that change is likely to produces personal benefits that offset the personal costs associated with realigning, fundamentally, the set of expectations he or she has about his or her status and roles in that arena. Of crucial importance here are his or her attitudes toward those who read that arena differently, and who, thus, have accepted the validity of a different worldview. The point of despair is, however, reached when it is realized that none of these situational logics can provide an acceptable cognitive map of that social arena, one that ensures beliefs and certainties coincide.

The final contention is that when a cognitively consistent person, ultimately, finds that none of the four distorting lens enables him or her to explain, interpret and predict what he or she is experiencing in a social arena, then that person must engage, alone and with like-minded others, in introspective and investigative processes that challenge and, ultimately, change their assumptions about that arena. From the resultant deeper situational knowledge gained of the material and ideational (immaterial) properties present in that arena flows new strategic directional guidance, which justifies a new set of strategic social actions by those involved:

- Where the material and ideational properties present in a social arena stand, individually and together, in a necessary (mutually reinforcing) and complementary (mutually supportive) relationships, and, thus, provide mutual benefits, the situational logic is one of protecting those necessary complementarities, which guides the conduct of social actions toward maintaining ideational purity and strengthening those complementary relationships, irrespective of the power distribution amongst those involved.
- Where the material and ideational properties in a social arena stand, individually and together, in a necessary but incompatible (logically inconsistent) relationship, and, thus, generate tensions, the situational logic is one of compromising to limit those incompatibilities, which guides the conduct of social actions toward correcting any contradictions and the reducing any incompatibilities, although who compromises most depends on the bargaining power and negotiating strengths of those involved.
- Where the material and ideational properties in a social arena stand, individually and together, in a contingent (actualized only if particular social actions occur) but incompatible relationship, and, thus, are potentially capable of generating mutually exclusivity and competitive tensions, the situational logic is one of eliminating the contingent incompatibilities, which guides the conduct of social actions toward removing such incompatibilities, although what survives and what is eliminated depends on the power of those involved to advance and to protect their own interests.
- Where the material and ideational properties in a social arena stand, individually and together, in a contingent but complementary relationship, and, thus, are potentially capable of generating non-threatening opportunities, the situational logic is one of exploiting those contingent complementarities by pure opportunism, which guides the conduct of social actions toward the actualization of such complementarities, although who gains or losses most depends on the relative power of the those exploiting the opportunities.

Chapter 2

RELATIONAL SITUATIONS IN THE WORLD OF PERSONS

This chapter delineates a finite set of contending coherent beliefs about how best to describe, explain and understand a social arena, and to what the social actions of others in that arena can best be ascribed. It begins by demarcating a social arena within the broader social context.

Marcel's (1952: 164) "world of persons"[10] is the aggregation of each constituent person's social domain, which contains the myriad of mutual- or common-interest relationships that he or she has with others, whether permanent or temporary (Bernard (1926: 438). Social relationships can, according to Mills and Clark (1982, see also Clark and Mills 1993) be bifurcate into communal relationships (the product of other-centered and close social interactions between intimates—family members and romantic partners—and friends) and exchange relationships (the product of self-centered and superficial social interactions

---

10 Each person in this world is taken in Lockean terms to be "a thinking intelligent Being, that has reason and reflection, and can consider itself as itself, the same thinking thing in different times and places; which it does only by that consciousness, which is inseparable from thinking, and as it seems to me essential to it" (Locke [1690] 2004: II, 27, S. 9). His or her essential properties would include, contentiously, a bodily form with sensorial capacities and the capacity for self-movement; a first-person consciousness, a self-awareness and a diachronic sense of thematic identity; the ability to reason, so permitting the external environment to be interrogated in a way that generates experiences that can be meaningfully interpreted to provide the basis of cognition and behavior (Rogers 1961); the ability to have relationships with other human beings; and the capacity to be a moral agent, capable of purposive action.

between acquaintances and strangers),[11] although, as Kelley and Thibaut (1978) postulate, interdependent individuals may, over an extended time frame, undergo a prosocial transformation that changes an exchange relationship into a communal one. Bernard (1926: 438–39) distinguishes between exchange relationships where face-to-face contact occurs[12] (giving rise to direct-contact assemblages, the members of which have a common purpose[13]), and exchange relationships where face-to-face contacts does not occur (giving rise to indirect-contact assemblages, the members of which have something in common, such as an attribute, but no appreciation of a common purpose). He further distinguishes between rational face-to-face contact settings (giving rise to rational-type direct-contact assemblages, characterized as purposive economic, political and social organizations[14] in which there are mutually recognized social relationships); and non-rational face-to-face contact settings (giving rise to non-rational-type direct-contact assemblages, characterized as gatherings where those engaged have a common purpose but no mutually recognized social relationships[15]). This study limits its scope to the exploration of social actions and focused interactions that are conducted on a face-to-face basis in a social arena delineated within a direct-contact assemblage that give rise to exchange relationships.

---

11 Morgan (2009) draws a similar distinction between friends and acquaintances, who he locates in space (such as neighbors, work-mates and professional advisors), and in time (such as fleeting, passing and coinciding encounters).

12 The process of face-to-face interaction Goffman (1959: 15) described as "the reciprocal influence of individuals upon another's actions when in one another's immediate physical presence."

13 A direct-contact assemblage can be one of Archer's (2000: 266) corporate agents, which has the capacity not only to articulate its own vested interests, but also to shape the environment for all its members, which enables it to active pursue those interests.

14 "There are many kinds of face-to-face associations, but the most numerous of these are the business associations and the multi-type organizations known as clubs. Of business, occupational, professional and other interest associations, such as corporations, firms of professional men, labor union locals, armies, etc., we need say but little. They are very common. They are also highly purposive in character. The behavior of their members is presumably controlled by highly rational considerations, and they make a considerable use of those aspects of science which apply most particularly to their objects in view" (Bernard 1926: 441).

15 Such assemblages lack of any permanency, definiteness of integration, or formality of organization, and can include gatherings of people for commercial, social, ceremonial and ritualistic transactions, and in audiences or crowds (rallies, demonstrations, or mobs):

> Crowds may be either voluntary or involuntary. That is, the members of the group may come together on purpose, or they may associate by accident, with all grades of aggregation and association between. It is usually some strong emotion or curiosity impulse which integrates a crowd. Emotion is especially dominant in the mob (Bernard 1926: 458).
>
> Membership is typically very fluid. However, those engaged understand its membership, leadership, and common purpose. The extent of participant activity differs according to purpose (Bernard 1926: 451–64).

Each such social arena is a network of people with whom a person can choose how best to engage or, indeed, not to engage, and constitutes a social engagement setting. This arena is located in time[16] and is changing through time; past events influence not only a person's perception of the emergent present but also the array of possible futures without necessarily determining them. The spatio-physical, temporal, sociocultural, economic and psychological factors present in this social engagement setting can impact consciously[17] or unconsciously[18] on a person's

---

16 Time permits a person to sequence and describe external events (Kant ([1781–87] 1956, Leibnitz [1716–1717] 1956). As time passes, it is lived through—consciously experienced—but it is not as a steady and homogeneous stream (Piaget [1946] 1969) and it not experienced the same way by different people. It is also a scarce resource that can be the object of social transactions.

17 A conscious mental state is, contentiously, "a qualitative subjective, first-personal, airy-fairy, and touchy-feeling phenomenon" (Searle 2004: 88), which has been equated to "the dimensions of truth" (Leader 2007: 16). Consciousness is a single, well-defined, unified field of first-person awareness that has the qualities of, at least, self-awareness, sentience, sapience, subjectivity, unity, and intentionality (in the sense of being able to attach meaning to an object, which requires a mental state that is able to refer to, or to be about, something other than its), which enables a person to perceive self as separate from its environment (Blackmore 2003, Flanagan 1992, Lehrer 1991, McGinn 1982, Searle 1983, 2004). A distinction can be made between phenomenal mental states (associated with conscious perceptual, bodily-sensational, imaginative, or streams of thought experiences); introspective mental states (associated with self's conscious direct examination of its own mental states and processes); and intentional mental states (associated with self's conscious hopes, aspirations and goals directed at objects) (Farthing 1992, Flanagan 1992). Explanations of consciousness are various (Searle 2004). Mentalism holds that consciousness is a mental state (Fodor 1981), either because it exists as a product of a mind that, itself, exists in a nonmaterial realm as a nonphysical substance (entity) that is separate from the body and that is both autonomous and causally efficacious—Descartes' ([1641] 1961, [1644] 1983) mind–body dichotomy—and cannot be fully explained in materialist terms (substance dualism) (Eccles 1994, Popper and Eccles 1977), or because the brain has nonmaterial (mental) as well physical properties (property dualism), which means that consciousness exists as a causally interactive mental property of the brain (Robinson 2003). Physicalism holds that the range of phenomena experienced as consciousness are the product of neurobiological states and processes taking place in the brain (Chalmers 1996, Kim 1998, Poland 1994)—as James (1890a: 231), a chronic sufferer of constipation (Walker and Zacharias 2007), remarked of consciousness: "whilst we think, our brain changes, and that, like the aurora borealis, its whole internal equilibrium shifts with every pulse of change." Biological naturalists hold that consciousness, as a real phenomenon, is "just a qualitative, subjective first person process going on in the nervous system" at "a higher level than that of neurons and synapses," which means that it cannot be reduced "to its neurobiological basis, because such a third-person reduction would leave out the first-person ontology of consciousness" (Searle 2004: 79, 87, 91). Mysterians "think that consciousness is a mystery that cannot be solved by our existing scientific methods; and some mysterians think we will never be able to understand how consciousness could be explained by brain processes" (Searle 2004: 102). See also McFarland 2007, McGinn 1989, Nagel 1986.

18 An unconscious (subconscious or metaconscious) mental state is a phenomenon that occurs without conscious awareness and as such that it defies any sort of introspection (Mollon 2000, Searle 2004) and can be contrasted to the temporary lack of any mental state—unconsciousness

cognitive disposition[19] toward a social action by interconnecting meaning, purpose and social action [20] (Audi 1993, McCelland and Fararo 2006). As Crumbaugh (1973: 29) observes:

(an "interruption of awareness of oneself and one's surroundings, lack of the ability to notice or respond to stimuli in the environment" (MedicineNet.com 2003)) To Freud ([1912] 1959, but see Grünbaum 1984), the unconscious is personal; the repository of suppressed and forgotten experiences and memories, which is the driver of human behavior over which a person has little control. To Jung ([1934] 1981, see also Hall and Nordby 1973), it is also the repository of inherited religious, spiritual, and mythological symbols and understandings, expressed through universal thought forms or mental images (archetypes) (collective unconsciousness):

a part of the psyche which can be negatively distinguished from a personal unconscious by the fact that it does not, like the latter, owe its existence to personal experience and consequently is not a personal acquisition. While the personal unconscious is made up essentially of contents which have at one time been conscious but which have disappeared from consciousness through having been forgotten or repressed, the contents of the collective unconscious have never been in consciousness, and therefore have never been individually acquired, but owe their existence exclusively to heredity. Whereas the personal unconscious consists for the most part of complexes, the content of the collective unconscious is made up essentially of archetypes (Jung 1934).

To Frankl ([1948/1975] 2000: 31) the unconscious can be "differentiated into unconscious instinctuality and unconscious spirituality."

19 This is a mental phenomenon that constitutes a propositional attitude (a relational mental state that connects a person to a proposition in a way that involves holding particular attitudes (expectancies and value) towards and/or intentions (hopes, aspirations and goals) about that proposition) (Cresswell 1985, Lycan 1990, Rey 1997). Mentalism holds that mental states—the interior life of first-person experiences—can affect (by unknown processes) neurobiological states and processes taking place in the brain. It axiomatically accepts that mental states give rise to actions. How this occurs (mental causation) is an unresolved issue (Jackson 1996), although Eccles (1994: 5) hypothesizes that "mental events act by a quantal probability field to alter the probability of emission of vesicles from presynaptic vesicular grids." Physicalism, which axiomatically accepts that the mind supervenes on the brain, making all mental states contingent upon physical phenomena (Firth 2007, Pylyshyn 2007), and considers, variously, that mental phenomena can be reconceptualized as behavioral phenomena, as all statements about mental phenomena are equivalent in meaning to statements about behavioral dispositions (logical behaviorism) (Hempel 1980, Ryle 1949); can be identical to, but not reducible to, a physical event, because mental phenomena are not regulated by strict physical laws (anomalous monism or predicate dualism) (Davidson 1980); can be defined as the type of brain states that produce the type of functions fulfilled by mental phenomena (functionalism) (Armstrong 1968, Block 1980, Putman 1980); can be the product of mental states that are identical with brain states (identity theory) (Place 1956); can be ascribed to neurobiological states and processes (reductionism); can be considered to be illusory and thus do not exist (eliminativism) (Feyeraband 1963, Rorty 1971) (material monism). The unresolved issue for physicalism is, of course, the accommodation of first-person mental experiences that are unobservable and only individually knowable by experience (Thorpe 1962: 21), which suggest an irreducible, subjective state of awareness that is intrinsically mental (Searle 2004: 91), a proposition that "is likely to be repugnant to some people because of its dualistic implications" (Thorpe 1962: 24). Action theory in philosophy, however, challenges this mind-brain dichotomy by arguing that "the act of will and the action of the body are not two different states objectively known, connected by the bond of causality; they do not stand in the relation of cause and effect, but they are one and the same thing" (Schopenhauer [1818/ 1844] 1969: I, 100) (dialectical monism);

> Man [sic] not only strives to perceive his environment as a meaningful totality, but he strives to find an interpretation which will reveal him as an individual with a purpose to fulfill … pointing up man's distinctive ability to find meaning not merely in what is, but in what can be.

The outcome of any social interaction is the development and sustainment of a set of mutually recognized relationships—a state of connectedness—between

---

and that "'willing' is not the name of an action; and so not the name of any voluntary action either" (Wittgenstein 1953: 613). Thus, "the tie between desire, decision, intention etc. and the so-called physical act is ... 'logical' and not 'contingent'." (Stroll 2006: 157, see also Brand and Walton 1976, Donagan 1987, Melden 1961).

20 The interaction of meaning, purpose and action places consciousness at the point at which perceptual inputs (from external cues, prompts or stimuli) interface with behavioral outputs (the action responses) —the Input-Output Picture of consciousness—which, according to Hurley (1998: 2), "confuses the subpersonal-level distinction between causal input and causal output with the personal-level distinction between perception and action." Mental phenomena (including intentional mental states) can, thus, shape and govern meaningful action (Mele 2003, Spiker 1989, see also Anderson *et al.* 1986, Kim 1993, but see Cunning 1999, Ryle 1949), on the premise that a person's mental states can be directed onto tangible or intangible objects (Brand and Walton 1976, Donagan 1987, Searle 1983). Gestalt theory (Koffka 1935, Wertheimer 1945) emphasizes that it is the construction of meaning that a person gives the external cue, prompt or stimulus that governs his or her meaningful action response to it. Social learning theory (Bandura 1977, 1986, Miller and Dollard 1941, Rotter 1954, 1982) holds, following Alder (see Crosbie-Brunett and Lewis 1993), that an action-taker's construction of meaning of, and his or her expectations, anticipations and predictions about, phenomena present in a social situation—social knowledge—has a significant influences on his or her actions in that situation, the mechanism involved being social learning reinforcement, punishment, extinction, and imitation (modeling). Action theory (Mele 1997, Holmstrom-Hintikka and Tuomela 1997) holds that desire and belief jointly cause an action. Reasoned action theory (Fishbein and Ajzen 1975) holds that the proximal cause of action can be found in intention, which is, in turn, the consequence of attitudes (the expectancy, and the value attached to the outcomes, of an action) and social norms (the complying with the wishes of significant others who believe that that action should be performed). Planned behavior theory (Ajzen 1991) adds a third causal factor, perceived behavioral control (the expected ease of performing that behavior), to which Ouellette and Wood (1998) have suggested adding previous behavior or habit as a causal factor. Mentalism thus overarches three broad theories of human behavior: cognitivism (behavior is the product of cognitive processes, such as perceptions, memory and decision making), that give rise to cognitions, such as beliefs, desires and motivations) (Heider [1958] 1982, Piaget 1955, 1968, Tolman 1922, 1948, Wundt [1874, 1902] 1904, [1896] 1897)); humanism (behaviour is connected to a person's inner feelings and self-image (Maslow [1962] 1968, Rogers 1961)); and psychodynamism (behavior is determined by the unconscious mind and memories of past experiences (Erikson 1963, 1964, Freud [1929] 1971, 1957, Jung 1969). In contradistinction stands physicalism, which overarches two theories of behavior: radical behaviorism (behavior is a reflection of the frequency of the reinforcement effects of environmental stimuli without reference to emotions, memories and motives) (Pavlov 1927, Skinner 1938, 1953, 1973, Watson [1924] 1930, see also Graham 2007, Zuriff. 1985); and neurobiological determinism (behaviour is the product of neurobiological states and processes) (James 1890a, Rutter 2006, Wilson 1976, 1978).

those involved.[21] This connectedness portrays their interactions, particularly the meaning-content of those interactions for their self-assessed subjective worthiness, their dependence on each other, and their mutual interdependence.[22]

21 Pinker (2002: 65) observes that "social reality exists only within a group of people, but it depends on a cognitive ability present in each person to understand a public agreement to confer power and status, and to honor it as long as others do."

22 Buber ([1923] 1958) argued that a person can adopt one of two attitudes toward another person: I-It or I-Thou. In an I-It relationship, a person perceives another person as an object having specific, isolated qualities and the relationship is one of separateness and detachment. In an I-Thou relationship, a person is aware of another person as having a unity of being with whom he or she can engage in a dialogue, with the resultant relationship being one of mutuality and reciprocity. The state of connectedness thus has degrees that are directly correlated with relative importance of the other person. Buber ([1923] 1958: 45) emphasized the importance of a person having someone who believe in him or her, which is a characteristic he describes as "confirming the other ... Confirming means accepting the whole potentiality of the other. I can recognize in him the person he has been created to become." For Lévinas ([1961] 1969), the face-to-face encounter with another is a privileged phenomenon in which the other person's proximity and distance are both strongly felt. "The Other precisely reveals himself in his alerity not in a shock negating the I, but as the primordial phenomenon of gentleness" (Levinas [1961] 1969: 150). There is in this encounter an instant recognition of the transcendence and heteronomy of the other, which installs in self a responsibility for the other:

I am responsible for the Other without waiting for reciprocity, were I to die for it. Reciprocity is his affair. It is precisely insofar as the relation between the Other and me is not reciprocal that I am subjection to the Other; and I am 'subject' essentially in this sense. It is I who support all ... The I always has one responsibility *more* than all the others (Levinas 1985: 95–98, emphasis in original)

Rogers (1961: 32) observed "the safety of being liked and prized as a person seems a highly important element in a helping relationship." He goes on: "if I accept the other person as something fixed, already diagnosed and classified ... then I am doing my part to confirm this limited hypothesis. If I accept him as a process of becoming, then I am doing what I can to confirm or make real his potential" (p. 48).

Chapter 3

THE RELATIONAL INDIVIDUAL

To any social arena, a person brings two identities: his or her personal identity[23]—the characteristics that makes him or her the person he or she is (Harré 1988)—and his or her social identity[24]—the set of mask[25] he or she adopts for

---

23 At a fundamental level, this embraces the characteristics that make a person "the same person across time and change" (Searle 2004: 205). These characteristics would include physiological continuity (the spatio-temporal continuity of a recognizable body); conscious state continuity (the continuous sequences of first-person awareness, because of the memory of consciously experienced past unique, personal experiences); and a sense-of-self continuity (the continuous first-person sense of what it is to be *me*) (Searle 2004: 196–206, see also Martin and Barresi 2003, Noonan 2003, Perry 1975, Rorty 1976).

24 Social identity theory holds that the membership of social groups is an important element of a person's concept of self. It is concerned with why individuals identify with, adopt shared attitudes with, and behave as members of, social groups. It involves three key concepts: categorization (the assignment of self and others to meaningful categories, so a person can know the categories to which he or she belongs and who else is in them); identification (the identification of the groups to which a person perceives he or she belong, the membership of which becomes an essential aspect of that person); and comparison (the evaluation of self by compare with similar others) (Tajfel 1981, 1982, Tajfel. and Turner 1979, 1986; see also Abrams and Hogg 1990, Capozza and Brown 2000).

25 Jung argued that each person has a set of masks that constitutes "a compromise ... between the demands of the environment and the necessities of the individual's inner constituents" (Jacobi 1962: 19). These masks have many hues, each designed to enable that person to play the role necessary to meet the demands of other people in different situations. Haselbach (1994: 45–46) elaborates on this idea: "Where life situations of individuals are segmented, where individuals fulfill different roles, where individuals have experienced, learned, and actually use different registers of behavior, we find plural identities. ... If ... we link 'identity' with development (of the personality), change (over time), interaction (with others), responsiveness and adaptation (to a variety of dissimilar situations encountered and to evaluations of these situations and of our responses by others, i.e. to the never-ending processes of calibration), we end up with plural identities of the individual and with a notion of identity, of those plural identities, that have a process character, something which one cannot possess but which is acted out, which one lives."

different group to which he or she belongings (Strauss 1959)—both of which have evolved over time in response to the challenges confronted in the natural, practical and discursive orders of the world in which they live.[26] Accounting for personhood—what it means to be a person (Harre 1998, Rorty 1976)—according to Archer (2003: 119–21), involves three explanations. The first is "explaining the emergence of self-consciousness [the consciousness of self as separate from the environment, which reflects the] primacy of practice ... [and] which is prior and primitive to our sociality" (Archer 2000: 121). The second is explaining the emergence of self-identity (his or her sense of uniqueness and direction: who he or she is; is not; wants to become; does not want to become; and is expected to become (Erikson 1963. 1964, Evans 1967)), which reflects a person's "a rich inner life ... [of which] our emotions are among the main constituents" (Archer 2000: 194)]. The third is explaining the emergence of social identity, which is "inextricably related to the emergent properties of the social structures and cultures in which we find ourselves" (Archer 2000: 258). As Foucault (1991) observed, a person tends to adopt in the construction of his or her own self-identity not only the way he or she identifies himself or herself, but also the way that he or she is identified by others[27] (see also Bourdieu 1976, 1990).

---

26 Archer (2000: 119, 311) postulates that a person's causal powers are the product of past engagement with the world as a natural order (body-environment relations), where the concern is physical well being; as a practical order (subject-object relations), where the concern is performance achievement); and as a discursive order (subject-subject relations), where the concern is self-worth.

27 Nietzsche reflected: "'I must *allow* myself to be known, then, and meanwhile know myself'" ([1886] 1998: 82, emphasis in original). Cooley ([1902] 1983) suggested that a person's solipsistical self concept depends on perceived responses of others: what he or she believes others think of him or her, so he or she is reflected in their behavior: "Each to each a looking-glass/Reflects the other that doth pass" (p. 184). His 'looking-glass' theory of self, postulated that a person imagines how he or she appears to others, interprets what their reactions are to those perceptions, and then self-evaluates them, giving rise to positive or negative feelings, which impact on the development of his or her self concept. Mead (1934) described the *me* stage of the self process as when a person sees him or herself through the eyes of significant others, through communications and symbols, which enables him or her to embed collective values in to his or her conception of self. Rogers (1961) argued that this reliance on others is the product of a person's strong need for their approval and a desire to have their unconditional positive regard (their unconditional and unreserved prizing of him or her).

Each social arena provides the context within which a person internalizes elements of his or her emergent self-identity, through the development of relationships with others. This, thereby, develops that person's emergent relational identity, as defined by reference to his or her significant social relationships (Ho 1995, Ho, Chan, Peng and Ng 2001). In the context of a group, this can lead to him or her identifying with ideas, beliefs and habits of its members (social identification) (Deaux 1996). All of these identities signify a person's personality[28] (his or her more or less stable cognitive, emotional and behavioral patterns, grounded in "biological inheritance, learned skills and the experiences through which he or she passes" (Rice 1969: 565) that distinguishes that person from another), which lie behind social actions, and which are observed by others across both social relationships and relational situations over time (Kassin 2003, Matthews *et al.* 2003, Ho [1998] 1999).[29] As Cattell (1965: 117–18) succinctly remarks, personality is "that which tells what [a person] will do when placed in a given situation."

When a person confronts a social arena he or she must decide whether to, whether to continue to, or how best to engage with other people in that situation, in the light of his or her perspective on who's who amongst the people in that situation and on what they, individually and collectively, can do for, or to, him or her. This engagement decision is contingent upon two factors. The first relates to how that person sees him or herself as a person (his or her self-concept[30]), in

28 Five personality perspectives can be identified: the psychoanalytic and neoanalytic perspective (personality is the product of the way in a person resolve unconscious and conscious tensions and conflicts (Adler [1929] 1969, Erikson 1963, 1964, Freud [1923] 1927, Horney 1937, Jung 1969, Kohut 1971)); the traits perspective (personality is the aggregation of a person's distinguishing qualities or characteristics (Allport 1961, Cattell 1979, 1980, Eysenck 1970)); the pure cognitive perspective (personality is product of the way a person thinks (Kelly 1955)); the humanistic-existential perspective (personality is the product of a person's creative, spontaneous and active subjective experiences (Maslow [1962] 1968, May 1958, 1967, 1883, Rogers 1961)); and the social-behavioristic perspective (personality is the product of what a person learns through experiences by (Bandura 1971, 1986, Rotter 1954, Rotter and Hochreich 1975, Skinner 1938, 1953, 1973)). For a philosophical perspective see Goldie 2004.

29 Psychological anthropologists, such as Benedict ([1934] 1989, [1946] 1989), Mead (1942) and Kardiner *et al.* (1945), sought to establish the nature of the interaction between the individual and his or her culture, and concluded, contentiously, that different cultures produce different socialization processes that, in turn, produce different personality types (Hsu 1961).

30 In the mentalist tradition, Rosenberg (1979) defined the self-concept as "the totality of the individual's thoughts and feelings having reference to himself [sic] as an object." Allport (1955: 40) refers to it as "proprium," which embraces "all aspects of personality that make for inward unity." In the behaviorist tradition, Skinner (1971: 199) considered that "a self is a repertoire of behaviors appropriate to a given set of contingencies" (see also Rovane 1998). Neuroscience, however, "suggests that the self is best understood as a sort of illusion that the brain creates (Butler-Bowden 2007: 5, see also Sacks 1985, Ramachandran and Blakeslee 1998). For a

terms of his or her bodily self (bodily experiences and senses—Hume's ([1739–40] 1978) bundle-of-perceptions perspective); self-identity (characteristics that give a sense of uniqueness combined with a sense of continuity and sameness); desired self (desired personal characteristics); self-extension (sense of identification with external objects, both physical and human); self-objects (mental representation of significant others to be copied, admired, idealized and mirrored); self-sentiment (prime, integrating motivations); self-esteem (feelings of self-worth); self-objectification (ability to perceive his or her capacities and limitations); presenting self (way of presenting self to others); self-image (learned role expectations and future role aspirations), which may not be consistent with his or her social image (what others perceive about him or her[31]) or social self (what he or she reveals to others); self-as-rational-coper (awareness of his or her problem-solving and goal-achieving capacities); self-as-knower (capacity to unify self); and true self (self-concept that is in harmony with his or her experiential feelings) (Allport 1955, Baumeister 1993, Bermúdez *et al.* 1995, Bem 1967, Cattell 1965, Kohut 1971, McGuire and McGuire 1982, Rogers 1961, Rosenberg 1979, Shoemaker 1963). The second engagement-decision factor relates to how that person sees him or herself in a social arena, in terms of his or her desired social role (role-making); the characteristic social impressions[32] he or she wishes to portray to others (role-playing); the response to his or her chosen role that he or she anticipates from others (role response), the role expectations of others (role-set), and the roles into which others cast him or her (altercasting) (Goffman 1959, 1961, Rosenberg 1986, Weinstien and Deutschberger 1963). The product is a set of discernments about self and others that may well be rarely questioned and quite taken for granted, which enable a person to construct an assumptive world—a "cognitive map of the world out there" (Young 1979: 33)—that best makes sense of that social arena—thereby providing him or her with the best way of comprehending "the way that humans choose between multiple possible explanations of sensory and other input as they seek to conform the

discussion of the genesis and intellectual history of the concept of self see Taylor 1989 and Seigel 2004.

31 "O wad some Power the giftie gie us /To see oursels as ithers see us!" Robert Burns, *To a Louse* (1786). The Johari window model of interpersonal awareness permits the identification of a person's blind spots (what is known to others about a person that is unknown to that person) and façades (what is known to a person that is not known to others) (Luft and Ingham 1955).

32 Goffman (1959) talks of impression management as the ways in which a person can seek to project particular self-image to others. He sought to explain how, by reference to theatrical metaphors, people in their social interactions strive to present an image of themselves in particular ways (dramaturgical analysis).

phenomenological with the real in order to act in such a way as to determine or respond to the world around them" (Snowden 2005).[33]

33 Adler ([1922] 1924, [1929] 1969, [1933] 1973) considered that a creative self has the capacity to create his or her own destiny, which involves interpreting his or her experiences and taking action on the basis of his or her guiding self-ideals (perceived goals that guide behavior) and style-of-life (unique ways of pursuing those goals). Piaget's ([1936] 1963, [1963] 2001, 1968) constructivist theory of knowing argues that a person actively seeks to makes sense of the world, rather than merely being conditioned by it. He emphasized cognitive structure, which changes through the processes of adaptation, that is, assimilation (interpreting events in terms of existing cognitive structure) and accommodation (changing the cognitive structure to make sense of the environment). Cognitive development, thus, involves adapting to the environment.

Chapter 4

MAKING SENSE OF A SOCIAL ARENA

The challenge that confronts every person grappling with a social-engagement decision is to make sense of the social arena in which that engagement is to take place. Inherent in any arena are "demand characteristics" or "demand qualities" (Wertheimer 1961), which are the demands that a situation place on those involved by posing questions the answers to which requires them to decided upon their possible and desirable courses of action. This requires each of them to make sense of that situation, thereby "becoming aware of a possibility [for action in it] against the background of reality" (p. 141). This entails cognitive ingenuity, given the elusive nature of sensory perception and of memory, which give rise more to an interpretation (or recreation) of the past than to a dependable record of it (Byatt and Wood 2007); given the intensely-felt human need to understand others, despite their authentic thoughts and feelings being inaccessible; and given that a person using his or her ordinary modes of thought[34] is not always able to hold cognitions[35] that fit together without contradiction.[36]

---

34 On the presumption that a person is reasonably rational and thoughtful, and strives to make sense of what he or she thinks, feels and does: "the evidence indicates that human choices are orderly, although not always rational in the tradition sense of the word" (Kahneman and Tversky 1984: 344).

35 These are the outcome of the mental processes, such as attention, memory, reasoning and perception (visual, aural and tactile), and constitute the forms of knowing, perceiving, judging, reasoning and planning, through which information is synthesized so as to give rise to thoughts, beliefs, expectations, attitudes and perceptions.

36 Cognitive consistency theorists (Festinger 1957, Heider 1946, [1958] 1982, Osgood and Tannenbaum 1955) argue that a person seeks to ensure that cognitive inconsistency is kept within tolerable limits of cognitive tension, which compels that person to alter his or her cognitive process in a way that makes his or her cognitions more consistent. The alternative is to be in a state of dual consciousness, whereby a person simultaneously holds two apparently

How a person chooses to describe, explain, and understand a social arena, and to predict the social actions of others in it, depends on the set of descriptive and normative propositions that he or she judges to be most appropriate for that arena. These shape how he or she understands not only its material environment—the material objects and phenomena present in it—but also its nonmaterial environment—the ideas that are product of transcendental acts of the perceiving human minds of those engaged in it. These propositions also shape how he or she explains the attitudes expressed and the social actions taken by others in that arena. Insights into the cognitive processes involved can be gained from Lewin's (1948, 1952, 1972) concept of life space (a dynamic Gestalt psychological environment[37] existing in a person's mind). This deals with the world "as the individual sees it" (de Board 1978: 51), and consists of "his [sic] conscious and unconscious goals, dreams, hopes and fears, his past experiences and future expectations.[38] The physical and social conditions are also important, limiting as they do the variety of possible life spaces and creating the boundary conditions of the psychological field" (de Board 1978: 53). A life space has four dimensions (de Board 1978): cognitive (existential or perceptual), affective (evaluation), relational (cathartic) and directive (intentional). These intermingle to provide the interface between a person's perception of a social arena, and his or her specific assumptions about it. This enables that person to produce an appropriate personal construct[39] of that arena: a hierarchically arranged sets of truths[40] (genuine

inconsistent sets of cognitions (Fenon 1961). For Johnson ([1995] 2000: 95, emphasis in original), this state "exists when people hold one set of BELIEFS based on mainstream CULTURE and a contradictory set of beliefs based on their experiences." For Smith (2000: 371), however, the contrast is "between the world as we experience it and the world as we come to know it through the conceptual frameworks that science invents."

37 This is a person's holistic mental environment, constituted as set of conscious experiences that make up a system of dynamic relationships (Koffka 1935, Wertheimer 1945).

38 Jung ([1934] 1981) argued the importance of uniting the conscious and unconscious states of a person's mind, so that his or her unique potential can be fulfilled (indivuation).

39 Insights can be gleaned form Kelly's (1955) personal construct theory. This examines the ways in which a person constructs meaning about anticipated events. Personal construct systems comprise core constructs (important firmly held beliefs that are central to self-identity), peripheral constructs (relatively unimportant and changeable constructs), loose constructs (poorly defined and unstable beliefs that lead to erratic and perhaps invalid predictions), nonverbal constructs (unarticulated assumptions), preemptive constructs (constructions the elements of which do not apply to other constructions), propositional constructs (permeable constructions), superordinate constructs (freely chosen constructs that control other constructs) and subordinate constructs (constructs controlled by other constructs). These construct categories are the idiosyncratic means by which a person orders his or her social roles, in order to understand and explain the world he or she experiences, and to guide practical action in concrete situations and relationships. Kelly postulated that "a person's processes are psychologically channelized by the ways by which he [sic] anticipates events" (1955, 1: 46);

knowledge), truth propositions (knowledge claims), models of the individual (explanations of what it is to be a human being), human nature suppositions (the basic attitudes of people toward others),[41] modes of reasoning (ways of acquiring genuine knowledge), and ethical principles (the basis for deciding what is moral conduct). These constituents become part of his or her immutable core values (enduring beliefs),[42] adaptive attitudes (learned dispositions),[43] or changeable opinions (unsubstantiated beliefs)[44] (Parsons 1995: 375). That person then uses this assumptive world to make sense of his or her interactions with others in that arena.

A person's assumptive world is assembled as a result of his or her interaction with other individuals. The product of that interaction, which builds up over time, is a particular meaning system that constitutes "whatever one has to know or believe in order to operate in a manner acceptable to [a group's] members" (D'Andrade 1984: 89). Such meanings can be representational (knowledge and beliefs about the world expressed as true or false propositions), constructive (understandings about what people agree counts as what), directive (needs or

---

that "a person anticipates events by construing their replications" (p. 51); and that "each person characteristically evolves, for his [sic] convenience in anticipating events, a construction system embracing ordinal relationships between constructs" (p. 59). To the extent that a person can understand another person's internal constructions of reality, he or she can predict what that person will do, and so be able to adjust his or her own social behavior accordingly (Kelly 1955).

40 "To say of what is that it is not, or of what is not that it is, is false, while to say of what that it is, or of what is not that it is not, is true" (Aristotle [350 BC/1924/1953] 1994–2000: 4, 7).

41 Pinker (2002: 139ff) identifies four anxieties that influence people's perception of human nature: that oppression and discrimination may be justified; that the improvement of the human condition may not be possible; that people may not be held responsible for their actions; and that life may not have a higher meaning and purpose.

42 Rokeach (1973: 5, see also 1968) defines a value as "an enduring belief that a specific mode of conduct or end-state of existence is personally or socially preferable to an opposite converse mode of conduct or end-state of existence."

43 Allport (1935, cited in Warren and Jahoda 1966: 24) considered an attitude to be "a mental and neural state of readiness, organized through experience, exerting a directive or dynamic influence upon the individual's response to all objects and situations with which it is related." To Eagly and Chaiken (1998: 269) it is "a psychological tendency that is expressed by evaluating a particular entity with some degree of favor or disfavor." It is a learned disposition: a cognitive response (a thought and belief), an affective response (a feeling), and a behavioral tendencies (an action predisposition). The French novelist and airman Antoine de Saint-Exupéry shrewdly observed that "The meaning of things lies not in things themselves but in our attitudes to them."

44 These can be defined as beliefs based on grounds short of proof, which are held by an individual to be probable. Of these, Bacon ([1597–1625] 1972: 7) wryly observes:

> Doth any man doubt, that if there were taken out of men's [sic] minds vain opinions, flattering hopes, false valuations, imaginations as one would, and the like, but it would leave the minds of a number of men poor shrunken things, full of melancholy and indisposition, and unpleasing to themselves.

obligations to do something) or evocative (distinct and well shared emotional states or feelings that are aroused[45]) (D'Andrade 1984: 96–101). They guide attitude formation and motivate social actions, thereby enabling a person to engage in a social arena as he or she imagines it to be (Geertz 1983). These cognitions may well be held without awareness of their hypothetical nature and with the presumption that that social arena really is the way internalized images depict it.[46]

The existence of shared basic assumptions is premised on groups of individuals agreeing on the best way of describing, explaining, understanding and judging the social arena in which they conduct their social relations. This allows them to construct a shared meaning about that situation, which provides them with the meaning-context for their social interactions. This is the product of discourse—in Foucaultian terms, "the practices that systematically form the objects of which [people] speak"—which can be drawn upon to explain or warrant social actions (Nightingale and Cromby 1999: 226). Discourse produces, according to Giddens (2001: 687), "a framework of thinking in a particular area of social life." Each discourse takes place within a distinctive cognitive structure and can be "tied to specific institutions and actors" (Hajer 1993: 43–46). It produces meta-narratives—universal stories—that organize and justify a plurality of different stories; that contain true elements, although they may be incoherent chronologically or contradictory in the messages they transmit; and that can be condensed into icons that constitute the essential elements of a story that suggest particular ways of interpreting the world. These universal stories become part of the unquestioned habits of mind, that stock of taken-for-granted, commonsense or tacit knowledge (or prejudices to Durkheimians) upon which social actions are based. They "operate through inclusion and exclusion as homogenizing forces, marshalling heterogeneity into ordered realms, silencing and excluding other

45 Emotions (Kegan 2007) are distinctive mental states, involving the interplay of culture and neurobiology, which are stimulated by emotion-eliciting events, and which have subjective or introspective elements (Turner 2007). They may be caused by physiological disturbances stimulated by such events (James 1884, see also Rolls 2006) interacting with their personal significance to the person concerned (Arnold 1969, Lazarous 1966), and their cognitive interpretation is informed by that person's past experience (Schacter and Singer 1962). They can manifest as emotional expressions on the face and body and in the voice. These, arguably, have cathartic effects associated with the interaction of the emotion's physiological manifestation, its motor expression and the subjective feeling it elicits (Calhoun and Solomen 1984, Kenney 1963, Sartre [1938] 1948).

46 Bacon ([1623] 1997) considered that people are inevitably imprisoned in their own theoretical frameworks, which cause them to be misled because of the way they view the world, akin to the plight of Plato's ([c360 BC] 1955) imprisoned cave-dwellers shackled by their illusions of the outside world.

discourses, other voices in the name of universal principles and general goals" (Storey 1993: 159). They are value oriented and intended to persuade. They contain both objective and normative meaning. Indeed, they become the social control frameworks "by which we justify our actions to others and call them to account to us for theirs" (Rayner 1991: 84).

Shared constructions of meaning must be "intersubjectively shared, so that everyone assumes that others see the same things they see" (D'Andrade 1984: 115),[47] thereby avoiding social parallax—a misconception of sameness caused by the existence of multiple understanding of reality (Finley and Norman 1997, Zizek 2006). Thus, as Shweder and Bourne (1984: 142) point out: "what one thinks about (e.g. other individuals) and how one thinks (e.g. "contexts and cases") may be mediated by the worldview premises to which one is committed (e.g. holism) and by the metaphors by which one lives" (see also Draaisma 2000, Lakoff and Johnston 1980, Sacks 1979).

Social relationships are, then, constitutive of who a person is, how he or she thinks, what he or she does, and who he or she is becoming. Making choices about the nature of the relationships a person wishes to have with others involves determining how he or she needs to make sense of a social arena. How this need is to be satisfied, in turn, determines how that person's chooses to interpret information received about that arena and about how others behave in it.

There are competing lens that a person can choose from to read a social arena in order to discover its logic for him or her. These provide the directional guidance he or she needs about whether or how best to socially interact with others in that arena. Embedded in that lens is an abstract basic structure: a set of interrelated assumptions held about how to comprehend the actuality of that arena, and about how to understand why social actions are carried out the way they are in that situation. Any such set of assumptions must be the product of a person's preferred dispositions on epistemology (what is knowable and how it can be known); ontology (what exists and what has causal capacity[48]); methodology (the

47 Intersubjectivity emphasizes shared cognition and consensus, leading to shared, common sense meanings jointly constructed by transacting people, which enables them to share both meaning and divergences of meaning (Crossley1996): "Using the same words is not enough to ensure mutual understanding: we must also use the same words for the same category of inner experiences; ultimately, we must have the same experiences in *common*" (Nietzsche [1886] 1998: 163, emphasis in original).

48 In contention in the social and behavioral sciences is whether in the social world causal capacity should be understood in terms of determinism (Earman 1986), which, essentially, means that a social phenomenon has causes grounded in dependency relationships with one or more other phenomena.

> The metaphysics of causation [is] about the nature of the causal relata [sic], including (1.1) whether they are in spacetime (*immanence*), (1.2) how fine-grained they are (*individuation*), and

nature of investigation[49] and explanation[50]); method of investigation (the techniques to be used to investigate specific phenomenon); theory (hypothetical causal explanations of specific phenomenon); and ethics (the moral principles that justify what constitutes acceptable standards of social actions[51]). This set of assumptions permits the assembling of the explanatory filter that guides that person's attitudes and social actions, thereby enabling him or her to engage

(1.3) how many there are (*adicity*) ... [and] about the metaphysics of the causal relation, including (2.1) what is the difference between causally related and causally unrelated sequences (*connection*), (2.2) what is the difference between sequences related as cause to effect, and those related as effect to cause or as joint effects of a common cause (*direction*), and (2.3) what is the difference between sequences involving the cause, and those involving mere conditions (*selection*)" (Schaffer. [2003] 2007, emphasis in original).

Causal or scientific determinism (see Butterfield 1998) posits a strictly mechanistic causal relationship in that every event has an unbroken chain of prior material occurrences: "all events and states of affairs are *determined* by antecedent causes and laws of nature" (Kabe 2002a: 284), that is, "the *world* is *governed by* (or is *under the sway of*) determinism if and only if, given a specified *way things are at a time t*, the way things go *thereafter* is *fixed* as a matter of *natural law*" (Hoefer 2003, emphasis in original). Searle (2004: 151) explains: "the sufficient causes of an event are those that, in a particular context, are sufficient to determine that that event will occur. When we say the causes were sufficient we mean, given that those causes occurred, in that historical context, the event itself had to occur" (Leibniz's ([1704/1764] 1996) Principle of Sufficient Reason—*Ausreichenden Grund*). Contrastingly, probablistic determinism holds that "causes raise the probabilities of their effects, all else being equal" (Hitchcock [1997] 2002). Alternatively, indeterminism holds that "some events [are] entirely [materially] uncaused, or nondeterministically caused [by events], or [are] caused by agents and not deterministically caused by events" (Clarke [2000] 2004).

49 In contention is the appropriate unit of analysis for the social and behavioral sciences—social wholes (methodological holism), situations (methodological situationalism), interpersonal relationships (methodological relationalism), the action-taking individual (methodological individualism), or the action-taking individual's behaviors (methodological behaviourism) or mental properties or states (methodological solipsism).

50 In contention in the social and behavioral sciences is whether explanation can or should be understood in terms of causation (this accounts for a social phenomenon by reference to a dependency relationship with one or more other material phenomena, such that when a material cause occurs the material effect inevitably, or probably, follows), belonging to Appiah's (2008) world of being (*sinnewelt*); reasons and motivations (this accounts for a social phenomenon by reference to the human motives that explain why it occurred), belonging to Appiah's (2008) world of reasons (*verstandenwelt*) with its overlay of moral justification; or purpose (this accounts for a phenomenon by reference to its functions) (functionalism) (Wright 1971).

51 The focus of ethics is on the meaning of normative terms such as 'good', 'right' and 'virtuous' (Blackburn 2003, Stingl, 1997, Williams 2006), which involves critical evaluating the validity of moral claims regarding the ethicality of social actions (Gini 2006). These moral claims, of course, govern the lives of individuals—they fashion self-identity—and they represent actuality (Hegel [1821] 1991: 190). Therefore, a person's ethics can be regarded as a self-policing mechanism, which can stimulate self-control, motivate adherence to matters of principle, accentuate feelings, and give rise to particular lines of thought. However, such a pattern of idealistic impulses may require each moral agent to confront, or to obfuscate over, inconsistencies in their social actions that might be the outcome of a compromise arising from the imperatives of objective or subjective necessity.

appropriately in the "selecting, organizing, interpreting, and making sense of complex social reality to provide guideposts for knowing, analyzing, judging, persuading, and acting" (D'Andrade 1984: 109).[52] Such framing[53] gives rise to "a stable mental state derived from a sense of continuity and order in events" (Bilton 1996: 665) (ontological security) by providing a "perspective from which an amorphous, ill-defined, problematic situation can be made sense of and acted on" (Rein and Schön 1993: 146; see also Goffman 1974: 10–11, Johnston and Klandermans 1995: 8). It has both cognitive-rational (objective meaning) and communicative-rational (normative meaning) components.

In essence, then, a person seeking to interpret and evaluate the web of beliefs about a social arena must contemplate two fundamental sets of truth-seeking issues. The first relates to the concept of knowledge, which focuses on the limits on how human affairs in that arena can best be known—described, explained and understood (Chisholm 1989, Lucey 1996, Sosa 1994).[54] Thomas and Znaniecki (1918–20) formulated the view that for a person there are two possible sides to the comprehension of any situation: an objective side, that which is independent of the perceiving person and which can be analyzed and explained rationally (objectivism)—*en-so;* and a subjective side, that which is the product of an immanent act in the perceiving human mind, conditioned by a person's mental states that give rise to his or her feelings or interpretations (subjectivism)—*pour-soi*—such that he or she "has to take social meaning into account and interpret his [sic] experience not exclusively in terms of his own needs and wishes but also in terms of the traditions, customs, beliefs, and aspirations of his social *milieu*" (p. 230). The dilemma then confronted is well defined by Nagel (1979: 196, see also 1986):

> The problem is one of opposition between subjective and objective points of view. There is a tendency to seek an objective account of everything before admitting its reality. But often what appears to a more subjective point of view cannot be accounted for in this way. So either the objective conception of the world is incomplete, or the subjective involves illusions that should be rejected.[55]

---

52 "The greatest adaptive advantage of man [sic] is his capacity to modify his behavior as a function of the way in which he perceives and understands a situation" (Tajfel 1969: 81).

53 Goffman (1974: 15) defines a frame as "definitions of a situation [that] are built up in accordance with the principal of organization which governs events—or at least social ones—and our subjective involvement in them."

54 "Truth in human relations is of this more intangible and dubious order: hard to seize, harder to communicate" (Stevenson 1879).

55 G. K. Chesterton ([1908] 2007: 97) captured the essence of this problem:

The second set of issues relates to what in a social arena can the social actions of another person best be ascribed: to factors that are present within that action taker (his or self-determined and authentic hopes, aspirations and goals) (Ross and Nisbett 1991); or to factors external to the action taker, namely, the group-elaborated (worked out) norms, roles, and practices that shape his or her hopes, aspirations and goals, which are grounded the social, cultural,[56] politico-economic and linguistic[57] *milieu*, and which constitute the group rules or code of conduct that give rise to "ordered social interrelationships, or the recurring patterns of social behavior") (Parker 2000: 125, see also Nozick 1981).[58]

The real trouble with this world of ours is not that it is an unreasonable world, nor even that it is a reasonable one. The commonest kind of trouble is that it is nearly reasonable, but not quite. Life is not an illogicality; yet it is a trap for logicians. It looks just a little more mathematical and regular than it is; its exactitude is obvious, but its inexactitude is hidden; its wildness lies in wait.

56 This comprises, according to Scruton (2007: 3–4) "those customs and artifacts which are shared, and the sharing of which brings social cohesion ... [more broadly] all intellectual, emotional and behavioral features that are transmitted through learning and social interaction, rather than through genetic endowment" It is depicted by Schein (1991) as shared meaning at three levels: shared basic assumptions about existence, shared norms, and shared language and symbols. It consists of "a 'tool kit' of rituals, symbols, stories, and world-views" (Johnston and Klandermans 1995: 7) or "mental products" (Pye 1968: 218). Spiro (1984: 323) elaborates: "Cultural propositions are developed in the historical experience of social groups ... [and they] are encoded in the collective, rather than private, signs ... [which have] noncultural situational, ecological, economic, political, biological, emotional etc. as well as cultural (ideational) determinants."

57 Language is a rule-based system of finite arbitrary sounds, gestures and symbols used to represent objects, concepts, emotions, ideas, and thoughts for the purpose of interpersonal communication (Searle 1969). It links thought—content-elements (meaning)—and sound—expression-elements (sounds and words); and involves a series of arbitrary but mutually intelligible linguistic signs, grounded in a historically constituted system of linguistic conventions (Culler 1976, Sebeok 1989) (natural language). Chomsky ([1955] 1975, 1965, but see also Pinker [1994] 1995) surmised that there is generically embedded in all humans a set innate principles of grammar—a universal grammer—shared by all natural languages (linguistic nativism). This constitutes an element of the modularity of the mind (the set of genetically embedded innate functional structures within the mind (Fodor 1983)). Pinker (2007: 3) argues that people have in their minds innate generative rules for linguistic combinatorial mechanisms and caches of emotions that constitute their innate conceptual frameworks (conceptual semantics), whose "design quirks give rise to fallacies, follies and foibles in the way that people reason about the conundrums of modern life." "Our words and constructions disclose conceptions of physical reality and human social life that are similar in all cultures but different from the products of our science and scholarship" (p. 4). Wittgenstein (1953) argued that the linguistic rules that shape knowledge acquisition are intimately shared and, therefore, constitute the very essence of social interaction, which means that making sense of what others say is the product of a complex of interweaving of speech and action.

58 Attribution theory in psychology seeks to account for how a person explains—attributes reasons for—the behavior of self or others (Jones *et al.* 1972). It distinguishes between reasons that are internal or external to the person whose behavior is being explained (Heider [1958] 1982). Such attribution can be based on the multiple observations of covariation of the behavior to be

To convert beliefs (knowledge claims or alleged truths) into genuine knowledge (truths or certainties), thereby adding to new knowledge, requires the application of a truth-standard (truth-criterion) that enable judgments to be made about what constitutes sufficient justification—sufficient evidence[59]—to warrant the status of truth being assigned to a belief (Kirkham 1992, Moser, 1989, Vardy 2003a). However, as James ([1897] 1979: 15) pointed out, "no concrete test of what is really true has ever been agreed upon."[60]

explained and the possible causes (covariation principle) (Kelley 1967, 1973) or on generalized causal propositional beliefs (causal schemata) (Kelley 1972). Attribution can be spontaneous (Weiner 1985). It can be prone to error or bias (Fiske and Taylor 1991, Kruglanski and Ajzen 1983), explainable in terms of motivational, cognitive, cultural and linguistic considerations (see, for example, Gilbert and Malone 1995, Hewstone and Augoustinos 1998, Miller *et al.* 1978, Tetlock and Manstead 1985). People tend to attribute behavior more to internal than to external factors, contrary to psychological evidence—the fundamental attribution error theory. A greater explanatory reliance on external information can, however, be found, when there is interest in learning about the situation, perhaps before a decision has to be made about entering a new situation (Krull and Erickson 1995).

59 Evidentialism holds that believing a truth claim is warranted if and only if the evidence supports so doing (Feldman and Conee 2004). Clearly, a truth proposition cannot be genuine knowledge if it is false. Does this mean that the evidence proffered as proof must be so secure as to be beyond all doubt, thereby giving rise to propositional certainty? Under the Platonic conception of knowledge, for a truth proposition to be genuine knowledge requires the evidence proffered as proof to give rise to propositional (absolute) certainty that can never become false. Descartes ([1641] 1975), in this tradition, held that nothing should be believed unless it is absolutely certain that it is true—*de omnibus dubitandum* (every thing is to be doubted)—(Cartesian doubt). This means that all beliefs should be treated as if they are false, which is a perspective that "depicts knowledge as if were identical with the kind of [tautological] certitude found in logic and mathematics" (Stroll 2006: 31), where knowledge is without factual content. The scientific conception of knowledge requires that, since all scientific explanations are factual generalizations based on past observations, the factual evidence proffered as proof can only ever be contingent, so "knowledge, from a scientific perspective, is a matter of the strength of the evidence in support of a particular assertion" (Stroll 2006: 31).

60 Indeed, Nietzsche posed the fundamental question: why is truth important? Why is there a "will to truth"? What is the value of this will? "Given that we want truth: *why do we not prefer* untruth? And uncertainty? Even ignorance?" ([1886] 1998: 5 emphasis in original). "However much value we may ascribe to truth, truthfulness, and altruism, it may be that we need to attribute a higher and more fundamental value to appearances, to the will to illusion, to egoism and desire" (p. 6).

Chapter 5

EPISTEMOLOGY AND TRUTH

Epistemology is concerned with the nature, extent, sources and legitimacy of knowledge. It investigates the nature and coherence of knowledge claims (Devitt 1984, Kirkham 1992, Moser 2002, White 1970). At issue, fundamentally, is whether:

- truth is a property that can be investigated;[61]
- truth is a unique extra-linguistic objective fact that is independent of the truth-seeker and awaits discovery;[62]
- truth is relative, because there are no intersubjective, generally recognized method for determining the truthfulness of a knowledge claim (cognitive relativism[63]), which makes the truth dependant upon the truth-standard applied, as established by the truth-knower's sociocultural and linguistic *milieu*, gender and thus his or her cognitive status and circumstances (feminist epistemology) (Alcoff and Potter 1993, Duran

---

61 Advocates of the deflationary theories of truth (redundancy theory, performative theory and presentential theory) (Kirkham 1992) assert that truth does not have a nature that can be investigated. To ascribe truth to a statement does not attribute a property called 'truth' to that statement, rather it asserts nothing more than the statement to which truth is ascribed:

It is worthy of notice that the sentence "I smell the scent of violets" has the same content as the sentence "it is true that I smell the scent of violets". So it seems, then, that nothing is added to the thought by my ascribing to it the property of truth. (Frege [1918] 1997: 326).

62 "The question whether objective truth can be attributed to human thinking is not a question of theory but is a practical question. Man must prove the truth, *i.e.*, the reality and power, the this-sidedness [*Diesseitigkeit*] of his thinking, in practice. The dispute over the reality or non-reality of thinking which is isolated from practice is a purely scholastic question" (Marx ([1845/1924] 2002: Sect 2).

63 This holds that no set of epistemic norms is metaphysically privileged over another (Kirk 1999).

1991), and his or her mental characteristics or states that give rise to personal enlightenment; or

- truth cannot be established (skepticism[64] and solipsism[65]), because, as Berkeley ([1710] 1962: 74) observed, the mind construes the world as it is experienced (sense-datum theory[66]) and there is "no necessary [causal] connexion" between the two, for the perception of an object—the idea of the object—cannot prove that the separate existence of the object "without the mind, or unperceived", thereby, reducing physical objects to mental entities (mentalist monism), thereby denying the possibility of any genuine knowledge, leaving just beliefs and opinions.

Different truth-standards can be applied, of course, in different situation, because what counts as knowledge depends on the situation in which the truth-seeker has to make truth judgments. Which truth-criterion is adopted depends upon how the truth-seeker wishes to establish and conduct his or her social affairs in that situation: "the criterias [sic] for 'truth' depends on what group you belong to" (Dahl 1999: 181).

64 This derives from a classical Greek noun, *skepsis*—meaning consideration, examination or inquiry. It is the proposition that no beliefs (knowledge claims or alleged truths) can be appraised to be certain, justified or reasonable (Unger 1975), which makes them indeterminate and, thus, judgments about material reality must be suspended (Pyrrhonism) (Annas and Barnes 1985, Hankinson 1995, Popkin 1979, Sextus Empicus [c.200] 1994). Any criterion used to judge beliefs can be challenged because a further criterion is needed to judge that criterion. Beliefs about external reality are based on sense knowledge—Thorpe's (1962) experiencing—are always personal, immediate and mutable. Nietzsche's ([1886] 1998) extreme form of skepticism—epistemological nihilism—maintains that nothing in the world has a real existence (Crosby 1988, Zupančić 2002): "existence must not be interpreted in terms of 'purpose,' 'unity,' 'Being,' or 'truth'" (Stack (1977: 17). For the Nietzschean nihilist, there is no true world at all, for all claims to knowledge are entirely relative to the vagaries of a person's thought and experience: "so what is truth?" Kierkegaard's related proposition is that "in regard to every other reality external to the individual it can only be known through 'thinking it'" (Stack 1977: 197, n. 19).

65 This is grounded in the principle that a person cannot know anything beyond self. It holds that only oneself alone (*solus ipse*) exists—the only center of consciousness—therefore, nothing at all exists apart from one's own mental states (metaphysical solipsism) (Russell 1948: Part III, Ch. 2).

66 This holds that any perceptual experience involves awareness of sense-datum, regardless of whether that sensory perception is an experience of the object being perceived—"the only object of our awareness is that experienced by the brain", which may be illusory (Searle 2004: 180, 181–84)—which means that all knowledge of the external world is grounded in potentially problematic sense data (Ayer 1953, Price 1932, Swartz 1965, but see also Searle 2004: 186–89, Austin 1962). The extreme position—methodological solipsism—holds that the content of a belief about the external world is fully determined by the mental properties or mental states of the believer (Wood 1962).

CONTENDING THEORIES OF TRUTH

A person can know a truth only if he or she holds a belief that a proposition—a statement held to be true—perhaps asserted by others—is true,[67] thereby making it a true belief (or genuine knowledge) for that person (BonJour 2002). Two truth-making principles can be identified. The first is the principle of causal explanation (statements of causation reporting lawful relations between one material phenomenon and another, so establishing an antecedently sufficient causal chain)[68] (Campbell *et al.* 2007, Rubin 1994). This is grounded on the world being material and existing independently of the mind, which means empirical enquiry methods can be utilized to develop causal explanations that "makes truth true" (Psillos 2002: 167). Nomothetic methods presume that a knowledge claim is proffered as proven on the basis of logical and empirically confirmed relations between material phenomena. The second is the principle of understanding (the acquisition of insightful and significant meanings to be attached to material and nonmaterial phenomena gained from discussion and reflection), which asserts that the world "must be understood from within rather than explained from without" (Hollis 1994: 16). Idiographic methods presume that understanding derives from both individual and group interpretations of the meaning—perhaps associating the correct ideas with particular words used, knowing the correct use of language, or discerning the communicative goals sought by the communicator—which can "range from what is consciously and individually intended to what is communally and often unintendedly significant"[69] (Hollis 1994: 17).

---

67 There is "no direct relationship between proof on the one hand, and what we can or cannot doubt on the other" (Baggini 2002: 36), which means that a proposition can be evidentially unproven but psychologically certain to a person because he or she believes it to be true without any doubt. Doubt, of course, is a state of mind—a state of indecision or hesitancy about accepting the truthfulness of a proposition.

68 This strictly mechanistic view of causal relationship was originally argued by Leucippus and Democritus, the ancient Greek atomists (Taylor 1999), who considered that everything happens in accordance with laws of nature (Russell 1946: 86)—or in Humean terminology "necessity"—"the necessary connexion among events" (Hume [1777] 1902: 75).

69 Flaubert captured the essence of this in *Madam Bovray* ([1856/1857] 2006):

> Emma was like all his mistresses; and the charm of novelty, gradually falling away like a garment, laid bare the eternal monotony of passion, that has always the same forms and the same language. He did not distinguish, this man of so much experience, the difference of sentiment beneath the sameness of expression. Because lips libertine and venal had murmured such words to him, he believed but little in the candour of her's; exaggerated speeches hiding mediocre affections must be discounted; as if the fullness of the soul did not sometimes overflow in the emptiest metaphors, since no one can ever give the exact measure of his needs, nor of his conceptions, nor of his sorrows; and since human speech is like a cracked tin kettle, on which we hammer out tunes to make bears dance when we long to move the stars.

There are five irreconcilable theories about truth (Blackburn 2005, Kirkham 1992).

- The correspondence theory sees truth as a knowledge claim that corresponds to, or is in agreement with some elements of, reality—an extra-linguistic fact—in a way that validates the proposition (Fumerton 2002, O'Connor 1994). It holds that "a belief is true when there is a corresponding fact, and is false when there is no corresponding fact" (Russell 1912: 129, see also 1948) (epistemological realism).
- The coherence theory sees truth as a knowledge claim that is logically consistent with, and mutually supported by, other knowledge claims, that attains a degree of knowledge-claim integration, and that offers the simplest explanations for multiple and divergent phenomena (Rescher 1973). It holds that a truth must fit into a system or network of mutually consistent propositions, although, on this basis, the whole truth must be in accord with the whole of reality, which provides it with a status that is beyond judgment (Bradley [1893] 2005), thus the substantiation of a truth occurs through other knowledge claims.
- The consensus theory sees truth as something agreed upon by some specified group of experts even if it fails to describe reality (Peirce 1877). It holds that a belief is true if those who have investigated it agree that it is true, although, within this notion it is implicit that not all beliefs can be assigned a truth value.
- The pragmatism theory, which sees truth as instrumental and contingent upon the success of the practical consequences of an idea (Dewey [1895–1898] 1972, James [1897] 1979, [1907] 1995, [1909] 1979, Peirce 1877, Schiller [1903] 1912, [1907] 1912).[70] It holds that a belief counts as true if it is useful to believe it to be true. As James ([1897] 1979} remarks: "our obligation to seek truth is part of our obligation to do what pays" (quoted in Russell 1946: 844).[71]
- The social constructivism theory considers truth to be socially constructed and thus contingent upon convention, human understanding,

70 "The pragmatic method ... is to try to interpret each notion by tracing its respective practical consequences. What differences would it make to anyone if this notion rather than that notion were true" (James [1907] 1995: 18).

71 On this, Russell (1946: 52) observed: "Modern definitions of truth, such as pragmatism and instrumentalism, which are practical rather than contemplative, are inspired by industrialism as opposed to aristocracy."

and social experience (Glasersfeld 1995).[72] It holds that a belief is true if it is substantiated by discourse, which means that what is deemed to be true is contingent.

These truth theories do not offer a precise and irreconcilable division between those based on their objectivity or subjectivity. However, some truth-criteria embrace the notion of explanation more than understanding and vice-versa: the correspondence and coherence theories place an emphasis on objective criteria, whilst the social constructivism theory comfortably espouses subjective criteria, with the pragmatism and consensus theories drawing upon both.

CONTENDING WAYS OF JUSTIFYING KNOWLEDGE CLAIMS

A knowledge claim can be justified or warranted in a seven ways:

- by evidence of sensory experience (*a posteriori* knowledge[73]) or of deductive reasoning (*a priori* knowledge[74]) (Kant [1781–87] 1956; see also Guyer 2006, Kitcher 1998);[75]
- by reference to self-justifying knowledge claims that are beyond doubt, as a result of a combination of experience—Russell's knowledge by acquaintance (Jager 1992, but see BonJor 1985)—and reason, which constitute a set of basic robust and unambiguous foundations—a set of

72 This relates to social constructionism (Berger and Luchman 1966, Gergen 1999, 2001, but see Searle 1995), which embraces those social theories that emphasize that social life is socially created; to cognitive pluralism, which is the proposition that there are a various ways that people individually and in groups can go about the business of reasoning (Wilson 1979); and to epistemic relativism, which is the proposition that what can be known is relative and, thus, one system of reasoning may be best for one group of people, perhaps in terms of reflective equilibrium or truth-generating capacity, while a quite different system might be best for another group (Goodman [1954] 1965).

73 A proposition is knowable *a posteriori* if it can be known to be true by means of inductive reasoning based on empirical experience or data.

74 A proposition is known *a priori* if it can be known to be true by means of deductive reasoning without reference to empirical experience or data.

75 Both these enquiry methods, to varying degrees, may provide criteria that validate or inform propositions that are advanced by all the truth theories. However, both the social constructivism and pragmatism truth theories confine and critique inductive inferences or deductive reasoning as they hold that outcomes of human subjectivity takes precedence over logic and factual objectivity.

foundational beliefs—that do not need further justification (foundationalism) (DePaul 2000, Moser 1989);

- by reference to sufficiently valid reasons that are grounded in cognitive processes of direct apprehension (sensory perception and memory) or of reasoning that has produced a high proportion of true beliefs (reliabilism) (Alston 1989, Goldman 1986, Shope 1983);
- by reference to the believer's willingness to act in accordance with that belief on the basis of the axioms of probability theory (probabilism) (Rosenkrantz 1977);
- by reference to the knowledge claim not being made defective as a source of knowledge by being overridden or defeated by additional, previously unknown evidence (epistemic defeasibility) (Shope 1983);
- by unanimous agreement that a knowledge claim is true by all who have sufficient relevant knowledge or experience to judge it (consensual pragmatism) (Mounce 1997, Murphy 1990, Scheffler 1974); and
- by reference to a knowledge claim producing beneficial results for believers, after all matters are considered (instrumental pragmatism) (Mounce 1997, Murphy 1990, Scheffler 1974).

What a person can know about social world depends, then, on the standards of truth that person chooses to apply when endeavoring to gain genuine knowledge of such phenomena. As Lowell (1984) observes, "truth, after all, wears a different face to everybody, and it would be too tedious to wait till all were agreed." Once chosen, a truth-standard determines how he or she describes, explains, and understands the social world. The fundamental issue is: "you cannot search for X, whatever X may be, unless you are from the outset equipped with a good enough notion of what X is to provide you with criteria by which to judge whether you have found what you are looking for" (Welbourne 2001: 14).

Chapter 6

THE EPISTEMOLOGICAL DICHOTOMY: NATURALISM AND HERMENEUTICS

The two approaches to epistemology offered by the philosophy of the social sciences are naturalism[76] and hermeneutics[77]. Naturalism assumes that the world—including each individual present in it—is real, material and objectively knowable (Bhaskar [1979] 1998: 2–3) and can be explained by the use of inductive inference and/or deductive logic that draws only upon material evidence or luminous premises. Hermeneutics, in contrast, assumes that the meaningfulness of the world—including each individual present in it—can only be understood ideationally as they are subjectively experienced by the perceiving minds: "man is an animal suspended in a web of significance he himself has spun, I take culture to be those webs, and the analysis of it to be ... an interpretive one in search of meaning" (Geertz 1973: 5). These two distinctive epistemological approaches are reflected in a variety of dichotomous terminology (Berlin 1976, Braybrooke 1987, Ruben 1998), notably, objectivism (reality is independent of the mind—that is, "independent of human conception, speculation or fantasy" (Stroll 2006: 10)) versus subjectivism (reality is a set of first-person mental discernments); materialism (reality is constituted as material objects and phenomena) versus idealism[78] (reality is constituted as ideas in the perceiving mind); or empiricism

---

76 This has connotations that relate to the regularities of nature, the discovery of which gives rise to natural laws.

77 This is derived from the Greek *hermêneuô*, meaning "to interpret or translate".

78 A more accurate term would be "idea-ism" (Singer 1983: 91). This postulates that nothing exist independently of mental experiences (Hoernlé 1927), and so nothing exists independently of an idea in a perceiving person's mind (mentalist monism). The mind is, thus, the most basic reality. This gives rise to: metaphysical idealism (ideas are the constituents of reality) (Berkeley [1710] 1962, [1713] 1948); subjective idealism (the mind is where ideas about reality exist and are

(knowledge is ultimately based on sensory experience) versus constructivism (knowledge is constructed by knowledge-seekers).[79] The social epistemological debate is on whether social knowledge should be understood individualistically (knowledge claims can and should only be justified by reference to objective sensory experience, to reasoned deductions, or even to subjective first-person mental discernments grounded in intuition[80], common sense[81], or revealed wisdom[82]) or socially (knowledge claims can and should only be justified by reference to expert authority or testimony[83], consensus or tradition (received wisdom)) (Hollis 1994, Natanson 1963).

perceived) (Berkeley [1710] 1962, [1713] 1948); transcendental idealism (the reality beyond empirical investigation—such as the Platonic Forms (Plato [390s-347 BC] 1997) (Theory of Forms)—timeless, stable, perfect, unchanging and intelligible ideal-forms of objects and concepts (such as Justice, Good and Beauty), the Cartesian mental substance (Descartes [1641] 1975), the Spinoxan God substance (Spinoza [1677] 1985), the Leibnizian monads (the non-physical, indivisible soul-like fundamental constituents of nature) (Leibniz [1714] 1973), and the Kantian noumena (Kant [1781–87] 1956)—can exist only as ideas in minds) (Kant [1781–87] 1956); absolute idealism (all of reality is embraced in a universal thought or experience; the Hegelian universal mind or rational consciousness (collective *geist*)) (Hegel [1807] 1977, [1816] 1969, [1817] 1991, [1817] 1970, see also Beiser 2005, Singer 1983); and theistic idealism (God is the source of ideas about reality) (Berkeley [1710] 1962, [1713] 1948), Plotinus (see Rist 1967), Spinoza [1677] 1985). Wittgenstein ([1922] 1961: 5.64) considered that idealism "coincides with pure realism."

79 Orwell in *1984* ([1949] 1983: 205) captures the essence of these dichotomies when he has government agent O'Brien explaining to Winston Smith:

> You believe that reality is something objective, external, existing in its own right. You also believe that the nature of reality is self-evident. When you delude yourself into thinking that you are seeing something, you assume that everyone else sees the same thing as you. But I tell you, Winston, that reality is not external. Reality exists in the human mind, and no where else.

80 Bergson saw intuition is as an "instinct that has become disinterested, self-conscious, and capable of reflecting upon its object and of enlarging it indefinitely" (quoted in Russell 1946: 821). The feminist thought that extols intuition over reason centers it on an investigator's self-identification with the outcomes from oppressive practices that have remained hidden in a framework of dominant enquiry mode constructed around preponderantly male norms (Harding 1986, 1991, Shepherd 1993). Shand (2002: 46) notes, however, that "intuitions are without exception sensuous, and therefore, no speculative knowledge is possible which reaches further than possible experience" (p. 46).

81 In the tradition of eighteenth-century Scottish realist philosophy, common sense—beliefs that come naturally to mind to all people, as responsible agents, based on memory, reason, moral sense and taste—carries its own authority, despite accepted perceptual fallibilities, because people, proceeding cautiously, are capable of knowing the world (Grave 1960, Moore 1959).

82 This is Aquinas' ([1259–64] 1905) truths of revelation: "Wisdom ... conferred by God as a particular endowment" (Rofe 2001).

83 As Welbourne (2001: 125) observed, "the concept of knowledge enters our repertoire of concepts on the back of testimony." See also Coady 1992.

NATURALISM

Naturalism adheres to the doctrine of objectivism (Peikoff 1993), which postulates that a knowledge claim is epistemologically objective—a matter of fact—if the evidence for determining its truth value is material in form and, therefore, can be established by generally agreed enquiry procedures involving inductive inference (inferring conclusions about a category of things from observations of particular things in that category) and/or deductive logic (drawing logically valid conclusions from a set of premises). Truth or falsehood should, therefore, be established solely by reference to material objects or phenomena (Mill [1843] 1988).

On Knowledge

Naturalist epistemology proposes two types of knowledge, differentiated on the basis of how a proposition can be known: synthetic—knowledge derived by inductive inference based on sensory experience (*a posteriori* knowledge); and analytic—knowledge derived by deductive logic without reference to sensory experience (*a priori* knowledge).[84]

Synthetic Knowledge

Kantian synthetic propositions contain *a posteriori* (empirical or sensory experience-based) knowledge that have been justified (found to be factually true) on the basis of inductive reasoning that involves empirical evidence (generalizing about a category from observed particulars in that category) (Hempel 1966)—empiricism—in the tradition of Galileo, Bacon, Locke, Berkeley and Hume (Atherton 1999).[85] Thus, the archaic statement "all swans are white" is synthetic, because it rests on assumptions about the observed characteristics of the physical world (Williams and May 1996: 25). Crucially, the truthfulness of synthetic knowledge claims is asserted after the collection of a body of facts to which inductive reasoning is applied to generate probable generalizations, which rest on the probability of previous patterns of material observation being repeated in the future (Greene 1999: 63–71). This gives rise to new knowledge (Russell 1946:

84 "The *a priori* /*a posteriori* distinction is epistemological and should not be confused with the metaphysical distinction between the necessary and the contingent [truths] or the semantical or logical distinction between the analytic and the synthetic [propositions]" (Baehr 2006).

85 This presumes that how an object is experienced is how it is when it is not being experienced.

222). Synthetic propositions are closely related to Leibniz's "truths of fact", or contingent truths (truth propositions that could be factually untrue) (Leibniz [1714] 1973, see also Jolley 2005), because they "would seem to be knowable only *a posteriori*, since it is unclear how pure thought or reason could tell us anything about the actual world" (Baehr 2006).

Hume, a skeptical empiricist, denied the objective value of the concept of causation. He argued that an assertion explaining one material phenomenon in terms of another is based on confused logic. To him, causation had three components: priority (a cause must precede its alleged effect), contiguity in time and space (a cause and its alleged effect must be spatio-temporally adjacent), and necessary connection (a cause must make its alleged effect happen) (Searle 2004: 137). On this basis, any proposition maintaining that it is a necessary truth that one material phenomenon must automatically follow another is, no matter how clever, based on a fallacious argument (Hume [1748] 1975: Sect. 12, Pt. 3)—his celebrated problem of induction (Searle 2004: 138–41, but see 142)—which led him to hold the proposition that causal pronouncements can only follow the empirical demonstration of constant conjunction. Two material phenomena, which exist at separate times, are, of course, discrete within human thought and one can be imagined without the other. Hume considered, however, that it is through a process of "habits of the mind" that people are influenced by previous observations into making connections between material phenomena independent of consistent external sensory perception thus, "custom, then, is the great guide of human life" (Hume [1748] 1975: S. 5, Pt. 1).[86] Therefore, it is axiomatic "how use doth breed a habit in a man!" (Shakespeare, *The Two Gentlemen of Verona*). The problem that dominates is whether an objective understanding of reality is achievable through the explanation and modification of sensory perceptions.[87]

Analytical Knowledge

Kantian analytic propositions contain *a priori* (non-empirical) knowledge that has been justified (found to be logically valid) by being logically deduced from a

---

86 Hume was predisposed to the notion that natural instincts, which, he considered, no thought process can produce or prevent, shaped knowledge. Ideas or sensory impressions are thought able to agglomerate amongst individuals leading to the association of ideas that produces a level of commonality in human sensory perceptions (Scruton 1984: 124).

87 Nietzsche ([1886] 1998: 16 emphasis in original) thought not: "... people are actually saying that the external world is created by our sense organs? But then our body, as part of the external world, would be the creation of our sense organs! But then our very sense organs would be—the creation of our sense organs! It seems to me that this is a complete *reductio ad absurdum* [reduction to absurdity]: assuming that the concept *causa sui* [self-caused] is something completely absurd. It follows that the outer world is *not* the creation of our sense organs—?"

set of premises (semantics and logic) without reference to experience—rationalism—in the tradition of Plato, Spinoza, Leibniz and Descartes (Pereboom 1999). Sense experience is discounted as a source of knowledge, thereby rejecting "the world of sense in favor of the self-created world of pure thought" (Russell 1946: 93; see also Descartes [1637] 1951: Part III): "There is nothing in the intellect that was not first in the senses, except the intellect" (Leibniz [1704/1764] 1996, Bk. II: 111).[88] Analytical knowledge grounded in the Platonic proposition that the most important truths are those available through reason (Plato [390s-347 BC] 1997: xiv], which means that they could never become false: "the Hellenic belief in deduction from luminous axioms derived from the mind of the philosopher" (Russell 1946: 58). Indeed, the Stoics held that "there are certain principles which are luminously obvious and are admitted by all men [sic]; these could be made, as in Euclid's Elements, the basis of deduction" (Russell 1946: 292): "It is and it is impossible for it not to be" (Parmenides, quoted in Freeman 2003: 11). They present syllogistic reasoning or self-evident tautologies, whereby the truthfulness of a knowledge contention logically follows from either a set of *a priori* premises or axioms (statements accepted without proof, from which all other statements of a system can be derived, for the sake of studying the consequences that follow from them) or from its very definition (the predicate is in the subject, which means its opposite implies a contradiction). Analytical *a priori* propositions, which cannot be refuted by experience because they are beyond the scope of the senses to confirm, present transcendental deductions that can lead to *a priori* truths. Such propositions are closely related to Leibniz's "truths of reason" ([1714] 1973) or logical necessities (propositions that must be true because their opposites are either contradictory or factually untrue), which means that all analytical propositions are necessary propositions but not all necessary propositions are analytical propositions (Stroll 2006: 32).

Analytical knowledge offers a profound and strong demonstration of cause and effect and thus causal explanation. The deductive logic of analytic propositions can provides irrefutable grounds for knowledge claims about certain relationships. But the strength of the causal relationships they identify derives from the coherence of the definitions held within their premises. Thus, the truth of analytic statements rests on mathematical or linguistic definitions, not on the observable processes of the physical or social worlds. The issue is, however, in Aristotelian terms, "how do we know the first premises from which deduction

---

88 Hume ([1739] 1978: II, 3, S. 3, Para. 4), to the contrary, believed that "reason is and ought only to be the slave of the passions, and can never pretend to any other office than to serve and obey them."

must start? ... we must begin with something unproven, which must be known otherwise than by demonstration" (Russell 1946: 222). Unfortunately, mathematical description cannot be equated with empirical regularity, which means analytic statements can be logically valid, because they necessarily follow from the premises, but empirically untrue, because one or more of the premises are empirically false (Williams and May 1996: 25).[89] Moreover, debate continues as to whether new knowledge is created by the deduction process. Russell thought not (1946: 222); Finch (1995: 152–53) agrees: "Deductions can be made in a system that has no content or meaning, provided the symbols are used consistently with each other. The deductive relations are also empty of meaning." But, under the deductive closure principle it is argued, to the contrary, that if A knows X to be true and A correctly deduces Y from X, then A also knows Y to be true, which is new knowledge (Williams 1991).

Traditions

Realism

This is the long-standing proposition, advanced by Plato, that the external world exists when not being experience, and has properties and relations that are entirely independently of any human knowledge of or beliefs about their actuality (metaphysical realism), which gives it cognitive authority (Putman 1987, 1988, Rorty 1997, Searle 1995). What the senses perceive about the external world, despite accepted perceptual fallibilities, is true (epistemological realism) and portrays that world accurately (direct or naïve realism[90]), evidenced by the fact that different people can perceive the same object in the same way in all essentials (Searle 2004: 190–91). Realism does, however, accept the existence of unobservables (scientific realism) (Psillos 1999, Russell 1940).

Realism, in the tradition of Thucydides, Machiavelli and Hobbes, is "a theory concerned to generate a scientific account of 'the facts as they really are' ... [and] excludes the consideration of normative issues from theory in favor of a purely explanatory endeavor, based on the notion of the separation of facts and values"

89 Of syllogistic reasoning, Russell (1946: 456) identified the following defects in the context of the Scholastic method in the twelfth century and its Platonic predecessors: "indifference to facts and science, belief in reasoning in matter which only observation can decide, and an undue emphasis on verbal distinctions and subtleties." Nietzsche ([1886] 1998: 13) is more condemning: synthetic *a priori* judgments should not 'be possible' at all: we have no right to them, in our mouths they are false judgments."

90 "Naïve realism leads to physics, and physics, if true, shows that naïve realism is false. Therefore naïve realism, if true, is false; therefore it is false" (Russell 1940: 15).

(Murray 1997: 730). A phenomenon can, thus, be explained by the discovery of its constituents and underlying processes, established by reference to objective truth-conditions (Alston, 2002, Devitt 1984, Dummett 1963, Wright 1987). Thus, meaning as truth depends upon factuality.

Rationalism

Rationalism can be understood through the axiom "placing trust in reason" (Bunge 1996: 306).[91] In its search for the truth, rationalism holds that reality is a system of cause and effect that can be deciphered by reason. It has two strands: radical and moderate. The dogmatic assumption of radical rationalism is that there can be only one perception of reality that accords with reason, which, by implication, leads to discomfiture with both empiricism and positivism (Bunge 1996: 306). Descartes' philosophy is grounded in the epistemological issues connected with skepticism. He attempts to allow explanation to be free from a skepticism that leads to confusion and conflict. Human ideas can be innate—knowable in the mind acquired by pure reason—and thus sealed with validity, or they can be established through sensation—rooted in fractious and self-important notions (but see Locke [1690] 2004: Bk. 2). The individual is, thus, the ultimate arbitrator of truth as each person reaches his or her own decisions about the validity of truths and knowledge (Descartes [1641] 1961, see also Williams 2005). The moderate strand is an adaptable doctrine that accepts that reason is necessary, but acknowledges that different individuals may interpret rationality in different ways to comprehend phenomena fully.[92]

Whilst the human senses are not entirely ignored under the doctrine of rationalism, they are regarded as inferior to explanations derived through a process of deductive reasoning, which asserts that the validity of a conclusion follows from the logical deductions drawn from the postulated premises. On this basis, deductive reasoning produces contingent truths that are reliant on, firstly, the truthfulness of the premises from which the *a priori* knowledge is deduced;[93]

91 This stands in contradistinction to the broader common-usage meaning of rational, as the use of the human intellect—involving reasoning and sense experience—to gain knowledge by seeking evidence for and against a knowledge claim (Chisholm 1989).

92 Insightfully, Mirowski (1991: 231 and 237) considers rationality to be a "sadly abused word ... a strange *potage*."

93 When grounded in religio-mystical postulates, rationalism gives rise to some challenging propositions about the world. Lossky (1951), a Russian neo-Leibnizian idealist, in his religious-philosophical system explored causality and perfection. He postulated that there were three levels of reality: the real, the abstract and the concretely-ideal (the Kingdom of Spirit inhabited by non-material ideal beings or substantival agents). "Thus, as Losskii [sic] points out, the 'world as a whole, including material nature, is the work of spirit or of beings that are akin to

and secondly, the validity of the *ceteris paribus* (other things being equal) assumptions, which is only applicable in a closed system. Rationalism thus maintains that truths about the "really existing intelligible world that underlies the appearance of changing particulars that we experience" (Shand, 2002: 69) can be discovered through the methodical application of deductive reasoning. This proposition is grounded in Descartes' observation that "it is only the things that I conceive clearly and distinctly which have the power to convince me completely" ([1641] 1961: 123). Thus, only the mind, divorced as it is from the body, can sanction certainty and truth: "I think, therefore, I am" [94] (Descartes, [1641] 1961: 82).

To a rationalist, the world is, of necessity, logical. As Spinoza ([1677] 1985) observes, this condition reflects the nature of God, so denial of the theorem that is derived from the accepted axioms is an illogical contradiction implying God's imperfection (see also Shand 2002: 87). Leibniz refined this principle to the acceptance of theorems after the application of sufficient reason by acknowledging that truths might be contingent, because God is under no compulsion to actualize all truths. Accordingly, it is enough for every fact to find its justification in a previous fact to justify fundamentally the necessary and logical process of causality. Thus, it is acknowledged that, although the world is perceived through a variety of perspectives, humanity can, through logic, still obtain "as much perfection as possible" (Leibniz, [1714] 1973: 187–88).

Rationalism addresses one important imperative: cause and effect become explainable concepts offering declarations of greater value than a process of observation that is unable to move beyond mere correlation. Nevertheless, strong rationalism can still be held to be insufficient to explain fully the world, for theories that are the product of reason still demands empirical verification of their premises or predictions for their validation.

---

spirit. ... Considering the whole world in its systemic unity there ... must exist a principle which 'is the source of the world's plurality and of its original unification' and which 'does not contain any plurality in itself, and ... therefore ... stands above all systems. This principle is properly named the 'Absolute' and as such is the subject of no positive definition. ... According to [Lossky's] hierarchical personalism, 'the world as a system united by the Supreme Substance, Sophia [the Spirit or wisdom of God], is composed of an infinite multitude of smaller sub-systems governed by the appropriate substantival agents' " (Sergeev 1999: 4 and: 8). McTaggart (1927, see also Greach 2001), a British Hegelian absolute idealist metaphysician and personalist, argued that ultimate reality—absolute reality—is spiritual, and theorized that this reality is a community of selves—each self constituting a spirit that is defined by its perceptions of self and others—and every self loves every other self whom it perceives directly or indirectly (S. 470).

94 Rendered in Latin as cogito ergo sum in Section 7 of Part I of Principles of Philosophy (1644) and in French as *je pense, donc je suis* in Part IV of *Méditations Metaphysiques* (1647).

Empiricism

This stresses the fundamental role of sensory experience as the foundation of all knowledge. To Lock ([1690] 2004), the human mind was a *tabula rasa*[95]—literally scraped tablet—awaiting inscription from aspects of experience. As he ([1690] 2004: Bk. 2, Ch. 1, Sect. 19) observed: "No man's knowledge here can go beyond his experience." Locke classified experiences as being of two kinds. The first kind are the external sensations that exist in external objects that awake sensible qualities in the observer's minds (Alexander 1985, Lowe 2005, McGinn 1983). These sensations he divided into primary qualities, which are "utterly inseparable" from the external objects that are their source—their fundamental (mind-independent) qualities (such as space-occupancy attributes); and secondary qualities, which are "nothing in the objects themselves but powers to produce various sensations in us by their primary qualities"—their sensual (mind-dependent) qualities (such as colors, tastes, touches, smells and sounds) (Locke [1690] 2004: Bk. 2, Ch. 1, Sect. 19). The second kind are the internal sensations, which can be termed reflection and which are responsible for the ideas—"whatever is the object of the understanding when a man [sic] thinks" (Locke [1690] 2004: Bk. 2, Ch. 1, Sect. 19)—produced as a result of sensation data. In a similar manner, ideas are subdivided into simple and complex, with the latter being compounds of a simple notion that cannot be reduced further, for instance, the idea of a color. Furthermore, an idea is understood as representing an epistemological relationship between two entities (the representative theory of perception[96]): the idea that the knower has of an object and the object itself (Shand 2002: 111–13). In this relationship, "all men are liable to error, and most men are, in many points, by passion or interest, under temptation to it" (Locke [1690] 2004: Bk. 4, Ch. 20, Sect. 17).

Berkeley ([1710] 1962) rejected the Humean notion of primary and secondary qualities in external objects and maintained that there is nothing but mind-dependent qualities, which makes ideas rather than physical matter that are the

95 As Locke ([1690] 2004: II, 1, S. 19) expressed it: "Let us then suppose the mind to be, as we say, white paper void of all characters, without any ideas. How comes it to be furnished? Whence comes it by that vast store which the busy and boundless fancy of man has painted on it with an almost endless variety? Whence has it all the materials of reason and knowledge? To this I answer, in one word, from experience." Helvétius in *De l'Esprit* (1758) argued the extreme position: complete environmental determinism. Evolutionary psychologists argue, of course, that the human mind could never be blank as if has been forged over time by the processes of Darwinian natural selection (see Pinker 2002)

96 "According to the representative theory of perception, we spend our conscious lives as if we are inside a movie theater. We can see pictures of the real world on the screen of the movie theatre, but we can never go beyond the inside of the movie theatre to see the real world itself, because the movie theatre is entirely in our mind" (Searle 2004: 185, but see also 186–89).

constituents of reality (metaphysical idealism) and that all ideas, as first-person mental thoughts, are of a subjective nature, hence the Berkeleyan proposition *esse est percipi*—to be is to be perceived (metaphysical subjectivism[97]). Thus, he observes that "they are neither finite quantities, nor quantities infinitely small, nor yet nothing. May we not call them the ghosts of departed quantities?" (Berkeley [1734] 2004: S. 35). So, Berkeley was committed to the notion that people's intelligible thought must refer to what they have comprehended through their personal experience; consciousness is thus prior to existence. This led him to conclude (1710 [1962]: 74), drawing upon Gorgias, the fifth century BC sophist (cited in Russell 1946: 98), that "if there were external bodies, it is impossible we should ever come to know it; and if there were not, we might have the very same reasons to think there were that we have now" (Warnock 1962). Whilst Berkeley neglected to address the designation of objects that are not perceived, his suppositions are comprehensive enough to permit a mild form of subjectivism to be part of his explanatory methodology.

Kant ([1781–87] 1956), in his search for the universal rules of understanding about the nature of experience, advance the view that the world of sensory experience is actively shaped by the mind, which categorizes and organizes all received sensory data in terms of space, time and causation, making the knowledge of objects the knowledge of appearances—things-as-they-are (phenomena), beyond which is the realm that is inaccessible to the senses, and thus only the thinkable—but unknowable—and metaphysically speculative, things-in-themselves (noumena).[98]

Early empiricism grounded causal explanation in the sensory perception of incorrigible empirical observation, whereby the world itself provides stimuli that are directly open to human sensory perception and do not require a pre-existent theoretical frame of reference. Evolving from this eighteenth century sense-datum theorizing, three fundamental suppositions are discernible, which, together, define contemporary empiricism (Scruton 1985: 123):

- that the only available basis of knowledge is facts grounded in sensory experience, but they are unable to generate further necessary truths, as

[97] This is "the view that the knowing subject creates its objects by an act of consciousness, essentially that existence finds its source in a form of consciousness" (Thorn 2001).

[98] Bradley's (1893) neo-Kantian distinction was between mind-constituted appearances (where objects with properties stand in causal relations in time and space), which he saw as incoherent and illusory, and reality (akin to Hegel's Absolute), which he saw as a single Cosmic Experience.

they can only establish what is known to be true and, by implication, what is not true; and

- that there cannot be *a priori* proof for any matter of fact, as knowledge is contingent upon sensory experience,[99] which means that the principle of induction is the only source of a factual proposition; and
- that propositions advanced after empirical enquiry are only true by virtue of their inherent ideas, which means that reason is nothing but the relationship between different notions.

As Hollis (1994: 45–6) remarks about empiricism:

> Its plausible starting point is that the world exists independently of us, that perception gives knowledge of some particular items of its furniture and that there is no way of knowing independently of experience what else it contains.

This epistemology is grounded in the principles of materialism (or physicalism); essentialism (whereby, for any specific kind of material object or phenomenon there is a set of characteristics or properties that any such object or phenomenon of that specific kind must have)[100] (see Hallett. 1991); and reductionism (whereby, complex material objects or phenomena can be explained by reference to, or as a consequence of, less complex material objects or phenomena). Thus, only human behavior, as opposed to human intention, can be the subject of empirical observation, as mental states or processes cannot be observed, and thus cannot be distinguished from, or made independent of, bodily material processes.

Empiricism contends that genuine knowledge rests on the Humean principle of induction (Hollis 1994: 45), "which seeks to reach principles inductively from observations of particular facts" (Russell 1946: 58). It offers causal pronouncements following the empirical demonstration of constant conjunction, or regular correlation. Systematic knowledge, then, is composed of

---

99 Russell [1912) conceived objects as logical constructions inferred from sense-data (inferential realism): "[T]he real table, if there is one, is not the same as what we immediately experience by sight or touch or hearing. The real table, if there is one, is not immediately known to us at all, but must be an inference from what is immediately known" (p. 46).

100 Fuss (1989: x—xii) argues that essentialism is most commonly understood as a belief in the real, true essence of things, the invariable and fixed properties which define the 'whatness' of a given entity ... Importantly, essentialism is typically defined in opposition to difference. ... The opposition is a helpful one in that it reminds us that a complex system of cultural, social, psychical, and historical differences, and not a set of pre-existent human essences, position and constitute the subject. However, the binary articulation of essentialism and difference can also be restrictive, even obfuscating, in that it allows us to ignore or deny the differences within essentialism.

generalizations based on observed regularities that enable prediction, and serve as contingent explanations based on the probability that future correlations between cause and effect would reflect the patterns observed in previous instances. Thus, many theories are labelled as laws that cannot be sustained by the epistemological limitations of the inductive inference from which they derive, let alone the apparent contingent nature of the universe proposed by Heisenberg uncertainty principle[101] (Rae 1986: 53–62). Laws, then, are merely theories with an unblemished predictive history: "beyond the constant conjunction of similar objects, and the consequent inference from one to the other, we have no notion of any necessity or connexion (Hume [1777] 1902: 82). Thus, theories provide as-if explanations of the world that may be true in so far as they are capable of exact prediction, but contingent in so far as they are ultimately unprovable (Hollis 1994: 59). As Gribbin (2005: 156) remarks: "Note that a theory can never be proved right. The best that can ever be said is that it has passed all the tests applied so far."

Central to early empiricist epistemology was the distinction between what Hume ([1777] 1902: Sect. 4, Part I) termed "matters of fact" and "relations of ideas," which reflects the Kantian distinction between synthetic and analytic knowledge. Thus, empiricist epistemology confronts a twin dilemma. It is unable to judge the truth or falsehood of analytical statements that are not grounded in observation, although such statements may offer a profound and strong demonstration of cause and effect, of causal explanation, and of prediction. With respect to synthetic statements derived by inductive inference, empiricism can offer reasonably reliable predictions, but only a weak and contingent correlation of cause and effect, which means it cannot identify unambiguous causal relationships (Williams and May 1996: 25). These uncertainties and ambiguities were captured by Newton's own admission (cited in Greene 1999: 57) that whilst he had identified the regular effects of gravity, he could not explain gravity itself:

> It is inconceivable that inanimate brute matter, should, without the mediation of something else, which is not material, operate upon and affect other matter without mutual contact. That Gravity should be innate, inherent and essential to matter so that one body may act upon another at a distance thro' a vacuum without the mediation of anything else, by and through which their action and force may be conveyed, from one to another, is to me so great an absurdity that I believe no Man who has in philosophical matters a competent faculty of thinking can ever fall into it. Gravity must be caused by an agent acting constantly

[101] This holds that it is impossible to know both the exact position and the exact velocity of an object at the same time (Cassidy 1991: 226ff).

according to certain laws; but whether this agent be material or nonmaterial, I have left to the consideration of my readers.

Epistemological Positions

Positivism

This emphasizes, in the tradition of Comte, Condorcet, Mill, Spenser and Taine, that genuine knowledge can be produced by reference to material evidence derive by means of observation and experimentation, comprehended within the bounds of science. It was originally associated with the empiricist principle of induction (Comte [1830–42] 1896, Condorcet [1795] 1955), but more recently it has come to embraced hypothetico-deductivism (empirically testing theory-grounded hypothesized deductions) and the inductive-hypothetico-deductive spiral or research wheel (empirically testing observation-grounded hypothesized deductions) (Cattell 1965, Friedman 1955, Lipsey and Chrystal [1953] 1995, Nesselroade and Cattell 1988, Wallace 1969, 1971). It encourages the use of statistical analysis to identify patterns in the observable behaviors of individuals and groups of individuals.[102] Under strict positivism, however, the explanatory burden must rest on the individual-level characteristics statistically associated with various forms of group behavior, and not on any unobservable processes related to the interaction of individuals within groups, such processes being excluded *a priori* by the empiricist epistemology of this methodology. It rejects unobservable processes as unknowable.

Verificationism

This stresses that the truth value of a knowledge claim is established by reference to supporting (confirming) empirical evidence (Hume [1748] 1975, Locke [1690] 2004, Quine 1951). This hypothetico-deductive model essentially commences with observation, and proceeds through deductive logic to formulate analytic assumptions that provide verifiable explanatory propositions the truthfulness of which can be tested using empirical evidence. It thus makes use of theory to hypothesize causal explanations, which, if they are consistent with observed outcomes, can demonstrate very high rates of successful prediction (Hempel 1966, Lipsey and Chrystal [1953] 1995).

---

102 Mills ([1959] 1970) took issue with what he called abstract empiricism in sociological research, arguing that numerical data needs theoretical and historical contextualization to give it sociological meaning (see also Bannister 1987).

Verificationism does not claim that the theoretical causal explanations derived from verified hypotheses have the status of confirmed knowledge claims. However, despite the pragmatic appeal of the hypothetical-deductive model, it remains an attempt to overcome the epistemological barriers to empirical explanation. The epistemological status of theory within the positivist tradition rests on the assumption that social knowledge can be attained through the techniques applicable to the physical sciences. However, the use of theory to manage the problem of explanation identified in naturalist epistemology has been subject to particular criticisms. These various criticisms, and associated developments, are well represented by the claims of the logical positivists for incorrigible verification as the only basis for genuine knowledge and Popper's (1935/1959) 2000) attack on the notion of pre-theoretical observations.

Logical Positivism

This stresses, in the tradition of Ayer, Carnap, and Schlick, that propositions are only meaningful to the extent that they can be empirically verified by means of observation and testing. It brings into focus the relationships between the constituent elements of a complex system of thought, and provides a mechanism by which the correlations between cause and effect offered by induction can be translated into a coherent, if unproven or unprovable, causal explanation. In its purest form, logical positivism (alternatively, logical empiricism or neopositivism) emerged as a response to the significant influence of Romanticism[103] on nineteenth century German philosophy of science. It was a school of thought, pursued during the early part of the twentieth century in the work of the Vienna Circle of philosophers, mathematicians and natural scientists, which aimed to connect positivism with empiricism (Frank 1949). Most particularly, it was concerned to overcome the rigid division between the physical or natural sciences (*geisteswissenschaften*) and the social or cultural sciences (*kulturwissenschaften*). Whilst the most vociferous criticisms of the logical

---

103 This was an eclectic pan-European movement in the arts and philosophy that began in Germany and England in the 1770s. It is characterized by its reaction against the age of reason with its emphasis on imagination, feelings, and intuitions (Abrams 1971, see also Higgins and Solomon 1993). It featured the philosophy of Hegel, Schelling, Schlegel, von Hardenberg, and Schleiermacher. It rebelled against the "barren rationalism of John Locke and the 'Age of Reason', partly ... to discover some principles of unity (or 'Oneness'), some common hidden truth perceived, cherished and guarded by ... representatives of the Hermeneutic tradition through the ages" (Newsome 1997: 178–79). It argued that the creative arts and the wisdom of the great religions could act as an inspiration to free people's subjective feelings and so inspire a vision of idyllic pre-industrial communities bound together in a union of blood and soil. Its emphasis was, thus, on an organic concept of nature (Silz 1929) and "upon mind as opposed to matter" (Russell 1946: 730).

positivists were directed against the hermeneutic epistemology of Dilthey and Heidegger, they also questioned the hypothetico-deductive model of the emergent verificationist form of positivism. The logical positivists contended that the problem of inductive inference, notably its incapacity to identify causal relationships, denied any epistemological legitimacy to the unverifiable theoretical statements that served as probabilistic guides to explanation. Rooted in radical empiricism[104] (phenomenalism[105]), they restricted knowledge claims to the analytic propositions of mathematics and the incorrigible evidence of sense experience (Lewis 1946).

Logical positivism sought to manage the distinctions, ambiguities and dilemmas posed by analytic and synthetic propositions, deductive and inductive inference, explanation and prediction through theory. Quite simply, deductive logic and inductive inference provide a mechanism by which the correlations between cause and effect offered by induction can be translated into a coherent, if unproven or unprovable, explanation (Ayer 1959). Its essential epistemological objectives are twofold: to establish a very clear demarcation between observation statements and theory statements; and to expunge from any enquiry process unverifiable theoretical explanations, particularly those based on the assumed operation of unobservable processes or phenomena (Carnap [1928] 1969: 108–9). This task was to be carried out by "their making the impossibility of metaphysics depends not upon the nature of what could be known but upon the nature of what could be said" (Ayer 1959: 11): if a statement cannot be verified it is meaningless. As Ayer ([1936] 1975: 28) remarked:

> The criterion which we use to test the genuineness of apparent statements of fact is the criterion of verifiability. We say that a sentence is factually significant to any person, if, and only if, he [sic] knows how to verify the proposition which it purports to express—that is, if he knows what observations would lead him, under certain conditions, to accept the proposition as being true or reject it as being false.

Hence, the precise distinction between the analytic and the synthetic resolves the tension within Hume's philosophy, which regards *a priori* propositions as matters of fact and the stuff of real existence. So, logical positivists can designate

---

104 "To be radical, empiricism must neither admit into its constructions any element that is not directly experienced, nor exclude from them any element that is directly experienced" (James 1912).

105 This postulates that knowledge claims about the physical world can be reduced to claims about possible sensory perceptions of it (Lewis 1946).

as trivial Hume's statement that "it is not contrary to reason to prefer the destruction of the whole world to the scratching of my finger" ([1739] 2004: Bk. 2, Pt. 3). Having established a separation between analytic and synthetic propositions, logical positivism, in attempting to offer a general set of methodological rules that would be the same for natural and social sciences, found, axiomatically, that "all metaphysical, ethical and theological doctrines are meaningless. This conclusion was inevitable, not because of any defect of logical thought, but because these strands of thought were unverifiable" (Scruton 1984: 278).

Ayer's ([1936] 1975) verification principle holds that a knowledge claim (proposition or statement) is meaningless either if it is not true by definition or if, in principle, its truth value cannot be empirically established, which requires all the evidence needed to establish beyond doubt its truth value to be available—his strong sense of empirical verifiability. This has its origins in the thinking of Wittgenstein, and lead to the necessity of distinguishing between observational and theoretical non-analytic statements. To resolve this dilemma, Ayer (1959) proposed limiting the concept of verification to verification in principle and weak or probabilistic verification, which requires only that some evidence be available to determine contingently a knowledge claim's truth value—his weak sense of empirical verifiability. This avoids both the trap of denying the meaningful premises in empirical propositions, which cannot be verified due to the existing limits of experience and the danger of conclusive verification or falsification when observation can only reach a conclusion that is more or less probable. So, for Ayer, thinking logically takes him to the conclusion that "all empirical observations are hypotheses because there is no way of absolutely confirming or refuting such propositions" (Shand 2002: 248). However, this prescriptive rule returns logical positivism to the contradiction that is central to the uncertainties of induction: "if an induction is worth making, it may be wrong" (Russell 1927: 83). Whilst knowledge is recognized as a causal explanation of observations that lead to empirical laws stating universal truths, nevertheless as these generalizations are only ratified through a positive experience how can their truth be guaranteed? (Scruton 1984: 126).

Logical positivists, thus, link knowledge to meaning and claim that only empirically verified statements have epistemological meaning (Carnap [1928] 1969). The logic of this position can be summarized as follows: if meaning is derived from knowledge, and knowledge from verification, then statements that cannot be verified, cannot be considered knowledge, and, therefore, cannot have any meaning epistemologically (Ayer [1936] 1975). This attempt to restrict the foundations of knowledge to hypotheses verified by observation alone, forced the logical positivists to abandon causal explanation. Thus, "denying not only that we could identify any form of natural necessity in the world but that, in principle, we could never come to know the real world" (Williams and May 1996: 27). The implication of this extreme empiricism is to require the abandonment of virtually the entire knowledge base of the physical, human and social sciences. This is because the predictive power of science rests not on the verified hypotheses grounded in theory, but on the causal relations imputed from the verification of these constitutive hypotheses. Further, the theories constructed to explain causal relationships—the source of the predictive power of empirical knowledge—are not merely rendered epistemologically curious (already accepted by Newton himself), but meaningless. Clearly, the observed capacity of theory to provide consistent prediction made this position untenable. Despite the heroic failure of logical positivism, it inspired a key development in naturalist epistemology: the recognition by Popper (Ackermann 1976: 43–64) of the theoretical nature of observation.

Falsificationism

This stresses that only a knowledge claim that can, in principle, be falsified (disproved) can, in principle, be true, and that the truth value of a knowledge claims is established by the absence of disproving empirical evidence (Popper ([1935/1959] 2000, 1979). Popper was concerned to refute what he considered the unfalsifiable contentions of self-referential systems of thought (such as Marxism and Freudianism) and the myriad collection of authoritarian political ideologies. He, therefore, shared the logical positivists' desire to find a methodological defense against unsubstantiated causal explanations of reality. However, his project required the possibility of truth-like explanation, and forced his adoption of a strongly realist position (Stokes 1998: 99–105).

Popper's falsificationalism argued for a deductive procedure under which the consistency of the proposed theoretical system must first be established before, as a second stage, its analytical and synthetic elements, can be distinguished. Then, the new theory can be compared to other theories, so as to ensure that it advances existing knowledge, before, as the final element in Popper's, the new theory is rigorously tested. As it can explain all the content of the existing theory, if it survives attempts to falsify it can be adopted as highly corroborated. However, this process does not result in the discovery of the truth, rather that the best unfalsified theory has been chosen. Therefore, Popper acknowledged, even though he is a metaphysical realist, that theories can only be tested in the idiom of current critical awareness of reality (Popper [1935/1959] 2000, 1979).

Although realism is an essential pre-requisite for the denial of particular claims to knowledge, Popper has still to confront the problem of inductive inference and the uncertainties of epistemology ([1935/1959] 2000: 111):

> The empirical basis of objective science has thus nothing 'absolute' about it. Science does not rest upon solid bedrock. The structure of its theories rises, as it were, above the swamp. It is like a building erected on piles. The piles are driven down from above into the swamp, but not down to any natural or 'given' base; and if we stop driving the piles deeper, it is not because we have reached firm ground. We simply stop when we are satisfied that the piles are firm enough to carry the structure, at least for the time being.

Fallibilism went further than the logical positivism in addressing these epistemological uncertainties. It holds that all knowledge claims are vulnerable during their unknowable provisional stage prior to certitude being established, which makes knowledge contingent and provisional. Not only did Popper deny the certainty of inductive inference, he also challenged the very observation statements it placed at the heart of genuine knowledge: "the belief that we can start with pure observation alone, without anything in the nature of a theory is absurd" (Popper [1962] 1969: 35). The core of his epistemological position is that human sensory perception, and therefore observation, is not only irredeemably theory-laden, but also essentially conjecturalist. As Ackerman (1976: 44) points out:

> On this view there is no immediate experience, as idealists hold; the feeling that we have some kind of direct perception is due to the facility given by our practised decoding of sensory information, as well as by innate genetically determined skills which have been honed by the process of evolutionary development. ... The mind frequently looks for clues to support *a priori* conjectures derived from evolutionary development and incorporated into hereditary transmission. The mind does not simply accumulate and then inductively test sense experiences.

In other words, sensory perceptions are conditioned by cultural and linguistic education. People possess a neurological tendency to extrapolate from these preconditions of experience and to search for expected patterns of sensory perception. Thus, the gamekeeper sees a dozen species of mallard, whereas the child sees 'cuddly ducks.' What people see is a function of what they expect to see: observation is shaped by expectation of phenomena based on previous knowledge and reflection. These theoretical preconceptions are ubiquitous and the very act of observation is constrained by the conjectural possibilities shaped by people's existing body of knowledge. The notion of incorrigible observation, then, appears as naïve. This has implications for the hypothetico-deductive model, as well as for logical positivism, because it makes observation itself a complex process of theoretical interpretation. The theoretical preconceptions drawn from extant knowledge—explanatory theories—can be used not only to devise meaningful tests, but also to define what constitute empirical corroboration. This process of corroboration is based on conjectures about the relationship of new sense data to existing structures of causal explanation. The result of these insights is to invert the propositions of the logical positivists: if meaning depends on knowledge, and knowledge depends on corroboration, and corroboration depends on theory, then meaning depends on theory. Thus, the pessimism of the logical positivists becomes fallibilism under Popper (Stokes 1998: 42).

Ultimately, then, Popper claimed that the process of causal explanation rests on the intersubjective agreement of those engaged in the causal-explanation enquiry as to what constitutes a definitive test of any hypothesis (Burke 1983: 64). Causal explanation—the explanandum—must be a logical consequence of its explanatory variables—the explicans—and falsifiable propositions derived from the logical relationship between the two must be posed (Ackermann 1976: 18). It is this requirement for clear statements of falsifiability that demarcates scientific and non-scientific knowledge: only non-falsified, but falsifiable, statements can be considered scientific knowledge.

As a consequence, knowledge proceeds through an iterative process of conjecture by which theories can only be fully falsified deductively, in the sense that they depend on the identification of deductively crucial observations that would be deemed to demonstrate the logical incoherence of particular clusters of theoretical contention. Falsification is, thus, not a wholly empirical process, but one that rests on methodological rules about the type of observation that should render a hypothesis null. Knowledge, therefore, is defined in terms of the capacity to determine the categories of falsification. As Ackermann (1976:18) argues:

> Falsifiability is a logical notion: a sentence or statement is falsifiable if it is incompatible with some clearly defined basic statements representing possible observations. ... Falsification is actually deciding that a falsifiable sentence is false—and this will depend on methodological rules which we adopt and which set out the decisions to be made as to whether a sentence is falsified given that certain observations are made.

The Popperian epistemological legacy is complex. First, he demonstrated the theoretical nature of observation, and the social and psychological dimensions of scientific enquiry. Second, he placed hypothetico-deductive model firmly within the realist framework of naturalism. However, his realism was based on the recognition of the immutability of epistemological uncertainty, which demands a suspension of judgment on unfalsifiable knowledge claims. This principle of verisimilitude drove him to a strict methodological falsificationism that precluded not only the final confirmation of theory, but also the *a posteriori* evaluation of theory, whereby a single instance of methodological falsification forced the rejection of the conjectured causal explanation. Ultimately, even methodological falsification falls subject to the logic of induction, since the demonstration of past falsifiability, however sophisticated the methodology, can only imply future falsification through inductive inference (Burke 1983: 59). In other words, the very epistemological uncertainties that inspired Popper's rigorous methodological falsification undermined the methodological solution he offered for them.

Implications

Kant ([1781–87] 1956) maintained that *a posteriori* knowledge of objects is of importance but "is of only practical application, since it has not the slightest effect in enlarging theoretical knowledge of these objects as insight into their nature by pure reason" ([1781–87] 1956: 58). Thus, causal explanation through *a posteriori* knowledge is limited to immediate appearances resulting in Kant concluding that "the highest good is a synthesis of concepts" ([1781–87] 1956: 117). This led him to propose ([1781–87] 1956) the possibility of synthetic *a priori* knowledge (beliefs that are not verifiable by experience or true by definition but are known with certainty to be true, thereby constituting new knowledge). To this end he recommended self-reflection over the effects of both rationalism and empiricism "on common sense" to "avoid the error of a crude and unpracticed judgement" ([1781–87] 1956: 167). Nevertheless, this assertion still leaves the dilemma that analytical *a priori* propositions cannot be proven empirically and synthetic *a posteriori* propositions can always be denied without contradiction, thereby making Kant's attempt to create a method of ratio-empiricism through synergy inconclusive. Peirce (1877), however, advanced the epistemological fusion proposition a century later with his absolute belief that the best possible interpretation of reality comes from the product of individual cognitive processes being subjected to systematic and rigorous testing. Thus, the deductive reasoning processes that are pivotal to the generation of *a priori* knowledge are held by Peirce to owe their elaboration to *a posteriori* reasoning. Indeed, Peirce (1877: 8) went further: "what is more wholesome than any particular belief is integrity of belief, and that to avoid looking into the support of any belief from a fear that it may turn out rotten is quite as immoral as it is disadvantageous." Similarly, the design of empirical research is informed by the content of theories making an irrefutable argument for the interdependence of both modes of reasoning.

While both the deductive and the inductive forms of naturalism address the problem of causality in different ways (Popper [1935/1959] 2000), neither can identify unambiguous causal relationships, although naturalism is able to offer reasonably reliable predictions (Williams and May 1996).

In view of the deficiencies in both inductive inference and deductive logic, they may well be relegated to the function of suggesting scenarios that might make the people aware of how reality may be explored. Furthermore, freed from the belief that each approach offers the best available enquiry method, it becomes possible to envisage them as complementary explanatory frameworks that enable people to reach a pragmatic solution on issue of truth in relation to a specific social phenomena, thereby contributing to their understanding of the social world.

HERMENEUTICS

Hermeneutics assumes that the social world lack fixity and certainty because it grounds knowledge in a person's conscious perceptions (Brentano [1874] 1995): "the social world must be understood from within, rather than explained from without" (Hollis 1994: 16, see also Baert 1998, Giddens 1990, 1991). The evidence for determining the truth value of social knowledge claim is subjective[106]—"truth from a human perspective" (Wiggins 1991: 120, see also Luntley 1995)—in that a person interprets social phenomena to decide their meaning (Hollis 1994). Thus, of course, such genuine knowledge may not correspond to material reality (Bretano [1874] 1973, see also Scruton 1984: 255–57).

106 Freud ([1929] 1971), Knorr-Cetina (1981) Harding (1986; 1991) and Shepherd (1993) maintain that subjectivism extends beyond the recognition of the relevance of human feelings, beliefs and interests.

On Knowledge

The doctrine of subjectivism postulates that a knowledge claim is epistemologically subjective if the evidence for determining its truth value exists only in the human mind, derived from practice, language and discourse (Winch [1958] 1990).[107] Thus, knowledge is unique to an individual. The truth or falsehood of a knowledge claim is, therefore, established solely by reference to its personal beneficiality, to the individual testimony of others, to the consensus view of others, or to self-justifying common sense or received, or revealed wisdom, which involves a process of personal reflection and rumination that draws upon material and immaterial evidence, that takes place within a sociocultural and linguistic *milieu*, and that involves the use of reasoning (not only induction and deduction, but also abduction [108] and retroduction[109]) as well as intuition.

Hermeneutics embraces:

- antirealism, which holds that reality does not exist independently of the mind, and that the truthfulness of a knowledge claim depends upon the circumstances that would justify its assertion (its assertability-conditions) (Alston, 2002, Devitt 1984, Devitt and Sterelny 1987, Dummett 1963, Wright 1987);
- relativism, which holds "that there are no grounds for postulating or investigating a reality independent of the knower; that there is no ultimate

---

107 Miller and Fredericks (1994: 93–94) observe: "the genuine problem of indeterminacy for the human sciences does not lie at the level of debates concerning 'hermeneutic' vs 'scientific empirical' views of human action, but rather at the level of specific methodological techniques that ultimately are the constitutive elements for determining the existence (or lack of it) of indeterminant translations ..., we are not arguing that the definition of methodology as the application of specific techniques and procedures is sufficient to resolve indeterminacy in all situations, but only that it is a necessary condition both to establish its existence and to demonstrate possible ways of reducing it." This suggest, as King *et al.* (1994) argue, that qualitative interpretive research methods should conform to the logic of inductive inference. Examples of conforming methodologies are Cressey's (1953: 22) analytical induction, which, focuses on the systematic, sequential and exhaustive examination of an array of cases to provide generalizations; and Glasser and Strauss's (1967) grounded theory, which argues for the generation of theory inductively from a body of qualitative data.

108 This form of reasoning is a thought process by which a causal hypothesis is inferred from a body of evidence about a phenomenon that would, if correct, provide the best explanation for that evidence (inference to best explanation) (Lipton [1991] 2004). It, thus, identifies the best explanation for a phenomenon, given all the evidence under consideration (Kapitan' 1992).

109 This form of reasoning involves drawing causal inferences from a body of evidence related to one phenomenon, to explain the cause of another phenomenon (Edwards 1967). It is contingent upon observed concomitances, which may be merely coincidental.

truth and, therefore, no grounds for presuming that any one truth claim is 'better' than any other" (Nightingale and Cromby 1999: 228, see also Baghramian 2004);

- perspectivism, which holds that "the external world is interpreted through alternative systems of beliefs and concepts and that there is no means of establishing that one view is necessarily "any better than another" (Nightingale and Cromby 1999: 227);
- multiculturalation of meaning, which holds that there are a multiplicity of interpretation of meaning reflecting the diversity of cultural contexts (Gergen and Thatchenkey 1998);
- indexicality, which holds that any interpretation of words and concepts is dependant on their relation with other words and concepts, and on the context of their use (Forbes 1989);
- reflexivity, which holds that the act of being self-aware, reflective, and hence reflexive, about the ways a knowledge seeker's personal values, experiences, interests and beliefs have shaped the knowledge obtained (Bartlett and Suber 1987): "the connection between knowledge and social life" (Giddens 2001: 697); and
- narrative knowledge, which holds that knowledge can take the form of story-telling, perhaps involving legends and myths—little narratives[110]—which provide a "network of powerful symbols that suggest particular ways of interpreting the world" (Midgley 2003: 1) that shapes meaning and justify knowledge claims (Lyotard 1979, Tsoukas 1998).

Hermeneutics contends that knowledge is generated by acts of ideation (the product of transcendental acts in the perceiving mind of a person engaged in reflection and rumination, conditioned by his or her mental characteristics or states that give rise to personal temperaments, interests, tastes, feelings, interpretations and prejudices, and shaped by the prevalent sociocultural and linguistic *milieu*). It rests on intersubjectively shared symbols that allow for the sharing (reciprocity) of perspectives (Schutz [1932] 1967). However, this pre-acquaintance of the individual with the social is both active and contextually variable, which makes it dependant on the relationship between sensory perception, memory and communications. This connects thought to object, and requires acts of reflexive interpretation to ensure the appropriate contextualization

110 This stands in contradistinction to modernism's totalizing meta-narratives and grand theories (Mills [1959] 1970), which postmodernists assert have lost credibility (Harvey 1992, Lyotard 1979).

of meaning (Blumer 1969, Garfinkel [1967] 1984; Wittgenstein 1953). To Garfinkel, an individual make sense of what others say by reflecting on actual, ordinary activities (practical actions, practical circumstances, commonsense knowledge of social structures, and practical reasoning) (ethnomethodology). This enables that person to work out what to do, as distinct from what to think (contemplative or theoretical thinking) (Byron 2004). To Blumer, drawing upon Mead's (1934, 1938) proposition that self awareness arises through the process of role-taking (social behaviorism) (Cook 1977), an individual takes meaning about the social world—every day life—by making sense of what others say through symbolic communications, which involve the interaction of language, identity and societal values, achieved by means of interactive processes that underpin the construction, negotiation, presentation and affirmation of self (symbolic interactionalism). To Wittgenstein (1953), deriving meaning about the social world and making sense of what others say is the product of the complex of interwoven speech and action that are ordered in praxis in a way that makes sense to the participants (language games).

If the social world can only be understood subjectively then, by implication, one person's truth is just as valid as another's, and so each person can create reality in a metaphysical domain that is incapable of being addressed by the naturalist methods of enquiry. The dichotomy between truth and reality is deemed an irrelevance and problems of objectivity do not arise (Bunge 1996: 330), because facts flowing from naturalist methods do not contribute much to the understanding of the social world. In this scenario, as Kant ([1781–87] 1956, see also O'Neill 1989) reasoned, any ultimate reality cannot be known. This imposes restrictions on "the scope of human reason" (Callinicos 1999: 31).[111]

What, then, is knowable is relative—both across time and across individuals (epistemic relativism)—which means that people in different groups (societies) have very different approaches to reasoning and to belief confirmation and belief systems (social relativism) (Hollis and Lukes 1982, Stich 1990).

111 Berkeleyan notions of subjectivism, which relied on God as the source of ideas or sensations in the mind, were reinterpreted by Husserl, who sought to isolate pure consciousness by means of a methodology that excluded reflexive and speculative thought from descriptions of mental conditions (Husserl [1929] 1981). Subsequently, Sartre rejected both an objectivist and subjectivist philosophy in developing a position of human intentionality of consciousness (Sartre [1960] 1976).

Traditions

Moderate Subjectivism

This holds that what a person can know about the social world is dependent on his or her reflective perceptions, perhaps defined and interpreted by comparing and contrasting them with the perceptions held by others (Dilthey [1883] 1988, Schleirmacher [1805–10] 1977).

Radical Subjectivism

This holds that what a person can known about the social world is the product of his or her engagement in social interactions and discourses that continually constructed and reconstructed his or her perceptions of that world (Murphy 1980).

Epistemological Positions

Epistemological Hermeneutics

This stresses the divining of the meaning of individual subjectivity through comparison and contrast with the meaning of others' subjectivity, in the tradition of Schleiermacher and Dilthey. Modern hermeneutics originated with the work of Schleiermacher ([1799] 1988; see also Palmer 1969, Richardson 1998, Sorrentino 1992), which combined the Kantian search for universal rules of understanding of experience with Romanticism's recognition of the uniquely human consciousness (Ricoeur 1981: 46). Thus, he attempted to develop a general system of interpretation of human meaning derived from the methods of theological exegesis and classical philology. The duality of the hermeneutic task was reflected in Schleiermacher's distinction between grammatical interpretations (which are concerned with the language rules that define the range of meanings available to the individual) and psychological interpretations (which are based on the meanings construed by individual authors within a culture) (Ricoeur 1981: 47). Whilst Schleiermacher continued to espouse the universality of general hermeneutic methodology, the primary focus of divination and comparison related to the psychological dimension of meaning at the individual level. However, the subjectivity of the individual was not directly accessible, and could only be approached through the individual in a social setting: "we never directly grasp individuality, but grasp only its difference from others and ourselves" (Ricoeur 1981: 47). Thus, Schleiermacher's epistemology can be characterized as structured subjectivity. This universal methodology for the investigation of interpretation requires a recognition of objective (critical) grammatical or cultural structures that enables the divination of individual subjectivity, through comparison with the meanings commonly held by others within a given culture, which enables the investigator "to understand an author as well as and even better than he understands himself" (Ricoeur 1981: 46).

The early hermeneutic epistemology pioneered by Schleiermacher was developed by Dilthey (1910). He located the distinctiveness of the human sciences in "a primordial capacity to transpose oneself into the mental life of others," through language, such that "man [sic] is not radically alien to man because he offers signs of his own existence" (Ricoeur 1981: 49). It is this social dimension of human consciousness that allows the unique relationship between object and subject within the human and social sciences. Knowledge of others is possible because social existence produces forms of life—regularized human activities, expressions, emotions and prejudices that are mutually intelligible to the participants within a particular culture or society. Indeed, these patterns of communicable feelings and discernments, or structured acquisitions (*acquis*), are essential to the construction of meaningful social life; they constitute the bed-rock of cultural phenomena, such as literature. Thus, an individual gains self-knowledge through interaction with the forms of life that constitutes human culture. Dilthey claimed that the very possibility of individual self-knowledge rests on the capacity for self-interpretation: self-knowledge[112] derives from the iterative interrogation of meaning based on the manner in which the forms of life apparent in historical society are returned to the individual by others. Thus, individual self-interpretations (knowledge claims) are the product of historically structured signs and expressions that become collectively meaningful (genuine knowledge) through mutual recognition. These processes of mutual recognition constitute the objectifications of life, or history. However, objectifications are dynamic and creative, as well as durable over time. As Ricoeur (1981: 52) remarks:

> Acquired meanings, present values and distant goals constantly structure the dynamic of life, according to the three temporal dimensions of past, present and future. Man learns about himself only through his acts, through the exteriorization of his life and through the effects it produces on others. He comes to know himself only by the detour of understanding, which is, as always, an interpretation.

112 Nietzsche, by his own admission, had "an ungovernable distrust of the *possibility* of self-knowledge" ([1886] 1998: 170, emphasis in original).

Existentialism

Kierkegaard, considered by many to be the father of existentialism, had as his project to contradict the notion of totality or the progression of understanding that proceeds from the self to the entire human species and, finally, to the "absolute idea" (Wahl 1949: 3). Crucially, he grounded epistemology in the self-knowledge of human beings ([1846] 1941). In doing so, he followed in the footsteps of Schopenhauer in the metaphysical idealist tradition.

To Schopenhauer the world is a manifestation of will—"the world is my idea" (Schopenhauer [1818/1844] 1969: 1) and "no will: no idea, no world" (Schopenhauer [1851] 1970: 56)—his doctrine of the primacy of will (see also Young 2005). He saw Kant's phenomenal world as the appearance or expression of will, while Kant's noumenal world he saw as the world of will. This latter world is not, however, beyond a person's ken. Indeed, he argued that "a way from within stands open to us to [the] real inner nature of things" (Schopenhauer [1818/1844] 1969: 5), which involves reflecting on the inner experiences of acts of willing. Once a person realizes that his or her inner nature is will, them he or she

> will recognise that same will not only in those phenomena that are quite similar to his [sic] own, in men and animals, as their innermost nature, but continued reflection will lead him to recognise the force that shoots and vegetates in the plant, indeed the force by which the crystal is formed, the force that turns the magnet … all these he will recognise as different only in the phenomenon, but the same according to their inner nature (Schopenhauer [1818/1844] 1969: 46).

Hence, "my body is the phenomenal form of my will [how the will appears in the phenomenal world], my will is the noumenal form of my body [the will is the inner nature of the body]: my body is 'appearance'' [*natura naturata*], my will 'thing in itself' [*natura naturans*]" (Schopenhauer [1851] 1970: 56). Will is, thus, the real world—the life force or the will to exist (*wille*)—of which the intellect is the servant not master: what a person believes, then, to be real is the basis for reasoning. The real world is, thus, the self who has an idea. All knowledge is based on immediate personal experience: "Our existence has no foundation on which to rest except the transient present" (Schopenhauer [1851] 1970: 52); and "that which has been no longer is; it as little exists as does that which has never been. But everything that is in the next moment has been. Thus the most insignificant present has over the most significant past the advantage of actuality, which means that the former bears to the latter the relation of something to nothing" (Schopenhauer [1851] 1970: 51).

Knowledge, then, is embedded in the lived existence of subjectively aware human beings. It is grounded in the belief that the individual has a private self—a private inner world with mental processes that use a private language[113] capable of determining the truthfulness of an experience (for example, deciding that an object is, as a matter of fact, red) independently of the experience itself (seeing an object that generates the sense-data associated with the color red) (see Humphrey 2006; for a philosophical rebuttal see Wittgenstein 1953, see also Gazzaniga *et al.* 2002, Kripke 1982, Price 1932). It follows from this existential isolation of individual consciousness that knowledge cannot be truly shared, merely that the knowledge of one person may shape the experiences that inform knowledge formation by another. Thus, the world of persons must contain a multitude of subjective truths grounded in first-person mental discernments, which render the notion of objective truth paradoxical, and thereby problematic (Warnock 1970: 8–9). As Kierkegaard [1846] 1941: 185) explained:

> When subjectivity, inwardness, is the truth, the truth becomes objectively a paradox; and the fact that the truth is objectively a paradox shows in its turn that subjectivity is the truth. For the objective situation (of entertaining a paradoxical thought) is repellent, and the expression for the objective repulsion constitutes the tension and the measure of the corresponding inwardness. The paradoxical character of the truth is its objective uncertainty.

The subjective constitution of knowledge has three key implications for objective knowledge. It must be illusory and science a myth, being merely the domination of another's knowledge, which must be inauthentic because it is externally generated. It must, therefore, as a proposition, be viewed as essentially political and, antithetical to genuine freedom.[114] It can, as a chimera, provide no objective basis for moral choice.

These consequences of subjective knowledge shape the nature of the human condition and, thereby, the context of knowledge acquisition. This existentialist imperative shapes epistemology: no clear distinction can be made between evaluation and description: "perceptions are altogether permeated with valuations

---

113 "Thought, says Plato, is a silent speech of the soul with itself" (Peirce 1984: 172).

114 To existentialists, such freedom is the freedom to search for one's self-identity, to leave behind persistent self-delusions (preferring commitment to uncertainty, fiction to doubt, assent to denial, and passing judgments to doing justice), rooted in bad faith; and to decide one's own fate, and so be able to determine one's own destiny, for which personal responsibility is accepted. This transcends both the classical understanding of freedom (being able to live an objectively desirable life) and the libertarian understanding of freedom (being free from the control, interference or exploitation of others).

(useful or harmful, hence acceptable or unacceptable)" (Nietzsche [1895] 1967: 78). Kierkegaard ([1845] 1940) notes the danger of the feeling of dread—the fear of nothingness—that derives from existential isolation can lead to the denial of both reality and meaning (see also Sartre [1943] 1957). Nietzsche sought to explain the myth of objectivity in terms of the essential human need to dominate the social and physical environment: "our cognitive apparatus is an abstracting and falsifying mechanism directed not toward knowledge, but toward mastery and possession" (Nietzsche [1895] 1967: 120). Heidegger saw the task of analyzing the problem of self-knowledge arising from the self in the everyday world being seen as an entity unconscious of its own existence. Thus he argued that "all conventional, objectifying representations of a capsule-like psyche, subject, person, ego or consciousness in psychology and psychopathology must be abandoned in favor of an entirely different understanding. The new view of the basic constitution of the human being may be called *dasein* or being-in-the-world" (Heidegger [1927] 1996: 47). This he defined as what it is that each person is, which is product of his or her factuality (the past through which his or her present is constituted), existentiality (his or her sense of freedom about the future) and fallenness (his or her capacity to focus on the mundane present moment by ignoring both the past and the future). To Heidegger, self knowledge required the recognition of past determinants, the acknowledgement of present concerns, and an alertness to future possibilities.

Sartre's conviction was that people must create their own meaning in what he saw as a meaningless world. His commitment was to the domain of human existence—its essences or intellectual constructs—the analysis of which he premised on an epistemological approach that begins with a detailed ontological analysis of Being. The initial task for this enquiry is to draw a distinction between what denotes the reality of the familiar forms, which make up everyday sensory perceptions (such as furniture, buildings and people), and what denotes reality within the metaphysical domain. This latter, higher level of reality consists of three modes of existence: being-in-itself, which applies to the Being that has no consciousness of existence (non-human inert objects); being-for-itself, which is the type of existence that individual consciousness has that leads to the making of choices about values and meanings that arise from the constant movement of intentional awareness; and being-for-others (*le pour-autrui*), which involves the process of intersubjective relations between individuals that provide them with fundamental understandings about their world. Predominately, understanding reality within the metaphysical domain only comes after the reality of familiar forms is understood.

Sartre can be identified with the immediacy of stripping away both sentimental and objective speculations about reality. Thus, he propounded the belief that only a reality divested of its various descriptions is accessible. In this space, Being is indefinable, unknowable and unattainable, thereby making reality speculation misleading in any quest for genuine human engagement (Shand 2002: 230–31). Knowledge, then, is, ultimately, unique to the individual.

Phenomenology

This stresses, in the tradition of Brentano, Husserl, Heidegger, Merleau-Ponty, Schutz and Sartre (Hammond *et al.* 1991), that objects are objects of experience, akin to Kant's phenomena, which makes reality relative and subjective. Understanding, thus, necessitates an investigation of the relationship between the objective and subjective realms, by drawing on the process by which an individual conceives and interprets aspects of his or her experience of the world as distinct and meaningful, on the basis of his or her experience of it constituted in and by consciousness, which requires the analysis and explication of the structures of conscious experience. Phenomenology has come to embrace (Embree *et al.* 1996, Moran 2000, Thévenaz 1962)

- realistic phenomenology, which explores meaningfulness by understanding the structure of consciousness and intentionality[115], as it is brought into being by consciousness (Husserl and Merleau-Ponty);
- constitutive phenomenology, which explores meaningfulness by understanding how the immediate experience of objects is constituted in a person's consciousness (Husserl);
- existential phenomenology, which explores meaningfulness by searching the immediacy of lived experience—by observing and analyzing *daseim* (being-there) and *lebenswelt* (lifeworld)—for the basic presuppositions of knowledge (Heidegger, Levinas, Marcel, Merleau-Ponty and Sartre);
- social phenomenology, which explores meaningfulness about what others say—as individually constructed meaning—by utilizing meaning contexts that reflects patterns of subjective meaning acquired through intersubjective everyday experiences (Schutz);

[115] "Every mental phenomenon is characterized by what the Scholastics of the Middle Ages called the intentional (or mental) inexistence of an object, and what we might call, though not wholly unambiguously, reference to content, direction towards an object … Every mental phenomenon includes something as object within itself, although they [sic] do not do so in the same way. On presentation, something is presented, in judgement something is affirmed or denied, in love loved, in hate hated, in desire desired and so on" (Bretano [1874] 1995: 35).

- generative historicist phenomenology, which explores meaningfulness by understanding how meaning grounded in personal experience is generated in collective-experience processes (Husserl);
- genetic phenomenology, which explores meaningfulness by understanding the genesis of meanings grounded in a person's stream of experience (Husserl); and
- hermeneutic phenomenology, which explores meaningfulness on the premise that all forms of human awareness are interpretive, thereby requiring the exploration of the role of language, the nature of questioning, and the phenomenology of human conversation, and of the significance in human understanding of prejudice, historically, and tradition, thereby embracing myth, religion, art, and language (Heidegger, Gadamer, and Ricoeur).

Bretano's [1874] 1973) original and fundamental contribution was the proposition that knowledge is provided by conscious perceptions that are mediated by intentionality, as the human mind could only be understood from the viewpoint of the first person. Husserl, Bretano's pupil, developed phenomenology with the aim, similar to that of Descartes, of "establishing a unified certain foundation for all knowledge" (Shand, 2002: 218, see also Smith 2006). Initially, he pursued this goal by studying logic, which led him to reject positivist explanations, as they relied on the mechanical application of reason to deduce logical consequences. Instead of universal naturalistic analysis restricted to the appearance of phenomena, Husserl advocated focusing on the understanding of essences through conceptualization and self-reflection (Husserl [1929] 1981; see also Gordon 1991: 612).

Intentionality, as a distinguishing feature of human mental processes, defines some mental acts (such as hopes, aspirations and goals), but predominant states of emotion (such as happiness or anxiety), can only be accommodated if temporary states of mind—moods[116]—are regarded as the object of intention (Shand 2002: 220).[117] Arising from this theoretical framework, phenomenology has discovered its unit analysis to be a mental act (methodological solipsism) that is capable of

116 Thayer (1996: 3) defines this as "a background feeling that persists over time," which is ephemeral and elusive by nature, which has energy and tension dimensions, and which does not always have an identifiable cause.

117 "The terminological expression … for designating the basic character of being as consciousness, as consciousness of something, is intentionality. In the unreflective holding of some object or other in consciousness, we are turned or directed towards it: our 'intentio' goes out towards it" (Husserl [1931] 1960: 15).

revealing the essence of knowledge, which constitutes its datum (Scruton 1985: 258). Phenomenological inquiry, then, is concerned only with the human experience; the past experiences that influence the meaning taken from the external world. In this paradigm, the world is knowable by a person through meanings that describe the appearances of objects and, unless this realm is transcended, at this level he or she would also perceive certain and necessary truths. So, a person can participate in a world informed by sense data that can assume some degree of intersubjectivity through language, culture and a pattern of common sense that has evolved from the commonalities of social experience internalized as recipes for social actions.

The heart of phenomenology is located in its method of reduction. The eidetic reduction sees past—or through—the particularity of undifferentiated lived experience that gives rise to concreteness of meaning, toward the iconic universal—*eidos*. The idea of this phenomenological essence is not some immutable human nature, for that would be committing the fallacy of essentialism. Husserl ([1929] 1981) could support the Cartesian position by maintaining a separation between the intrinsic elements of a person's mental states from extraneous encumbrances. The presuppositions a person possesses concerning the designation of mental phenomena are to be bracketed off or suspended from his or her belief or judgment, so as to allow him or her to deliberate on pure phenomena. Such an enhanced reflective awareness, which is facilitated by his or her own intuitive intellectual vision, excludes existing theories and assumptions to achieve a phenomenological attitude that can comprehend the essence of the reduced objects of consciousness (Shand 2002).

The phenomenological method of bracketing contributes to an enhanced understanding about the way an individual may interact when involved in activities that are geared to achieve other people's objectives, and about how these background expectancies can produce practices that phenomenologists consider positivists mistakenly attribute to normative or rule-guided social actions. This attribute is the outcome from an approach that is *a priori* by nature, as essential meanings are apprehended by excluding, or making them prior to, all information from our habitualized layered consciousness. Even the individual ego[118] must be bracketed off and replaced by the transcendental ego, which "simply places an

118 In terms of the Freudian set of mind metaphors, the ego is a set of functions in the rational part of the mind that provide realistic direction for impulses by seeking to balance primitive short-term drives (the pleasure-seeking id) with long-term consequences (the monitoring and regulating superego) (Freud [1923] 1927, 1936, see also Cramer 1991, Freud [1936] 1948).

existentially independent reality under intelligible categories or concepts and so makes that reality an object for consciousness" (Shand 2002: 228).[119]

Husserl prioritization of the idea of essence, recognizable in his method of bracketing, makes phenomenology a branch of eidetic science, which is concerned with people's recollection and retention. He takes the stream of consciousness[120] to be chaotic and temporally naïve: "Indeed, when I immerse myself in my stream of consciousness, in my duration, I do not find any clearly differential experiences at all" (Schutz [1932] 1967: 133). Mental life presupposes an act of ideation, whereby the individual reflects on the passage of time and events, and identifies experiences that are discrete, and placed in the past, present or future (Husserl [1928] 1931: 140). Acts of ideation are constituted by the attentional activities of the ego, notably retention (whereby experience is captured within the stream of consciousness) and recollection or reproduction (whereby retention is constituted as meaningful memory) (Husserl, [1928] 1964: 51–52). The exact distinction between retention and recollection is provided by Husserl ([1928] 1964: 161):

> Retention itself is not an act of looking back which makes an object of the phase which has expired. Because I have the phase which has expired in hand, I live through the one actually present, take it—thanks to retention—'in addition to' and am directed to what is coming. ... But because I have this phase in hand, I can turn my regard toward it in a new act which—depending on whether the living experience which has expired is being generated in a new primal datum (therefore, is an impression), or whether, already completed, it moves as a whole 'into the past'—we call a reflection (immanent perception) or recollection.[121]

The pre-phenomenal objects of retention and recollection constitute multi-characteristic (polythetic) acts of discrete individual experience. These are synthesized by the reflective glance into single-characteristic (monothetic)

---

119 It is axiomatic that Husserl's transcendental ego cannot form part of existentialist philosophy, as the subjectivism within this doctrine of intentions suggests that objects can be moved into a passive and pure realm of consciousness, which in existentialist thought cannot exist.

120 "Consciousness ... does not appear to itself chopped up in bits. Such words as 'chain' or 'train' do not describe it fitly as it presents itself in the first instance. It is nothing jointed; it flows. A 'river' or a 'stream' are the metaphors by which it is most naturally described. In talking of it hereafter, let us call it the stream of thought, of consciousness, or of subjective life" (James 1890b).

121 This distinction is summarized by Schutz ([1932] 1967: 49):

> It is, therefore, by virtue of retention that the multiplicity of the running-off of duration is constituted: the present Now differs from the earlier Now if only because retention, as the being-still-conscious of the just-having-been, is carried out in a Now in whose constitution it partakes. On the other hand, the identity of the object and objective time itself is constituted in recollection (reproduction).

configurations of meaning, which make up a person's stock of knowledge, constituted as schemes of interpretation, or meaning-contexts; the taken for granted assumptions and meanings attached to experience (Schutz [1932] 1967: 75–77).

Knowledge is, thus, always indeterminate, tentative, and incomplete and always inclined to question assumptions by returning repeatedly to lived experience. It involves "the ordering of a lived experience within the total configuration of experience [through] a synthesis of recognition, [and the association of a lived experience with] an objectification already on hand within the store of experience" (Schutz [1932] 1967: 83). However, whilst knowledge is stratified through the continuing process of retention and recollection, immediate perceptions and interpretations reflect the current use made by the ego of objectifications, or meaning contexts, derived from past retention and recollection. Thus, "the meaning of a lived experience undergoes modifications depending on the particular kind of attention the ego gives to that lived experience ... the meaning of a lived experience is different depending on the moment from which the ego is observing it" (Schutz [1932] 1967: 73–74). Knowledge is not only unique to the individual, but unique to the individual at a specific point in time: it is, thus, both subjective and relative.

Phenomenology, by acknowledging the possibility of objective knowledge, accepts the objectivity of Kant's analytical knowledge: mathematics and semiotics offer unproblematic knowledge systems derived from the notion of non-contradiction: "A sign has an 'objective meaning' within its sign system when it can be intelligibly coordinated to what it designates within that system independently of whoever is using the sign or interpreting it" (Schutz [1932] 1967: 123). Crucially, however, phenomenology also proposes a synthetic objective knowledge based on the notions of reciprocity (Simmel [1908] 1950) and intersubjectivity. Indeed, the explication of objective knowledge represents a primary ambition of the phenomenological project, and involves the following argument: "Constituted as it is within the unique stream of consciousness of each individual, [intended meaning] is essentially inaccessible to every other individual" (Schutz [1932] 1967: 99). However, "the listener notices that the speaker is expressing certain subjective experiences of his [sic] and in that sense may be said to notice them; but he himself does not live through these experiences—his perception is 'external' rather than 'internal'" (Husserl [1928], cited in Schutz [1932] 1967: 10). The objective meaning of a statement in German can be established by any individual cognizant of the grammar and vocabulary of the German language, however the assumed consciousness of the speaker encourages the observer to seek the "intended meaning" of the statement itself:

what the speaker meant by the statement (Schutz [1932] 1967: 112). Whilst the observer cannot penetrate the exact meaning of another's statement, face-to-face conversation can allow the gap between objective and subjective meaning to be bridged with varying degrees of approximation. Simultaneous social relations increase the observer's capacity to grasp the meaning contexts indicated by the objective terminology offered by the speaker (Schutz [1932] 1967: 128), assisted by past experience of the speaker, appropriateness of response, bodily gestures and the apparent success or failure of clarification. Thus, the possibility of subjective knowledge depends on the observer's proximity to the speaker's complete field of expression. According to Schutz ([1932] 1967: 166):

> First of all I grasp the 'objective meaning' of your words, the meaning which they would have had, had they been spoken by you or anyone else. But second, of course, there is the subjective meaning, namely, what is going on in your mind as you speak. In order to get your subjective meaning, I must picture to myself your stream of consciousness as flowing side by side with my own. Within this picture I must interpret and construct your intentional Acts as you choose your words. To the extent that you and I can mutually experience this simultaneity, ... to that extent we can live in each other's subjective context's of meaning.

Thus, the spatial relationship—the horizon—between the observer and speaker determines the relationship between objective and subjective knowledge. Phenomenology distinguishes between consociates, contemporaries, and predecessors: the possibility of subjective knowledge essentially fades with the horizon, to be overtaken by either objective knowledge or objectifications, ideal-types derived from the life experience of the individual. Objective knowledge emerges as the *sine quo non* of epistemology: it is the only assured, though limited, basis for social knowledge. Subjective knowledge offers definitive understanding of social actions, but is only partially accessible through the approximation of simultaneity. The intended meanings of remote contemporaries and predecessors can only be approached through an analysis of the objective meaning of the cultural artifacts they produce, or through the application of schemes of interpretation or meaning contexts "already on hand within the store of experience" (Schutz [1932] 1967: 83). Thus, a person's taken-for-granted stock of knowledge, or natural attitude (Schutz [1932] 1967: 83), reflects patterns of subjective meaning acquired through interaction with consociates, which are then utilized to interpret the meaning contexts implied by the objective cultural artifacts offered by contemporaries and predecessors.

Linguistic Epistemology

Whilst the hermeneutic tradition generally recognized the epistemological salience of language, linguistic epistemology *per se* only emerged with the work of Ludwig Wittgenstein ([1922] 1961, 1953, [1956] 1978). Whereas phenomenology conceptualizes language as an objective mechanism for the approximate communication of subjective meaning (Berger and Luckmann 1966: 51), Wittgenstein reversed this epistemological logic and argued that the objective rules of language are prerequisite of knowledge itself: "That the world is my world shows itself in the fact that the limits of my language (of the only language I can understand) mean the limits of my world" (Wittgenstein, [1922] 1961: 5.62, but see Pinker [1994] 1995). Language gives pictures of the world and consists of pictures of reality. The limits of language are the limits of thought: "What can be said at all can be said clearly, and what we cannot talk about we must pass over in silence" (Wittgenstein [1922] 1961: iv). Furthermore, the linguistic rules that shape knowledge acquisition are intersubjective and, therefore, "the very existence of concepts depends on group-life" (Winch [1958] 1990: 44). These propositions imply that the natural attitude (Husserl [1931] 1960) is rooted in the objective reality of language rules.

Linguistic epistemology stresses the importance of learning the rules of language that govern the social meaning associated with any social action (Wittgenstein [1922] 1961). These language rules vary from culture-to-culture, and from time-to-time. They shape knowledge acquisition, because they are intersubjectively shared and rooted in a taken-for-granted stock of tacit knowledge. Whilst two or more individuals can undertake new activities, and agree new linguistic conventions, this merely indicates the group-dependency of language and meaning. Indeed, "speaking of language is part of an activity, or a form of life" (Wittgenstein 1953: 23; see also Garver 1994). A person understands what other do linguistically in everyday life—when, for instance, they give orders, ask a question, or translate from one language to another—as distinct and meaningful phenomena, because they satisfy certain definitional rules, which serve to constitute them in the context of a particular form of life.

The relationship between language and reality (Devitt and Sterelny [1987] 1998) is the focus of Wittgenstein's three major contributions to epistemology. His *Tractatus Logico-Philosophicus* (1922) builds on the logic of Frege ([1884] 1980) and Whitehead and Russell ([1910–13] 1925–27). It views ordinary language as ambiguous, due the multitude of objects associated with individual words, and the root of philosophical confusion. His logical atomism, which conceives the world as a collection of discrete atomistic factual propositions—simple, independent and irreducible constituents of meaning (the picture theory of meaning)—that required linguistic clarity, sought to establish an ideal logical syntax, whereby:

> In order to avoid these errors [caused by sentences in ordinary language having a misleading surface form], we must employ a symbolism which excludes them, by not applying the same sign in different symbols and by not applying signs in the same way which signify in different ways. A symbolism, that is to say, which obeys the rules of logical grammar—of logical syntax (Wittgenstein [1922] 1961: 3.325, see also Griffin 1964).

It, thus, utilized mathematical logic in the attempt to construct an ideal language able to overcome the ambiguities associated with ordinary language.

In contrast, the later Wittgenstein (1953, 1969) privileged ordinary language—thought is limited by language—and made the intelligibility of language rules the key both to meaning. —meaning of a word is grounded in its use in the language, which links it to behavior and context—and to epistemological certainty. Crucially, he argued that to grasp the meaning of the word "swan" is not to grasp the essence of "swanness," but rather to apply correctly the everyday definition of the term at a given cultural moment. The essence of the latter Wittgenstein is captured by his rejoinder to philosophy: "Don't think, but look!" (1953: 66). He explained language and its conceptions of meanings (Finch 1995: 57–58) as imperatives (rules, obligations and commands); as constructions (concepts, uses and science-mathematics); as customs (ceremonies, myths and rituals); as physiognomies (pictures, design and art-architecture); and as activities (such as commanding, questioning, recounting or chatting).

Language rules are considered to have acquired epistemological significance because, as Wittgenstein (1953: 119) states:

> The aim of philosophy is to give a correct description and thus to arrive at an accurate understanding of the world, and (2) such a description is not scientific in nature. ... Philosophy is a battle against the bewitchment of our intelligence by language.

The use of the word "rule" and the use of the word "same" are interwoven (as are the use of "proposition" and the use of the term "true") (Wittgenstein 1953: I, 225). Hence: "The rule can only seem to me to produce all its consequence in advance if I draw them as a matter of course. As much as it is a matter of course for me to call this colour 'blue'" (Wittgenstein 1953: I, 238).

Implications

The dilemma for hermeneutics is that the knowledge it generates is not only socioculturally specific and subject to severe relativism, but also dynamic and open to constant revision. The former makes explanation contingent on culture, whereas the latter makes prediction problematic. There is, therefore, no "best" or "most justified" mode of reasoning in the search for genuine knowledge (Davidson 1984, Goodman 1965, Hollis and Lukes 1982, Mackie 1977).

TRUTH AND THE SOCIAL WORLD: AN EPISTEMOLOGICAL PERSPECTIVE

The concept of truth is fundamental to people's social existence, as it determines what they can known and what they can learn about the social world in which they find themselves. Their social interactions require them to be able to determine the truthfulness of the knowledge claims that others assert to be true. However, beyond this expansive supposition, lies the uncomfortable realization that truth can be comfortably interpreted by those who have a predilection toward multifarious standards of truthfulness. Thus, social knowledge claims need to be treated as provisional and contingent, as argued by fallibilists (such as Peirce, Popper). This provides a foundation for consideration of how contending epistemological standpoints can acknowledge the fundamental legitimacy of alternative perspectives.

Following Peirce (1932a, 1932b, see also Mounce 1997: 42), a distinction must be made between truth (the condition that must be meet if a particular knowledge claim is to be accepted as true) and reality (everything, whether observable or not, that is accessible or understandable by any system of analysis). Within the human conceptualization of truth and reality, there are multiple methodologies that can be used to adjudicate on what constitutes genuine knowledge, which should not be confused with Feyerabend's (1975) contemporary assertion that the limitations of all methodologies only leads to the one rule "anything goes." The distinct explanation-focused naturalist epistemology—grounded in realism with its focus on objective truth-conditions—stands in contradistinction to understanding-focused hermeneutic epistemology—grounded in antirealism, with its focus on assertability-conditions. But they are not substitutes. The total separation of truth and reality would, as Williams and May (1996: 105) note, "open up the whole question of the relationship between values and scientific practice." The pragmatic alternative (Peirce 1932a, 1932b) is to adopt the position that individuals reach common meanings that constitute the truth, whilst also being part of reality and reality being part of them (Habermas 2003). Such a proposal avoids the paradox within relativism, or the idea that beliefs or judgments do not need to meet independent standards, by maintaining that, through the assiduous and continuous testing of theories, truth can gradually evolve toward reality. Thus, naturalist and hermeneutic epistemologies co-exist as the epistemological foundations upon which people describe, explain and understand their social domain in the world of persons.

Chapter 7

ONTOLOGY AND REALITY

Ontology[122] is the philosophical investigation of existence or being. The task of understanding ontological notions begins with the distinction between pure philosophical and applied scientific ontology. Pure philosophical ontology "is concerned with the meaning of the concept of being, with the question why there is something rather than nothing, and the modal ontological status of the actual world" (Jacquette 2002: 3–4). It is, thus, a foundational study that proceeds to the assertion of the existence of particular theoretical entities:

> Pure philosophical ontology, indispensable as groundwork, is only the first major step toward a complete fully integrated ontology. When we know what it means for something to exist, we can then proceed to the details of applied scientific ontology, defending the choice of a particular domain of existent entities (Dale 2002: xi)

Applied scientific ontology aims to determine the ontological questions and answers relevant to "specific areas of thought and discourse whose meanings require the positing of a particular choice of entities" (Jacquette 2002: 5). Ontology, thus, seeks to provide a consistent account of the world in its totality and of the status of the categories of phenomena that possess causal efficacy. It considers the veracity and reliability of explanations based on different notions of causality.

What has the power of producing a human action has long been the concern of philosophy (Hobbes [1642] 1949, [1651] 1996, Hume [1748] 1975, Kant

122 This is derived from the classical Greek *ontos* meaning "being" and *logos* meaning "reasoned speech."

[1788] 1906, see also Dennett 2004, Fischer 1989, 1994, Hasker 1999, Hospers 1966, Kane 1996, 2002a, Peters 1997, Searle 2001 2006, Slimansky 2002, Singer 2001, Strawson 1986, Wegner 2003, Wolf 1994). In the words of the twelfth-century Persian poet, Jalalu'ddin Rumi (1956: 77): "There is a disputation that will continue till Mankind is raised from the dead between the necessitarians and the partisans of free will." Free will is the proposition that a person is free to determine and control his or her own actions, because he or she has the capacity to perform actions consciously (knowingly and responsibly[123]) and voluntarily (unconstrained by the freedom-limiting punitive, oppressive, coercive, compulsive, manipulative or social conditioning factors over which he or she has no control) that are chosen from an array of alternative courses of action, which means that he or she "could have chosen or acted otherwise" (Kane 2002b: 5). This stands in contradistinction to determinism (Butterfield 1998), which seeks to explain social actions in terms of determining conditions over which the action-taker has little or no control. Such determining conditions can be bifurcated into those that are *external* to the action-taker, such as fate or destiny (logical fatalism), the mystical forces or God's will (divine determinism[124]), the stars (astrological determinism[125]), the environment in which the action is to take place

123 Pettit (2001: 12) considers that "to be fully fit to be held responsible for a certain choice is to be such that no matter what you do, you willfully deserve blame should the action be bad and fully deserve praise should the action be good. … And your action in a given case will be free so far as it materializes in a way that enables you to count as fully fit to be held responsible." Thus, to be held responsible for a choice of action, the action taker must have been aware of the alternatives courses of action at the time of making the decision, must have been capable of evaluating those options, and must not have been the victim of unwelcome duress (pp. 13–14).

124 This posits that a person's actions are determined by divine agency, a manifestation the divine nature of all-powerful God. Occasionalists (such as Ibn Muhammad al-Ghazali, La Forge and Malebranche) believe that God is the only true causal agent, one who is able to cause both bodily and mental states by exercising, on occasions, his necessary efficacious power (Fakhry 1958, Malebranche [1774–75] 1980, Nadler 1993, but see also Teresa and Kolodieichuk 2007). Spinoza's ([1677] 1985) belief in divine determinacy is grounded in the proposition that there is only one substance—God (theistic monism)—and thus a person's physical body and thoughts are simply aspects of the infinity of God, which means that his or her actions are a necessary manifestation of God, hence there is no room for free will, although a person may consider him or herself to have free will simply because he or she is conscious of his or her actions, and unaware of their causation by God.

125 This posits that a person's actions are determined by the motion and relative position of celestial bodies:

> One school of [classical astrological] thought (exemplified by Vettius Valens) (late second century A. D.), held that the lives of individuals are strictly destined by the agency of the heavenly bodies … [which] can infallibly forecast all details of each life (Inwood 2003: 341).

To this proposition, d'Ascoli (1487) added, according to Milman ([1855] 2006: 469), "the [determining] stars themselves were subject to the enchantment of malignant spirits."

(environmental determinism[126]), or the situation in which the action is to take place (situational determinism or situationalism[127]), economic processes and relations (economic determinism), the group beliefs, tendencies and practices that an action-taker adopts to become integrated into that group (social determinism), culturally specific cognitive structures expressed cultural acts and artifacts (cultural determinism), and thought- and behavior-shaping language the language used to shape the way an action-taker creates meaning about, and behaves in, the world (linguistic determinism)—or those that are *internal* to the action-taker—such as his or her psychological makeup (psychological determinism[128]), physiological or neurobiological makeup (physical, physiological or neurobiological determinism[129]) or heredity (hereditarianism[130]), which determines the genetics makeup (genetic determinism[131]). There are two strands of determinism. Hard determinism holds that consciously performed actions are subject to predetermination and thus have antecedently sufficient prior cause such that every event is the necessary outcome of its specific preceding causes, which are, in turn, the inevitable consequence of yet previous causes: "the occurrence of the determined event is *inevitable* or *necessary*, given the determining conditions" (Kane 2002b: 5, emphasis in original). This makes free will just an illusion. Soft determinism accepts, following the Humean conceptualization of causation, that "causation does not give rise to compulsion or constraint or indeed to any form of necessity" (Stroll 2006: 160), and thus it permits space for the causal capacity of free will. As Schopenhauer ([1839] 1999) epigrammed: "A man can surely do what he wills to do, but he cannot determine what he wills." This makes soft determinism compatible with free will (compatibilism) in that free will can be

---

126 This posits that a person's actions are determined by the reinforcement effects of environmental stimuli. Indeed, Watson ([1924] 1930) boasted that given a dozen healthy children he could mold them into an adult of his choice.

127 This posits that a person's actions are determined by the nature of the particular situation in which particular actions are to take place (Harré 1980, Mischel 1968, 1973).

128 This posits that a person's actions are determined by mental states or events that are the product of psychological laws (Berenson 1976: 116–17, Lucas 1970: 78–83), which means that he or she must always act in accordance with either their strongest desire (orectic psychological determinism) or their best reason (rational psychological determinism). Popper's (1945: 89) psychologically reductionist psychologism holds that "all laws of social life must be ultimately reducible to the psychological laws of 'human nature'."

129 This posits that a person's actions are determined by physiological (neurobiological) processes occurring in the brain (Lucas 1970: 84–89).

130 This posits that that a person's actions are determined by any human property that is capable of being inherited or genetically transmitted from one generation to another.

131 This posits that a person's actions are determined by his or her inherited genetic make-up, with particular genes being responsible for particular behaviors (Wilson 1976, 1978).

exercised in the absence of freedom-limiting conditions (constraints or impediments that prevent actions being taken) (classical compatiblism). Thus, free will is the freedom to act in whatever way a person is inclined and able to do in any situation, which means he or she could have chosen to act differently if so willed (Neilson 2002, Skinner 2002). To be able to have chosen to act differently in any situation, however, requires freedom of will, whereby a person is able to will whatever he or she wishes to will. This is compatible with determinism only on the presumption that what matters is that a person takes ownership of, or is committed to, the wills he or she has—regardless of the sources from which they were acquired—and is free to act accordingly (hierarchical motivation) (Frankfurt [1971] 2002). In contrast, incompatibilism hold that free will is incompatible with determinism, because, if determinism is true then as consequence a person is not *causa sui* and, thus, not *solely* responsible for the way he or she is—so he or she is not a genuinely free agent, which means that free-will either exists, because determinism is not true (libertarian incompatibilism), or it is an illusion, because determinism is true (hard determinism). Indeterminism posits that a person has free will because his or her actions are exempt from prior-event causality (libertarian free-will or metaphysical freedom), because, in the dualist tradition, his or her mental states either are not strictly materially determined (naturalistic libertarianism) or are totally exempt from material determination (supernatural libertarianism), which means actions are the result of personal desires, intentions and beliefs, without reference to any events, processes or states of affairs relating to the action-taker (agent-causation or immanent causation) (Chisholm 2002)—thereby making actions attributable to reasons or motives that explain but either do not cause those actions[132] (simple indeterministic libertarianism), or do not inevitably cause them[133] (event-causal libertarianism) (Kane 2002b, [2001] 2002c).

---

132 This construction of indeterminism avoids the need to explain how intentional mental states can cause physical actions (mental causation).

133 This construction of indeterminism is consistent with the proposition that reasons for action are its causes, albeit, not inevitably and thus only indeterminately.

Chapter 8

The Ontological Dichotomy: Structure and Agency

In the social sciences the ontological debate has focused on whether social actions can best be ascribed, in reductionist terms, to the internal agental dimension of social actions; or, in holist terms, to the external structural dimension of social actions. These contending ontological positions impose different methodological constraints on the explanation and understanding of the social world and the actions people take in it (Kincaid 1996).[134]

Agency

Agency posits that social actions can best be ascribed to an action-taker's self-determined set of hopes, aspirations and goals, which identifies the courses of action that he or she judges to be personally acceptable and required. The presumption is that the action-taker can self-determine these intentional mental states, because he or she is capable of individual self-rule[135] and individual

---

134 Hollis (1977) critically reviews the various metaphysical views of human nature—"models of man"—embedded in sociology, economics, and psychology, and identifies and addresses the challenge of articulating a "model of man" that can accommodates an autonomous self who can be the subject for empirical explanation.

135 This requires the action-taker to have deliberative and choice independence (that is, to be free from the interference of others in the determination of desires and choice prefereces); and to have self-rule capacity (that is, to have the ability to think rationally, to exercise self-control, and to be free from debilitating pathologies and self-deception) (Arneson 1991, Dworkin 1989, see also Berofsky 1995, Haworth 1986, Meyers 1989, Young 1986).

authenticity[136], albeit with the limits of his or her intrinsic properties[137]. In terms of an action-taker's social action choice, then, agentists would adhere to the tenets of free will. They would be incompatibilists in terms of the determining conditions external to the action-taker (such as, the environmental, situational, socio-cultural, economic and linguistic conditions), thereby giving those determining conditions no capacity to shape the content of action-taker's hopes, aspirations and goals and, thus, to influence the course of action he or she chooses to follow. They would, however, be compatibilists in terms of determining conditions internal to the individual (such as, psychological, physiological or hereditary conditions), thereby giving those determining conditions a constraining or enabling capacity to shape the content of action-taker's hopes, aspirations and goals, and, thus, a constraining or enabling capacity to influence the course of action he or she chooses to follow. As Mill expressed it ([1859] 1963, Vol. 8: 879): "human beings in society have no properties but those which are derived from, and which may be resolved into, the laws of the nature of individual men" (see also Bentham [1789] 1970: ch. I, sec. 4). This means that "individuals ... act more or less appropriately in the light of their dispositions and understanding of their situation" (Watkins 1968: 270). This reduces the causal status of a social phenomenon to an epiphenomenon: "a mere aggregate consequence of individual activities, incapable of acting back to influence individual people" (Archer 1995: 4).

On the Social World

Agency ontology is firmly grounded in ontological individualism, the proposition that whilst individuals exist, social wholes (collections of individuals, such as families, groups, organizations and societies) do not. It embraces nominalism (particulars are all that exist, making universals—features that are shared by many different particulars—merely ideas or concepts that have no independent existence[138]) (Armstrong 1978, 1989, 2000, Ockham [c1329] 1974);

136 This requires the action-taker to have substantive independence, to have procedural independence, and to be able to be critically self-reflective, which means having the capacity to reflect upon and endorse a set of desires (Benson 1987, Christman 1989, 1991, Frankfurt [1971] 2002, Haworth 1986, Stoljar 2000, Wolff 1970).

137 These can be properties associated with the body, which reflects its biological inheritance, or with first-person awareness, which is grounded memories of consciously experienced past personal experiences and an acquired sense-of-self.

138 Universals, nominalists argue, cannot be material, because the only feature that particulars have in common is that they are covered by the same term, therefore it is language, rather than

social atomism (discrete individuals are the constituents of social wholes, knowledge of which is limited to what is knowable about those individuals)[139] (Watkins 1957, Weissman 2000); and reductionism (all complex systems can be fully understood in terms of their components) (Charles and Lennon 1992, Ryan 1970).

Metaphysical Individualism

This holds that the existence of the social wholes is contingent on the social nature—the patterns of social relationships—of the individuals whose social actions come together to sustain their existence. Thus, a social whole is nothing more than a mereological sum—the aggregate of its members. Social wholes and phenomena can, thus, be reduced to the social actions of individuals.

Methodological Individualism

This[140] (Elster 1982, Hayek 1942, 1943, 1944, 1953, Watkins 1952, 1968, Weber ([1921] 1968, Mises [1949] 1996, [1962] 2006) holds that human social life is best, or most appropriately, understood by analysis at the microscopic level of the social actions of individuals who constitute the basic units of social wholes.[141] Thus, facts about the social wholes and social phenomena—social facts—can be completely explained or predicted, in a reductionist way, by the reference to the facts about its constituent members—their traits and intentions—essentially, their wishes, desires, beliefs, or will—that give rise to their social actions, which Parsons' (1937: 43–51) referred to as "the action frame of reference" in social-scientific explanation. This means that social phenomena can only be explained by showing how they result from social actions that are the product of the intentional mental states that motivate the action takers.[142] Indeed,

independent reality, that underlies perceived likeness: "a whole which has parts has no reality of its own, but is a mere word, the reality is in the parts" (Roscelin of Compiègn cited in Russell 1946: 457).

139 "The properties of the mass are dependent upon the attributes of its component parts" (Spencer [1851] 1995: 1).

140 The term methodological individualism was first used in English by Schumpeter (1908).

141 On this proposition Elster 1982: 463) commented: "To explain social institutions and social change is to show how they arise as the result of the actions and interaction of individuals. This view, often referred to as methodological individualism, is in my view trivially true."

142 Not to so show, Watkins (1957: 106) argued, is to provide only an "unfinished or half-way explanations" of social phenomena, although, as Udehn (2001: 216) observes, simply because social phenomena can be explained in a particular way "does not imply the methodological rule that they should be explained this way." Moreover, explanations at the at the level of intentional mental states, the so-called "rock-bottom explanations," may well be effected by cognitive biases that function almost entirely at a subintentional level (Sperber 1997), thereby giving rise

without knowing *why* people take the social actions they do, there can be no understanding of why social phenomena occur. As Weber ([1921] 1968: 13) remarked: "collectives must be treated as solely the resultants and modes of organization of the particular acts of individual persons, since these alone can be treated as agents in a course of subjectively understandable action."[143] This led Popper (1974: 14) to assign the social world primarily to a theoretical realm dealing with ideas and problems; nothing more than a mereological sum—the aggregate of its members. Therefore, those who undertake to study the social world from this ontological position would adopt a process that proceeds from the position of the micro (elucidating the action-takers' hopes, aspirations and goals that explain social actions) to the macro (so as to explain the patterns of social interactions that build up groups and social networks that make up the social world and give rise to the social phenomena in it).

Traditions

Individualism

This tradition, which has its origins in diverse ideas of Hobbes, Locke, Rousseau, Kant, John Stuart Mill, Humboldt, Godwin, Nietzsche, Proudhon, Stirner, Sartre and Hayek, privileges the individual over the social (Bunge 1996, McCann 2004), and places emphasis on personal autonomy, personal liberty and the need for the collective to justify any imposition of restrictions on that liberty.

Unqualified individualism postulates that all explanations of social actions must be expressed solely in terms of agent-caused intentional mental states (hopes, aspirations and goals). This is in the reductionist-atomism tradition, following Hobbes and Menger (Lukes 1968, Udehn 2001), premised on individual psychology being fully a-social or pre-social; as Hobbes ([1642] 1949: 8: 1) asserted: "consider men [sic] as if but even now sprung out of the earth, and

to deeper levels of explanation. Physicalist would, of course, assert that genetically-determined physiological and neurological structures and processes offer the only "rock-bottom explanations" of human behavior and thus of social phenomena.

143 Parker (2007: 2) points out that methodological individualism should not be confused or conflated with individual agency, positivism, rationality, and homeostatis. Whilst Weber ([1921] 1968) sought to privilege the causal efficacy of action-theoretic mechanisms (Alexander 1987) to enhance understanding of social phenomena, he did not privilege the individual over the social in terms of the content of action-takers' intentional mental states: "it is a tremendous misunderstanding to think that an 'individualistic' *method* should involve what is in any conceivable sense an individualistic system of *values*" (Weber [1921] 1968: 18, emphasis in original).

suddainly [sic] (like Mushromes [sic]) come to full maturity without all kind of engagement to each other." Agent-causation requires personal autonomy—grounded in self-rule and authenticity—with emphasis placed on the reasons for undertaking social actions being an expression of his or her authentic self, independent of his or her place in a metaphysical or social order. This means that the specific contents of the action taker's intentional mental states are completely self-determined—limited only by his or her intrinsic properties—and thus not depend at all on the environmental or situational considerations (narrow mental content) (see Fodor 1987, 1991, Kripke 1979, Loar 1988, White 1991, but see also Burge 1979, 1986, 1989, Putnam 1975, Stalnaker 1989, 1990, Wilson 1995). To achieve such control over their intentional mental states requires a person to be able to access and understand his or her our own such mental states, without being able to draw inference from observing those mental states, and without having anything or anyone to mediate between his or her self-ascribed beliefs and the object of those beliefs (Russell 1917). This presumes that an action taker has the capacity to critically reflect on his or her intentions, which generates self-knowledge (Cassam 1994, Wright, *et al.* 1998) that, with the first-person authority with which they are held, privileges a presumption of truth (Jackson 1973, but see Ryle 1949, Wright 1989).

Libertarian individualism (Hayek 1948, 1960, Humbolt [1791] 1969, Locke [1690] 2004, Milton [1644] 1949, Nock [1924] 1991, Nozick 1974, see also Vallentyne and Steiner 2000a, 2000b) holds that agents have the right to full self-ownership[144], thereby making all human interactions voluntary, reflecting their right to act in a self-interested manner.[145] According to Locke ([1689] 1960: 287 emphasis in original) humans are naturally in "a *State of perfect Freedom* to order their Actions … as they think fit … without asking leave, or depending on the Will of any other Man." Hayek (1960) recognized the supreme importance of individual autonomy—rightful self-governance—or negative freedom.[146] He

144 This holds that agents have full rights over the use of their body; full rights to transfer those rights to others; full payment immunities for the possession and execution of those rights (Vallentyne 2001: 1–2).

145 A distinction can be drawn between left-wing, right-wing, and paternal libertarianism. All three schools hold that agents are full self-owners. Right-libertarianism, however, holds that natural resources can be privately appropriated as a matter right, whereas left-libertarianism requires that such private appropriation is permissible only with the permission of, or after compensation has been paid to, society (Vallentyne 2001: 1). Libertarian paternalism accepts that people can be nudged into doing what is in their best interest by a re-arrangement of the "choice archicteure" that sets their choice decision context (Thaler and Sunstein 2008).

146 Berlin (1969) drew the distinction between negative and positive freedom. Negative freedom is the right of self-determination: freedom from control, interference or exploitation, identified with the Hobbesian idea of the absence of constraint or obstacles (see also Miller 1991). It is

propounded true individualism, "which regards man not as highly rational and intelligent but as a very irrational and fallible being, whose individual errors are corrected only in the course of a social process, and which aims at making the best of a very imperfect material" (Hayek (1948: 9). A little later he adds: "the famous presumption that each man knows his interests best ... is neither plausible nor necessary for the [true] individualist's conclusions" (p. 15).

Existential individualism (Heideggar ([1927] 1967, Kierkegaard [1845] 1940, Nietzsche [1871] 1993, [1878] 1994, [1883] 1968, [1886] 1998, Sartre [1943] 1957, Schopenhauer [1813] 1974, [1818/1844] 1969) holds that people need to live in the way they find most valid and fulfilling, which requires them to have freedom—what Camus ([1942] 2005: 55, emphasis in original) called "the freedom to *be*"—the inescapable condition required for any action and experience—to search for their own self-identity. There is a recognition that the individual is a self-determining agent who is ultimately accountable for his or her own destiny and character, and who engages in struggle to achieve an authenticity. To Kierkegaard ([1845] 1940), the awareness of individuality, temporality and nothingness means that a person is characterized by concern, marked by both fear of death and anxiety about nothingness, which when confronted creates an opportunity for that person to create his or her own human nature. Heidegger called for individual authenticity, so that a person's true self can be revealed (Heideggar ([1927] 1967). For Sartre ([1960] 1976), the notion of authenticity focuses on the need for a person to make choices in the full awareness that he or she can create his or her own character. Whilst he ([1943] 1957) recognized that there are the facts about a person that cannot be changed at any given point in time by acts of will—his or her facticity, an act of will can change his or her situation and thus the prevailing set expectations of self and others.

Utilitarianism

This tradition, grounded in the works of Bentham, Bernoulli, John Stuart Mill and Spencer, holds that that all explanations of social actions must be expressed

based on three premises: that individuals require the private space to identify appropriate personal goals and ambitions; that personal goals and ambitions have value only if they are freely chosen; and that voluntary action—choice and personal responsibility—enables individuals to meet important spiritual needs. Positive freedom is the right to be able to take control of one's life: freedom to choose and realize desired outcomes, achieved by empowerment, which is an inherently collective pursuit, identified with Rousseau's notion of moral self-government. It is also based on three premises: that all individuals have capacities or latent, but desirable, qualities; that positive freedom consists of the realization of these capacities, which may therefore be conceptualized, in the broader sense, as personal autonomy; and that social conditions are the decisive influence on the realization of these capacities.

solely in terms of states of mind about the actual or expected utility[147] of its consequences: "Nature has placed mankind under the governance of two sovereign masters, *pain* and *pleasure*. It is for them alone to point out what we ought to do, as well as to determine what we shall do" (Bentham [1789] 1970: 2, emphasis in original). This is utilitarianism's pleasure principle[148]—(psychological utilitarianism[149]). Bentham ([1789] 1970) considered that social actions are made explicable by reference to a hedonic or utility calculation,[150] premised on the proposition that an individual seeks to enhance his or her pleasure and avoid any pain, following the Epicurian tradition, which Frankl ([1948/1975] 2000: 89) describes as the "will to pleasure." Thus, the maximization of personal well-being is the only goal that people are motivated to pursues (psychological hedonism or egoism), and, indeed, should pursue (evaluative hedonism), as established by what they perceives as giving value to any pursuit (reflective hedonism).[151] Personal sacrifices for others—altruism (Scott and Seglow 2007)—can only be justified by reference to their own self-interest, which, of course, converts a sacrifice into a gain. Mill, whilst unequivocal about the appropriateness of utility calculation, argued that some pleasures are of a discernable finer quality than others, so he applied the following condition ([1861] 1968: 14): "but it must be utility in the largest sense, grounded in the permanent interests of man as a progressive being. Those interests I contend, authorize the subjection of individual spontaneity to external control, only in respect to those actions of each, which concern the interest of other people." Mill, thus, refined the doctrine of

147 Bernoulli ([1738] 1954) considered that utility (usefulness, desirability or satisfaction) is individually experienced intuitively, and, thus, would differ between individuals.

148 "By the Principle of Utility is meant that principle which approves or disapproves of every action whatsoever according to the tendency which it appears to have to augment or diminish the happiness of the party whose interest is in question" (Bentham [1789] 1970: 2).

149 This is manifest as Edwards' (1954) theory of subjectively expected utility and von Winterfeldt and Edwards' (1986) theory of multi-attribute utility, and is an important constituent of Ajzen and Fishbein's (1980) theory of reasoned action, Ajzen's (1991) theory of planned behavior, and Rotter's expectancy-reinforcement value theory (Rotter 1954, 1981, 1982, Rotter *et al.* 1972).

150 Bentham's utility calculus "sum up all the values of all the pleasures on the one side, and those of all the pains on the other" ([1789] 1970: 4). He measured the amount of pain in accordance with seven criteria—intensity, duration, certainty, extent, propinquity, fecundity and purity—and took into consideration the merits of various kind of pleasure (such as, those associated with sensation, possession, skill, friendship, reputation, power and malevolence) and demerits of various kind of pain (such as, those associated with want, disappointment and regret) (Bentham [1789] 1970).

151 What brings meaning to this endeavor is the human essence of striving to persevere in being—*conatus*—which generates a self-conscious desire in a person (Hampshire 2005). Therefore, when needs are satisfied by the striving of the individual, his or her well-being is enhanced in the process (Scruton 1984: 57).

utilitarianism by recognizing differences in the quality and quantity of particular anticipated pleasures, for he considered intellectual gratification to be more important than physical sensations, and that altruistic social actions could satisfy individual desires. Utilitarianism, thus, sustains the supremacy of individual hedonism and egoism.

Personalism

This tradition has its antecedents in the philosophical, theological and psychological thoughts of Grote, Lotze, Newman and Schleiermacher, but is firmly grounded in late nineteenth and twentieth century works of Bowne, Brightman, Buber, Lotze, Maritain, Mournier, and Scheler (Bengtsson 2006, Burrow 1999). It defends both the concept and the reality of persons, and resists all forms of depersonalization, thereby affirming the absolute value of human beings and the significance, uniqueness, and inviolability of those characteristics they possesses that uniquely shape their cognitions, behaviors and social actions and interactions—their personalities.[152] "To Personalism, personality is the supreme value" (Flewelling 1915: 23). Thus, persons and their interpersonal relationships should be placed at the center of social theory and practice. It denies both individualism's emphasis on mutual isolation and the sociobology's reduction of a person to his or her biological processes.

Sociobology

This tradition has its historical roots in Darwin's theory of evolution (Darwin [1859] 2006, see also Darwin [1871] 2004, [1872] 1965, Delger 1991, Dennett 1984, 2004, Peters 1997, Richards 1987) and his principles of natural selection (see, for example, Ardrey 1961, 1967, 1970, 1976). It holds that the origin and maintenance of behavior can be explained by physiological structures and processes that are the product of successful environmental adaption intergenerationally transmitted by the process of natural selection) (Wilson 1976). Human beings—as biological organisms[153] that are the outcome of cooperation amongst mutually compatible but selfish genes intent on executing strategies, even altruistic ones, to replicate themselves—are "survival machines, robot vehicles blindly programmed to preserve the selfish molecules known as genes"

---

[152] As Protagorasn remarked: "Of all things the measure is man, of the things that are, that [or 'how'] they are, and of things that are not, that [or 'how'] they are not" (Freeman 1983: DK80b1). In other words, a person's sensory perceptions and beliefs are true for that person.

[153] Frankl ([1948/1975] 2000: 95–96) quoting an uncited source suggests that a man [sic] is "nothing but a complex biochemical mechanism powered by a combustion system which energizes computers with prodigious storage facilities for retaining encoded information."

(Dawkins 1976: iv).[154] Behavioral geneticists (Rutter 2006), however, are beginning to consider that nature and nurture are not incompatible and that what is important is the interaction between the two. Genetic make-up, in this context, creates propensities, which unfold differently because of environmental factors. A person does not, by and large, carry genes for different patterns of behavior for life. This means that a person is not mechanistically at the mercy of his or her genetic make-up—biology is not destiny—but rather that that make-up makes him or her more or less susceptible to the consequences of particular factors in his or her environment. In other words, although physiological events occurring in the brain appear to be biologically determined, they might be explained by how the body has experienced the world.

Evolutionary psychology advances the more specific proposition that human behavior can be explained by reference to neurophysiological structures and processes[155] (Buss 1999, but see also Richardson 2007). Their reductionist-essentialist proposition is that the causes of human behavior can be found in a person's neurobiology of the brain[156] (neurobiological or physical determinism) (Wilson 1976, 1978, but see Rutter 2006). Epiphenomenalists (such as Huxley, James, and Maudsley) take this proposition to the extreme by arguing that neurobiological processes taking place in the brain are the sufficient and complete cause of human behaviors, a bi-product of which is the human mind experiencing mental states (Caston 1997, Hyslop 1998, James 1890a, Rivas and van Dongen [2001] 2003).[157]

---

154 For a review of the sociobiology discourse see: Arnhart 1998, Barkow *et al.* 1992, Hauser 2006, Hinde 2002, Wilson 1976, 1978; but see Francis 2004, Gould 2002, Lumsden and Wilson 1981, Pinker 2002, de Waal 2006; and also Brenan 2003, Caplan 1978, Dennett 2002, Kitcher 1885, Lewontin *et al.* 1984, Ridley 1997, 2003.

155 Dostoevesky's ([1880] 1948: 664) Dmitri Kazamazov describes his understanding of neural functioning in a way that captures the imagination:

> Imagine: inside, in the nerves, in the head—that is, these nerves are there in the brain ... (damn them!) there are sort of little tails, the little tails of those nerves, and as soon as they begin quivering ... that is, you see, I look at something with my eyes and then they begin quivering, those little tails ... and when they quiver, then an image appears ... it doesn't appear at once, but an instant, a second, passes ... and then something like a moment appears; that is, not a moment—devil take the moment!—but an image; that is, an object, or an action, damn it! That's why I see and then think, because of those tails, not at all because I've got a soul, and that I am some sort of image and likeness. All that is nonsense! Ratkin [a visiting academic] explained it all to me yesterday, brother, and it simply bowled me over. It's magnificent, Alyosha, this science! A new man's arising—that I understand ... And yet I am sorry to loose God!

156 The metaphors for that have been used to characterize the brain include: an enchanted loom (Sherrington [1937–38] 1978: 178)) and cerebral scripts and scores (Sacks 1985: 148).

157 La Mettrie (1748) anticipated this somewhat earlier:

> In fact, if what thinks in my brain is not a part of this organ and therefore of the whole body, why does my blood boil, and the fever of my mind pass into my veins, when lying quietly

Social Action Attributions

Social Actions Grounded in Rational Self-interest

This is premised on a social action being the product of a self-interested utility calculation (Sen 1987). It is grounded in the work of Hobbes, Manderville and Machiavelli. The starting point for understanding human behavior is, according to Hume [1739–40] 1978: II, 3), *pathos*—passions, desires, tastes and preferences—taken to be beyond logical disagreement and moral dispute, for the individual—and only the individual—can determine and define the requisites of the good life. How these passions are satisfied is the realm of *logas*—reason or instrumental rationality: "Reason alone can never be a motive to any action of will ... reason is and ought only to be the slave of passions and can never pretend to any other office than to serve and obey them" (Sect. 3). Each person has, according to Rand (1965, see also 1957), a rational egotistical belief in self-determination. He or she is presumed to be isolated, self-determining "Robinson Crusoe" agent (Urry *et al.* 2007: 96), with the necessary hopes, beliefs and desires needed to take self-interested and self-seeking social actions, unaffected in any way by what others say and do. Free will permits a person to choose what is best for him or her (metaphysical libertarianism) (Kane 2002b).[158] Social actions can, thus, best be ascribed to a person's self-interest calculations[159] (rational-choice or rational-action theory[160] (Arrow 1954, Buchanan and Tullock 1962, Downs 1957, but see Tversky and Kahneman 1981, 1986) or bounded rationality[161] (Kahneman

in bed, I am forming the plan of some work or carrying on an abstract calculation? ... In short, if the nerve-tension which causes pain occasions also the fever by which the distracted mind looses its will-power, and if, conversely, the mind too much excited, disturbs the body ..., if an agitation rouses my desire and my ardent wish for what, a moment ago, I cared nothing about, and if in their turn certain brain impressions excite the same longing and the same desires, then why should we regard as double what is manifestly one being?

Yet as Nietzsche observes: "The yearning for 'freedom of the will' in the superlative metaphysical sense that unfortunately still prevails in the minds of the half-educated, the yearning to bear complete and final responsibility for one's own actions and to relieve God, the world, one's ancestors, coincidence, society from it—this is really nothing less than being the same *causa sui* and, with a daring greater than Münchhausen's [Raspe's adventure-hero in Baron Münchhausen's Narrative of his *Marvellous Travel and Campaigns in Russia* (1785)] dragging yourself and into existence" ([1886] 1998: 21)

159 Expected utility theory proposes that a rational action is the action that yields the highest expected utility of all possible actions, after allowing for the probability of the occurrence of each possible action's outcomes (Fishburn 1982, Savage 1954)

160 "The crowning glory of this rational choice theory is the construct of 'general equilibrium' ... [which] contains no testable propositions. This makes its status as a scientific theory extremely questionable." (Urry *et al.* 2007: 96–97).

161 "Agents are postulated to have only partial rather than complete information, and the amount of information available may vary across agents. There is still a universal rule of decision making,

2003)) or to his or her self-interested responses, under conditions of uncertainty, to the decisions of others, when costs and benefits of those responses depend upon the uncommunicated decisions made by others[162] (game theory (Cournot [1838] 1927, von Neumann and Morganstern [1944] 1953, but see also Howard, 1971, 1999)).

Social Actions Grounded in the Search for Identity and Authenticity

This is premised on a social action being grounded in a person's search for his or her essence—essential characteristics or a sense of who he or she is—and for self-fulfillment, which is achievable by giving priority to his or her immediate personal experience of aloneness, death, and moral responsibility, thereby stressing his or her perception of being alienated from self and others (see Guignon 2004). It is grounded in the existential notion that individuals simply exist—"existence comes before essence" (Sartre [1946] 1973: 44): "Man [sic] simply is. Not that he is simply what he conceives himself to be, but he is what he wills, and as he conceives himself after already existing—as he wills to be after that leap toward existence. Man is nothing else but that which he makes of himself" (Sartre [1946] 1973: 28). So, the existence-precedes-essence process recognizes a person as having jurisdiction over his or her own awareness of the purposeful possibilities of his or her actuality. To May (1967: 8, see also, 1953, 1983), "the human dilemma is that which arises out of man's [sic] capacity to experience himself as both subject and object at the same time:" a product of people simultaneously living in world of biological needs and drives (*umweld*), the world of interrelationships (*mitweld*), and world of self-awareness and self-relatedness (*eigenwelt*). It is, then, up to them to use their unbridled freedom to decide their own fate, and so determine their own destiny—their purpose for being—for which they alone are responsible. Social actions can, thus, best be ascribed to a person's search for authenticity.

namely that agents maximize, subject to the information which they have" (Urry *et al.* 2007: 97).

162 It is crucial to recognize that, strictly construed, game theory has never sought to offer a general theory of rational social action. Indeed, the standard definition of a game-theoretic equilibrium—the Nash solution—explicitly excludes any communication between the players and when communication occur it does not work (Heath 2001).

Implications

Agency's dilemma is that it can apparently explain the empirically strong correlation between individual social action and free choice, but it cannot explain outliers that are not the product of individual intention (Williams and May 1996).

STRUCTURALISM

Structuralism posits that social actions can best be ascribed to group-elaborated (worked out) norms, roles and practices, as these identify the courses of action judged to by a group to be acceptable and required, which constitute the prevailing group rules or code of conduct. The presumption is that the action-taker's hopes, aspirations and goals can be molded by these group elaborations.[163] In terms of an action-taker's social action choice, structuralists would adhere to the tenets of soft determinism—albeit with the rhetorical overlay of hard determinism. As soft determinists, they would be compatibilists, in that the action-taker can, ultimately, exercise his or her free will, constrained or enabled by his or her internal determining conditions (such as, psychological, physiological or hereditary conditions), to diminish or reject the capacity of these group-elaborations to shape the content of his or her hopes, aspirations and goals and, thus, to influence the course of social action he or she chooses to follow. However, these group-elaborations are considered to be such that they overwhelm voluntarism (individuals being the self-determining agents of their actions) as the reasons for social actions (structural determinism). Social actions are, thus, taken to be "only comprehensible in relation to his or her [the action-taker's] social formation and existence" (Bryant 1985: 19, see also Robey 1973).

On the Social World

Structuralism adheres to ontological holism (Armstrong 1989, Simmel 1910–11), which holds that social wholes exist as independent entities formed by or within systems of relations amongst their constituent membership. This is firmly grounded in immanent realism (that universals are abstractions that permit the

---

163 Hence the view that "structuralism is a set of principles for studying the mental superstructure" (Harris 1979: 166) and "all our human properties and powers, beyond our biological constitution, [are] the gifts of society" (Archer 2000: 4).

grouping of the likenesses of particulars into a single whole, so as to represent that which is necessary to their constitution, and that exist outside the mind[164] (Armstrong 1978, 2000)). As Durkheim ([1895] 1962: xvii) observed: "whenever certain elements combine, and thereby produce, by the fact of their combination, new phenomena, it is plain that these phenomena reside not in the original elements but in the totality formed by their union."[165]

Metaphysical Holism

This holds that the social wholes both exist, and are more than their mereological sum, in that they consist not only of individuals, but also of their interrelationships:

> All structuralists recognize as fundamental the contrast between structures and aggregates, the former being *wholes*, the latter composites formed of elements that are independent of the complexes into which they enter. ... [The] elements of a structure are subordinated to *laws*, and it is in terms of these laws that the structure qua whole or system is defined. ... These laws confer on the whole as such *overall properties* distinct from the properties of its elements (Piaget 1970: 7, emphasis in original).

These interrelationships give rise to social institutions grounded in shared norms, roles, and practices.

Methodological Holism

This holds that human social life is best, or most appropriately, understood by analysis at the macroscopic level of the social institutions, values, practices and processes.[166] This can extend to an analysis of the social context in which

---

164 This stands in contrast to transcendental realism, which holds that universals represent an objective reality that exists outside the mind and are prior to, and independent of, particulars (Loux 2002).

165 Hegel [1806] 1998, [1807] 1977) saw an integral relationship existing between the personal and the social when he postulated that minds are an abstraction from, and a participant in, the social (group) mind (the independent collective mind of a social group): "I that is a We, and the We that is an I" (Hegel [1807] 1977: 177). He argued that an organic (rational) community is one in which individual and collective interests are rationally in harmony. This manifests as a state—whose citizens choose to obey and support it as the ultimate form of society—making it a Divine idea—the social mind incarnate. Hegel considered that conditions of full selfhood can be met only in such a law-governed social situation. For an exploration of the impact this Hegelian concept has had on social-psychological theorizing see Farr 1996, Karpf 1932.

166 Parker (2007: 2) points out methodological holism should not be confused or conflated with subjectivism, nonrationality, or historicism (the proposition that history can be resolved into a single narrative direction).

action-takers formulate the intentional mental states that give rise to their social actions (see Ryan 1970): "most people are shaped to the form of their culture because of the malleability of their original endowment" (Benedict [1934] 1959: 278); "we are forced to conclude that human nature is almost unbelievably malleable, responding accurately and contrastingly to contrasting cultural conditions" (Mead [1935] 1963: 280); and "much of what is commonly called 'human nature' is merely culture thrown against a screen of nerves, glands, sense organs, muscles etc." (White, quoted in Delger 1991: 209). As Bhaskar ([1979] 1998: 25) remarks: "societies are irreducible to people," which means they cannot be identified with human intentions, cannot be reduced to human intentions, cannot be explained in terms of human intentions, and cannot be reconstructed from human intentions. Durkheim ([1895] 1962: 105–6) makes the point:

> If we begin with the individual in seeking to explain phenomena, we shall be able to understand nothing of what takes place in the group. Individual natures are merely the indeterminate material that the social factor molds and transforms. Their contribution consists exclusively in very general attitudes, in vague and consequently plastic predispositions.

This means that individuals are considered to have little capacity to determine their lives. It is, moreover, axiomatically taken to be difficult, if not impossible, for one person to transform social institutions and processes (Baert 1998: 11). Therefore, those who undertake to study the social world from this ontological position would adopt a process that proceeds from the position of the macro (elucidating the socio-cultural, economic and linguistic factors that shape the patterns of social interactions that build up groups and social networks that make up the social world and give rise to the social phenomena in it) to the micro (so as to explain the action-takers' intentional mental states that give rise to social actions).

Traditions

Natural Laws and the Natural Social Order

This tradition is grounded in Comte's ([1830–42] 1896) positivist[167] philosophy, which sought to identify the invariant laws governing a society, in acknowledgement of the interrelated nature of social phenomena, and which

---

[167] Comte used this term in the sense opposite to negativist rather as a synonym for empiricism.

asserted that, apart from brief transitory periods, a society reflects the necessary order that is in nature—its basic uniformities or regularities (natural laws). This drew upon three propositions. The first was voiced by Aristotle ([350 BC/1924/1953] 1994–2000) and Plato ([390s–347 BC] 1997), who postulated that real or natural kinds of groupings are posited by nature rather than arbitrary classifications imposed as a result of the feelings of individuals: "knowledge is of invariant or unchanging universal necessary truths" and that these necessary truths must be married to "ontologically suitable objects" (Shand, 2002: 33). The second was offered by Quesnay, who argued in *Le Tableau Économique* (1758) that "all social facts are linked together in the bond of eternal, immutable, ineluctable, inevitable laws, which individuals and government would obey if they were once known to them" (cited in Randall 1940: 323). The third was proffered by Condorcet ([1795] 1955), who asserted that socioeconomic phenomena can be explained by mathematical methods. There was a social order, Comte argued, with natural laws that governed relationships between institutional and cultural forms, which made society an organic whole. He conceived that there these natural laws could explain social phenomena by reference to autonomous structures that were discoverable by the application of positivist thinking.[168]

Historical Materialism

This tradition is premised on the primacy of economic processes and relations as determinant of how particular forms of society are responsible for observed social phenomena—the materialist conception of history (Marx and Engels [1845–46] 1932, see also Labriola [1896] 1908). Plekhanov ([1897] 2004: Sect. V, emphasis in original) explains:

> Thus, man makes history in striving to satisfy his needs. These needs, of course, are originally imposed by nature; but they are later considerably modified quantitatively and qualitatively by the character of the artificial environment. The productive forces at man's disposal determine all his social relations. First of all, the state of the productive forces determines the relations in which men stand towards each other in the social process of production, that is, their *economic*

---

168 In Comte's ([1830–42] 1896) view, human intellectual development had moved historically through three mutually exclusive phases: (1) the theological phase: when knowledge of nature was based on super-natural absolute knowledge—objects have their own will (animism), divine wills are imposed on objects (polytheism), and the will of God is imposed on objects (monotheism); (2) the metaphysical phase: when knowledge of nature was based on abstract thought grounded in abstract principles or forces of origin; and (3) the positive phase: when knowledge of nature is based on the discovery of laws of phenomena, achieved by the application of reasoned observation.

> *relations*. These relations naturally give rise to definite interests, which are expressed in *Law*. "Every system of law protects a definite interest," Labriola says. The development of productive forces divides society into classes, whose interests are not only different, but in many—and, moreover, essential—aspects are diametrically antagonistic. ... Lastly, *social relations*, determined by the given state of productive forces, give rise to common *morality*, the morality, that is, that guides people in their common, everyday life.

Development and change in human societies is attributable to the way in which individuals as workers—the proletariat—collectively engage in work and their actual social actions and material life conditions. As Marx ([1859] 1999: i) observed:

> In the social production of their existence, men inevitably enter into definite relations, which are independent of their will, namely relations of production appropriate to a given stage in the development of their material forces of production. The totality of these relations of production constitutes the economic structure of society, the real foundation, on which arises a legal and political superstructure and to which correspond definite forms of social consciousness.[169]

Structural Functionalism

This tradition is premised on social systems being coherent, bounded and fundamentally relational constructs, functioning like organisms with individuals working together to maintain and reproduce them. Its "primary concern is with explaining the existence and continuity of structural elements, in terms of their contribution to the rest of the system" (Donaldson 1985: 28). It is grounded in the work of Parsons, Radcliffe-Brown and Malinowski. To Parsons (1951: 5–6), a social system is:

> a plurality of individual actors interacting with each other in a situation which has at least a physical or environmental aspect, actors who are motivated in terms of a tendency to the 'optimization of gratification' and whose relation to their situations, including each other, is defined and mediated in terms of a system of culturally structured and shared symbols.

Structural functionalism places particular emphasis on function (notably, systemic adaption, goal attainment, integration and pattern maintenance),

[169] Lukács ([1923] 1971) saw Marx's proletariat as both the subject and object of history and as embodying class consciousness as revolutionary subjectivity.

interdependence, consensus, equilibrium, and evolutionary change within a social system. Social order[170] (relatively stable patterns of institutional arrangements, interactions and customs that are capable of continually reproducing those conditions necessary for their continued existence) (Wrong 1994) is considered to be grounded in voluntary social cooperative action (Wrong 1994, see also Saussure [1916] 1974). "People act on the basis of their values; their social actions are oriented and constrained by the values and norms of individuals around them [the normative order]; and these norms and values are the basis of social order" (Knapp 1994: 191–92). A social system, thus, consists of parts, each of which have their own functions and work together, because individuals share values and norms that permit generally agreed upon means for accomplishing ends, so as to promote social stability.

Anthropological Structuralism

This tradition is premised on the proposition that the underlying meaning embedded in human thought can be discovered by examining expressed cultural acts: "[anthropological] structuralism [places] emphasis on cultural universals embedded in the psychic unity of humankind" (Barnard 2003: 132).[171] It is grounded in the work of Lévi-Strauss, Needham and Leach. Lévi-Strauss ([1962] 1963) considered, in the dualist tradition, that a human being is, at one and the same time, an organism and as an intellect, with the latter being the source of human nature—*l'esprit humain*.[172] As his object of analysis, he took the intellect, which, according to Leach (1970: 42), he conceived as "a kind of algebraic matrix of possible permutations and combinations." This is an unconscious mental state to which he attributed the characteristics of order, regularity and pattern. Systems of beliefs and customs are considered to be the basis for understanding these

---

170 According to Strauss (1978: 56), social order is "something at which members of any society, any organization, must work. For the shared agreements ... are not binding for all time ... review is called for ... the bases of concerted action (social arrangement) must be constituted continually, or 'worked out'."

171 "For the structuralism that Lévi-Strauss developed … the almost countless discrete elements that together make up a culture constitute a sign system. … The discrete bits of culture that we can distinguish are not meaningful in themselves, but draw their meaning from the sign system in which they function and, more in particular, from their differences from other signs" (Bertens 2001: 61).

172 To Lévi-Strauss ([1958/1963] 1969: 140, 142) explanations relating to the human spirit needed to transcend human emotions:

> Actually, impulses and emotions explain nothing: they are always results, either of the power of the body or the impotence of the mind. In both cases they are consequences, never causes. The latter can be sought only in the organism, which is the exclusive concern of biology, or in the intellect, which is the sole way offered to psychology, and to anthropology as well.

cognitive structures. They determine how a person relates to the group norms, roles and practices. This means, ultimately, that patterns of social interaction are manifestations of cognitive structures into which systems of beliefs and customs are embedded (Lévi-Strauss [1958/1963] 1974).

Linguistic Structuralism

This tradition is premised on language being a set of rules to which any individual speaking that language must submit, which shapes his or her cognitions and behaviors. It is grounded in the work of Saussaure and Bloomfield. Saussaure ([1916/1959] 1974) focused on the underlying system of language (*la langue*), namely: semiotics—how the elements of language (pre-verbal, vocal, rhythmic and sign elements) related to each other at particular points in time (synchronically) rather than throughout their historical development (diachronically)—and symbolism—how language is rule governed and subject to social and culture influences—and their interplay. He argued that linguistic signs comprise the signifier—the form the sign takes (such as the sound pattern of a word)—and the signified—the concept the sign represents (such as the meaning of the word). As a group convention, these language rules enable a person within a language group to acquire meaning about the nature of social interactions, social relationships and social phenomena from making sense of what others say. Bloomfield (1933, see also Hall 1987), contrastingly, advocated the study of linguistic phenomena in sociocultural and historical isolation, emphasizing the development of formal models of language, the importance of empirical description, and the need to deal objectively with physically observable social phenomena. He developed a behavioristic approach to linguistics.

Post-structuralism

This tradition is premised on individuals being shaped by sociological, psychological and linguistic structures that, in turn, have been shaped by rule-governed systems over which they have no control (Belsey 2002, Williams 2005). It is grounded in the work of Foucault, Derrida and Lacan. Foucault (1966, 1969) argued that the human condition cannot be explained by reference to any underlying objective social structure, because no social environment can be investigated objectively, as it is impossible to step outside the discourse that gives a meaning to the collectively elaborated rules, norms, customs and practices. Derrida (1976, 1978), influenced by Heidegger and Nietzsche, argued that any discourse has multiple interpretations, making the possibility of a final and complete interpretation impossible. To Lacan, the individual is the creation of language, which enables him or her to experience the world meaningfully (Dor

2001). A person's understanding of his or her body and the world at large is grounded in the language he or she has acquired. This gives language a major role in the way he or she constructs meaning, and allows the Freudian unconscious, which Lacan considered is structured like a language without a grammar, to enter into that understanding and dissolve essential distinctions between the subjective and the objective:

> For Lacan, Freud's central insight was not ... that the unconscious exists, but that it has structure, that this structure affects in innumerable ways what we say and do, and that in thus betraying itself it becomes accessible to analysis (Bowie 1979: 118).

The self is considered by post-structuralists to be incoherent, disjointed, and decentered. It is a mere site in which various sociocultural constructs and discursive formations are created and sustained by the power structures within a given sociocultural environment. Any meaning attached to the social world is derived from self-reflexive discourses that acknowledge the inherently fragmented, diverse, tenuous, ambiguous and culture-specific nature of knowledge, which is always changing and contestable, so it can never have a finality and completeness.

Social Action Attributions

Social Actions Grounded in Economic Participation

This is premised on the Marxian proposition that social actions have their roots in the relations of production: "the mode of production of material life conditions the social, political and intellectual life processes in general." (Marx [1859] 2001: 7) (economic determinism[173]). Because individuals are, essentially, productive beings who, by their very nature, cooperate in a process of collective, freely chosen labor, they are the product of the prevailing mode of production, which, in turn, is the product of the nature of the dominant economic structure—capitalism, socialism and communisms (Marx and Engels [1848/1969] 2002), see also Cohen 1988, 2001, Dupré 1966). As Marx ([1859] 1999: i) observed: "The mode of production of material life conditions the general process of social,

[173] Althusser (1962, [1965] 1969), drawing upon Marx and Engel's ambivalence about any reductionist interpretation of their work, advanced the propositions that social wholes at a certain place and stage in their development have economic, political, ideological and theoretical sets of practices, each with their own relative autonomy, according to the limits set by their place in the totality, and each thus contributing to the structural causality of the social whole (structural Marxism).

political and intellectual life. It is not the consciousness of men [sic] that determines their existence, but their social existence that determines their consciousness." Thus, "man is not an abstract being squatting outside the world ... the real nature of man is the totality of social relations" (Marx [1845] 1989: 66) but rather "individuals are ... embodiments of particular class-relations and class interests" ([1867] 1993: I, 10). Marx maintained that social actions are determined by economic pressures that shape the structural relations in everyday life. Under capitalism, these relations are based on conflict between an exploitative class—important economic others—with its profit imperatives, and workers' interests, which are focused on improving their economic condition. The resultant class conflict provides a theoretical approach that brought about by class struggle. This higher dialectic "consists not merely in producing and apprehending the determination as an opposite and limiting factor, but in producing and apprehending the positive content and result which it contains; and it is this alone which makes it a development and immanent progression" (Hegel [1821] 1991: 60).[174] This analysis offers a framework that explores long-term historical transformation and social evaluation, which also appraises of the notion of individual identity in the context of collective consciousness (Hobsbawn 1997: 83, see also Durkheim [1895] 1982). Social actions can, thus, best be ascribed to powerful economic pressures.

Social Actions Grounded in Social Participation

This is premised the propositions that "the beliefs, tendencies and practices of the group taken collectively" (Durkheim [1895] 1982: 54)—the social facts that materialize in particular physical environments—are able to shape its members' cognitive structures and, thereby, their social actions (social determinism). The human mind is taken to be a *tabula rasa*, and thus it "has no inherent structure and can be inscribed at will by society or ourselves" (Pinker 2002: 2, Dahrendorf 1968). Durkheim ([1895] 1982) argued that basic categories of thought—mental representations of the world—arise from social participation[175] (his theory of the social origin of mind) (Bergson 2004). These representations "are not only external to the individual but are, moreover, endowed with coercive power, by

174 Hegelian dialectical logic holds that any given thesis (an initial situation) contains within itself contradictory aspects—its antithesis (a negation of that initial situation), which requires a movement towards a resolution—a synthesis (a unification of thesis and synthesis) (Hegel [1816] 1969).

175 Durhkeim ([1912] 2001) talked of collective representations ("the ideas, beliefs, and values elaborated by a collectivity and that are not reducible to individual constituents") (*Gac Sanit* (online) 2006: 335).

virtue of which they impose themselves upon him, independent of his individual will" (Pinker 2002: 2), so determining the way a person articulates, denotes, and interpret social relationships, thereby inhibiting and stimulating social actions. The key to the transmission of social facts is socialization (the process whereby people acquire and internalizes the rules of behavior and system of beliefs, values and attitudes that equip him or her to identify and function as a member of a social group[176]) (Durkin 1995). This produces a collective conscience—"the body of beliefs and sentiments common to the average member of a society" (Durkheim ([1895] 1982: 126)—that creates a sense of group belonging and hence a feeling of moral obligation to live up to its expectations:

> When I fulfill my obligations as brother, husband, or citizen, when I execute my contracts, I perform duties which are defined, externally to myself and my acts, in law and in custom. Even if they conform to my own sentiments and I feel their reality subjectively, such reality is still objective, for I did not create them; I merely inherited them through my education (Durkheim [1895] 1962: 1).

This adaption process takes place when a person move into social environments that have their own group rules and norms defined, sanctioned and propagated by important others, the violation of which attracts penalties. Social actions can, thus, best be ascribed to group values and attitudes an action-taker adopts in order to become integrated into that group.

Social Actions Grounded in Cultural Participation

This is premised on Lévi-Strauss's belief that underlying all social actions are fundamental universal cognitive structures that are culturally specific in their contents (Lévi-Strauss [1958/1963] 1974) (cultural determinism). These deep structures produced and reproduced meaning within a culture—a system of symbolic communication expressed in a culture's practices, phenomena and activities (such as mythology, kinship, food preparation, religious rites, games, literary and non-literary texts, and entertainment). Understanding these deep structures can only be achieved by reducing them to their relevant constituent parts, thereby permitting the discovery of their operating principles (Lévi-Strauss

[176] Eysenck (1967, 1970) considers that although a person has genetically determined predispositions towards particular behaviors, such behaviors can be changed—new behaviors learnt—as a result of socialization, because of the rewards or punishments dispensed by authority figures. Individuals, however, differ in the extent to which they learn and conform to social rules, with rule violation being most problematic for an introvert (the quiet, introspective person who prefers a well-ordered life oriented towards the inner reality of the self) to whom the idea of violating rules creates a sense of guilt and anxiety (Eysenck and Eysenck 1985).

[1958] 1968). This constitutes the "deep grammar" of a culture, which originates in the human mind of its constituent members as learnt language and cultural practices that operate unconsciously on them. Social actions can, thus, best be ascribed to culturally induced cognitions (ideas, beliefs and a way of life) and patterns of social behavior (customs and practices) that give a person's life meaning and order (see, for example, Alexander 2003).

Social Actions Grounded in Linguistic Participation

This is premised on the proposition that the use of a particular language shapes the way people think about and behave in the social world[177] (linguistic determinism):

> The categories and types that we isolate from the world of phenomena we do not find there because they stare every observer in the face; on the contrary, the world is presented in a kaleidoscopic flux of impressions which has to be organized by our minds—and this means largely by the linguistic systems in our minds (Whorf 1956: 214).

And:

> Human beings do not live in the objective world alone, nor alone in the world of social activity as ordinarily understood, but are very much at the mercy of the particular language which has become the medium of expression for their society. ... The fact of the matter is that the 'real world' is to a large extent unconsciously built upon the language habits of the group (Sapir 1958: 69)

Harré (1980, 1983) considered that human reality has a practical (physical) and an expressive (conversational) dimension, of which the latter tends to be dominant: "the fundamental human reality is a conversation" (1983: 20). "I take the array of individuals as a primary human reality. I take the conversations in which those individuals engage as completing the primary structure, bringing into being the social and psychological reality. Conversation is to be thought of as creating a social world just as causality generates a physical one" (Harré 1983: 65). "Nothing [is] in the mind that was not first in the conversation" (Harré 1983: 116). He (1988: 42) advanced the proposition that "the private experience of a human being is shaped and ordered in learning to speak and write ... That ordering is expressed in language and other intentional, norm-gathering practices."

---

177 In nineteenth-century Germany, Herder, Hegel, and von Humbolt recognized the importance of language as the medium by which a society shaped its members (Markova 1983).

Language, then, is a dynamic activity that affects, and is affected by, cultural practices (Barthes [1975] 1977), making it a collectively derived objective cultural artifact: "One lives in a public world where one learns to use language in accordance with the prevailing social use of words. These practices instruct us in how to use terms applying to such things as tables, other people, astral bodies, and various institutions" (Stroll 2002: 119). This makes speech-acts (Searle 1969, Tsohatzidis 1994) or acts of communication (Austin 1962) "the primary entities in which minds become personalized, as private discourses" (Harré and Gillett 1994: 36), and thus "the minds of individuals are privatized practices condensing like fog out of the public conversation into material nuclei, their bodies" (Harré 1988: 50). Harré and Gillett (1994: 36) develop this point: "[The] structures of discourse in which psychological phenomena, such as remembering, displays of emotion, avowals of attitudes, attribution of causality and responsibility, and so on, are created under the control of conventions of right or wrong performance." Social actions can, thus, best be ascribed to the language people use to shape the way he or she thinks about—creates meaning—and behaves in the world.

Implications

Structuralism's dilemma is that it might be able to explain the empirically strong correlation between people's social actions and the group of which they are part, but it cannot unambiguously explain outliers derived from acts of choice by free individuals unencumbered by social norms and practices (Williams and May 1996).

Truth and the Social World: An Ontological Perspective

Where social enquiry is conducted within a social setting, those in truth-regulating groups and networks, who are concerned that truths-claims about what exists and what has causal capacity in that setting, are in a position to reject such truth claims because they are based on a "false" ontological premises, without offering any adequate analysis that overturns their case for being genuine knowledge. This is particularly apparent where it is firmly held that "science cannot attain objective, representational knowledge" (Bohman 1991: 131), either because the "facts" it offers are as relative and vague as any other singular elucidation, or because the premises underpinning the enquiry hypotheses are indeterminate.

Chapter 9

THE CONTENDING SOCIAL-REALITY DISPOSITIONS

Comprehending the actuality of a social arena—its social reality—requires a person to hold a standpoint or disposition on how it can best be known and to what social actions within it can best be ascribed. There is an incontrovertible epistemological bifurcation. There are those who adhere to naturalist epistemology and, thus, consider a social arena to be exclusively material in form with objectively factual qualities, which gives rise to objective data, from which conclusions can be drawn about what is, and can be, known with confidence about that social arena and about the reasons for social actions of those present in it. Then there are those who adhere to hermeneutic epistemology and, thus, consider a social arena as having both material and immaterial qualities, which produces first-person mental discernments, which gives rise to subjective data, from which can be drawn the meaning that they and others attach to a social arena and to the social actions of those present in it. There is also an incontrovertible ontological bifurcation. There are those who adhere to agency ontology and, thus, believe that social actions can best be ascribed and predicted on the basis of what action-takers' self-determined set of hopes, aspirations and goals. Then there are those who adhere to structuralist ontology and, thus, believe that social actions can best be ascribed and predicted on the basis of group-elaborated norms, roles and practices that molds an action-taker's hopes, aspirations and goals.

From these dichotomies can be deduced an inclusive set of configurations of epistemological and ontological assumptions that produces a synoptic classification that is both mutually exclusive and exhaustive (in Kierkegaardian terms, it does "exhaust its object"[178] (Kierkegaard [1843] 1941: 56): naturalist structuralism, hermeneutic structuralism, hermeneutic agency and naturalist agency (see Figure 1.1).[179] Each of these dispositions establishes distinctive and coherent, but mutually incompatible, ways of comprehending a social arena. This permits the categorization of contending standpoints on how the social world can best be described, explained and understood and to what social actions within it can best be ascribed, according to their epistemological and ontological assumptions (Dixon 2003). It also permits the categorization of ideas (concepts and theories) (Dixon and Dogan 2002, 2003a, 2003b, 2003c, 2003d, 2004, 2005; Dixon, Dogan and Carrier, 2005; Dixon, Dogan and Kouzmin, 2005; Dixon and Hyde 2003, Dixon, Sanderson and Dogan, 2005, Dixon, Sanderson and Tripathi, 2006, 2007).

This social-reality disposition framework demarcates a logical configuration of epistemological and ontological dispositions. They are monolithic categories, each being defined in terms of the features common to all members in each category. In any classificatory exercise there is always the danger of reification, when an abstract category becomes concrete as if it *is* reality. Whitehead (1925: 75 and 77) referred to this phenomenon as the fallacy of misplaced concreteness, which is recognized and acknowledged.

Grounded as it is in rationalism, this social-reality disposition framework presents the deductive conclusions drawn from *a priori* axioms that constitute a set of fundamental, robust and unambiguous foundations. This means that the framework is logically true, because it is premised on the definitional certitude of epistemological and ontological dichotomies. Empiricists can, of course, declare the ascendancy of the correspondence theory over the coherence theory of truth and, then, assert that the framework can only be judged to be true—corresponds to reality—on the basis of convincing evidence that individuals are cognitively consistency. The empirically established existence of cognitive inconsistency does not, of course, refute the logical truth of this social-reality dispositions framework.

---

178 Of classification, Kierkegaard ([1843] 1941: 56) remarked:

> A wit has said that one might divide mankind into officers, serving-maids and chimney sweeps. To my mind this remark is not only witty but profound, and it would require a great speculative talent to devise a better classification. When a classification does not ideally exhaust its object, a haphazard classification is altogether preferable, because it sets imagination in motion.

179 William of Ockham, with razor in hand, would undoubtedly be satisfied as plurality should not be posited without necessity——the principle of parsimony: *pluralitas non est ponenda sine necessitate* (Adams 1987).

Naturalist Structuralism

This disposition is grounded in two propositions. The first is that a social arena is entirely material in form with objectively factual qualities. These can be described, explained and predicted by reference to objective data, the truth-value of which can be only established by generally agreed objective enquiry procedures involving inductive inference and/or deductive logic that draws only upon material evidence or luminous premises. From these factual qualities, conclusions can be drawn about what is, and can be, known with confidence about that social arena and about the reasons for the social actions taken by those present. The second proposition is that that arena exists as perceptible, structurally functional and stable patterns of interpersonal relationships, which give rise to social institutions that reflect interdependence and can sustain social order. This means that the social actions of those present are best, or most appropriately, explained by analyzing the economic and social factors that shape the perceived patterns of social interactions by molding the social roles and social practices that influence, if not determine, the intentional mental state that give rise to social actions. Those engaged in this arena are considered to have no capacity to control how they conduct their interpersonal transactions. This is because the rules of behavior and the system of beliefs, values and attitudes that define what are the socially accepted courses of action and, accordingly, their and others' social roles, are taken be beyond the capacity of an individual to change, being exclusively sanctioned, propagated and enforced by those engaged in that arena who others have come to accept as having the authority to do so. Thus, when confronted with the need to make sense of a social arena, the user of this lens draws conclusions about that arena, and about his or her position in it, after analyzing the material objects and phenomena he or she perceives, probing the norms expressed, and weighing up the observed social roles and practices adopted by the important others present. This then establishes the form of social interaction that he or she believes to be necessary in order to be acceptable to the important others present.

Hermeneutic Structuralism

This disposition is grounded in two propositions. The first is that a social arena is subjectively experienced by those who engage in it, the meaningfulness and significance of which is socially constructed by a process of self-reflexive discourse amongst those engaged, one that acknowledges that knowledge can never be final and complete. This involves the intersubjective sharing of authentic testimonies that draw upon their encounters with the material and their feelings and discernments, the truth-value of which can only be established by reference to consensus. From these social constructs, conclusions can be drawn about what is, and can be, known with confidence about that arena and about the reasons for the social actions taken by those present. The second proposition is that that arena exist as a site in which various sociocultural constructs and discursive formations are created and sustained, giving rise to sets of common beliefs, worked-out norms, and agreed social roles and practices, all of which bestow meaning to those present, who would, otherwise, be incoherent, disjointed, and decentered. This means that that the social actions of those present are best, or most appropriately, understood by reflecting on sociological, psychological and linguistic factors that influence, if not determine, the cognitive structures that give rise to social actions. Those engaged in this arena are considered to have the capacity to influence how they conduct their interpersonal transactions. This is because they are taken to be able and willing to engage fully in the discourse processes that give rise to the rules of behavior and the system of beliefs, values and attitudes that define what are the socially accepted courses of action, and, accordingly, their and others person's social roles. Thus, when confronted with the need to make sense of a social arena, the user of this lens draws conclusions about that arena, and about his or her position in it, after engaging in discourse with the other actors present that enables him or her to socially construct the meaning of his or her first-person experiences in that arena, and of the motivations behind the observed behavior adopted by the others present. This then establishes the form of social interaction that he or she believes to be necessary in order to be accepted by those present with whom they share a set of common understandings and values.

Hermeneutic Agency

This disposition is grounded in two propositions. The first is that a social arena is subjectively experienced by those who engage in it, the meaning and significance of which is individually constructed on the basis of self-knowledge, which is the product of reflecting on inner, lived and conscious inimitable first-person experiences, which draw upon their encounters with the material and their feelings and discernments, the truth-value of which can be established by reference to the personal beneficiality of that experience. From these individual constructs, conclusions can be drawn about what, if anything, is, and can be, known with any confidence about that arena and about the reasons for the social actions taken by those present. The second proposition is that is all that is knowable about that arena is the existence of self, with the almost inevitable sense of the immediate personal experience of aloneness, death, and even moral responsibility, and of the on-going challenge of living a life in the most valid and fulfilling way possible in the face of what fate and destiny may have in store. Those engaged in this arena are considered to have, at best, the potential capacity to influence how they conduct their interpersonal transactions. This is because they can never fully predict even their own social actions, because whilst they may accept that they can, if they so wish, choose to draw upon their power of will actualize their potential, they may also accept that the struggle to achieve the desired self-identity and authenticity that such an act of will involves may proved to be too much. Given they consider that no one can ever understand another's social actions, they are inclined toward self-referentiality in their social relationships. Thus, when confronted with the need to make sense of a social arena, the user of this lens draws conclusions about that arena, and about his or her position in it, after he or she has individually constructed the meaning of his or her inimitable first-person experiences in that arena, and of the motivations behind the observed behaviors adopted by the others present. This then establishes the form of social interaction that he or she believes to be necessary in order to be tolerated by those present.

NATURALIST AGENCY

This disposition is grounded in two propositions. The first is that a social arena is entirely material in form with objectively factual qualities. These can be described, explained and predicted by reference to objective data, the truth-value of which can be only established by generally agreed objective enquiry procedures involving inductive inference and/or deductive logic that draws only upon material evidence or luminous premises. From these factual qualities, conclusions can be drawn about what is, and can be, known with confidence about that social arena and about the reasons for the social actions taken by those present. The second proposition is that that arena's existence is contingent on the known patterns of social relationships amongst those present, whose social actions come together to sustain its existence. This means that that the social actions of those present are best, or most appropriately, explained, essentially, by the reference to their revealed wishes and desires. Those engaged in this arena are considered to have the capacity to determine how they conduct their interpersonal transactions. This is because they are taken to be able and willing to author their social actions and social relationships, which they consider to be exclusive domain of their own self-determined set of hopes, aspirations and goals. Thus, when confronted with the need to make sense of a social arena, the user of this lens draws conclusions about that arena, and about his or her position in it, after analyzing the material objects and phenomena he or she perceives, and probing the motivations behind the observed behavior adopted by the others present. This then establishes the form of social interaction that he or she believes to be necessary in order to exploit the self-interested material opportunities that he or she has identified and evaluated.

Chapter 10

CONCLUSION

This chapter has explicated and critically reviewed the competing ways that a social arena can best be coherently described, explained and understood and that social actions within it can best be ascribed It has identified, from the epistemological and ontological dichotomies drawn in the philosophy of social sciences, a set of four mutually exclusive and mutually incompatible social-reality dispositions: naturalist structuralism, naturalist agency, hermeneutic structuralism and hermeneutic agency. These constitute the contending lens through which a cognitively consistent person can choose to frame a social arena. This, it must be emphasized, is not to suggest that such a person would necessarily have the same epistemological or ontological preferences in all social arenas. Indeed, the very point is that he or she can choose the lens through which a particular arena is to be observed and interrogated. Once a social-reality disposition has been adopted for a particular social arena, then there are a set of core values, attitudes and opinions that flow from it, which become the salient constituents of that person's cognitive system when he or she is in that arena. This brings to the fore how a person chooses his or her preferred lens.

BIBLIOGRAPHY

Abelson, R. P., Aronson, E., McGuire, W. J., Newcomb, T. M., Rosenberg, M. J., and Tannenbaum, P. (eds.) 1968. *Theories of Cognitive Consistency: A Sourcebook*. Chicago: Rand-McNally.

Abrams, D. and Hogg, M. A. (eds.) 1990. *Social Identity Theory: Constructive and Critical Advances*. New York: Springer-Verlag.

Abrams, M. H. 1971. *Natural Supernaturalism Tradition and Revolution in Romantic Literature*. New York: W.W. Norton.

Ackermann, R. 1976. *The Philosophy of Karl Popper*. Amherst, MA: University of Massachusetts Press.

Ackrill, J. L. 1981. *Aristotle the Philosopher*. Oxford: Oxford University Press.

Acton, H. B. 1971. *The Morals of Markets*, London: Longman.

Adams, J. S. 1965. "Inequity in Social Exchange." In Berkowitz, L. (ed.), *Advances in Experimental Social Psychology* (Vol. 1). New York: Academic Press.

Adams, M. M. 1987. *William Ockham*. Notre Dame, IN: University of Notre Dame.

Adler, A. [1922] 1924. *The Practice and Theory of Individual Psychology* (tr. Radin, P.). London: Kegan Paul, Trench, Trubner.

Adler, A. [1929] 1969. *The Science of Living* (ed. Ansbacher, H. L.). Garden City, NY: Doubleday Anchor.

Adler, A. [1933] 1973. "On the Origins of the Striving for Superiority and of Social Interest." In Ansbacher, H. L. and Ansbucher, R. R. (eds.), *Superiority and Social Interest: A Collection of Later Writings*. New York: Viking.

Adler, A. [1938] 1943. *Social Interest: A Challenge to Mankind*. London: Faber & Faber.

Adorno, T. W., Frenkel-Bruns, E., Levinson, D. J. and Sanford, R. N. 1950. *The Authoritarian Personality*. New York: Harper.

Adorno, T. W. and Horkheimer, M. [1947] 1972. *Dialect of Enlightenment* (tr. Cumming, J.). London: Allen Lane.

Ajzen, I. 1991. "The Theory of Planned Behavior." *Organizational Behavior and Human Decision Processes* 50: 179–211.

Ajzen, I. and Fishbein, M. 1980. *Understanding Attitudes and Predicting Social Behavior*. Englewood Cliffs, NJ: Prentice-Hall

Alcoff, L. and Potter, E. (eds.) 1993. *Feminist Epistemologies*. New York: Routledge.

Alderfer, C. P. 1972. *Existence, Relatedness, and Growth*. New York: Free Press.

Alexander, J. 1987. *The Micro–Macro Link*. Berkeley and Los Angeles, CA: University of California Press.

Alexander, J. 2003. *The Meaning of Social Life: A Cultural Sociology*. Oxford: Oxford University Press.

Alexander, P. 1985. *Ideas, Qualities and Corpuscles*. Cambridge: Cambridge University Press.

Allport, G. W. 1937. *Personality: A Psychological Interpretation*. New York: Holt.

Allport, G. W. 1955. *Becoming: Basic Considerations for a Psychology of Personality*. New Haven, CT: Yale University Press.

Allport, G. W. 1961. *Pattern and Growth in Personalities*. New York: Holt, Rinehart and Winston.

Alston, W. P. 1989. *Epistemic Justification: Essays in the Theory of Knowledge*. Ithaca, NY: Cornell University Press.

Alston, W. P. (ed.) 2002. *Realism and Antirealism*. New York: Sage.

Althusser, L. 1962. "Contradictions and Overdetermination" (tr. Brewster, B.). Available at http://www.marxists.org/reference/archive/althusser/1962/overdetermination.htm.

Althusser, L. [1965] 1969. For Marx (tr. Brewster, B.). Harmondworth, Gt. Lon., UK: Penguin. Available at http://www.marxists.org/reference/archive/1965/index.Althuss-er/htm.

Altman, Y. and Baruch, Y. 1998. "Cultural Theory and Organizations: Analytical Methods and Cases." *Organizational Studies* 19 (5): 769–85.

Anderson, R. J., Hughes, J. A. and Sharrock, W. W. 1986. *Philosophy and the Human Sciences*. New York: Barnes and Noble.

Anderson, S. M. and Cole, S. W. 1990. "'Do I Know You" The Role of Significant Others in General Social Perception." *Journal of Personal Social Psychology* 59 (3): 384–99.

Annas, J. and Barnes, J. 1985. *The Modes of Scepticism.* Cambridge: Cambridge University Press.

Antonak, R. F. 1988. "Methods to Measure Attitudes Toward People who are Disabled." In Yuker, H. E. (ed.), *Attitudes Toward Persons with Disabilities.* New York: Springer.

Appiah, K. A. 2008. *Experiments in Ethics.* Cambridge, MA: Harvard University Press.

Aquinas, St. T. [1264] 1974. *Selected Political Writings* (ed. d'Entreves, A. P.). Oxford: Blackwell.

Aquinas, T. [1256–59] 1952. *Disputed Questions on Truth.* Chicago, IL: Regnery.

Aquinas, T. [1259–64] 1905. *Summa Contra Gentiles* [*On the Truth of the Catholic Faith Against the Unbelievers*] (abridged) (tr. and ed.Rickaby, J.). London: Burns and Oates. Available at: http://www2.nd.edu/Departments/Maritain/etext/gc.htm.

Aquinas, T. [1266–73] 1948. *The Summa Theologica* (trs. Fathers of the English Dominica Province). New York: Benziger.

Archer, M. S. 1989. *Culture and Agency: The Place of Culture in Social Theory.* Cambridge: Cambridge University Press

Archer, M. S. 1990, "Human Agency and Social Structure: A Critique of Giddens." In Clark, J., Modgil, C. and Modgil, S. (eds.), *Anthony Giddens: Consensus and Controversy.* Basingstoke, Hamp., UK: Falmer Press.

Archer, M. S. 1995. *Realist Social Theory: A Morphogenetic Approach.* Cambridge: Cambridge University Press.

Archer, M. S. 1996. "Social Integration and System Integration: Developing the Distinction." *Sociology* 30 (4): 679–99.

Archer, M. S. 2000. *Being Human: The Problem of Agency.* Cambridge: Cambridge University Press.

Archer, M. S. 2003. *Structure, Agency and the Internal Conversation.* Cambridge: Cambridge University Press.

Archer, M. S., Lawson, T., Collier, A., Norre, A. and Bhaskar, R. 1998. *Critical Realism: Essential Readings.* London: Routledge

Ardrey, R. 1961. *African Genesis: A Personal Investigation into the Animal Origins and Nature of Man.* London: Collins.

Ardrey, R. 1967. *The Territorial Imperative: The Social Contract: A Personal Inquiry into the Evolutionary Sources of Order and Disorder.* London: Collins.

Ardrey, R. 1970. *The Social Contract: A Personal Inquiry into the Evolutionary Sources of Order and Disorder.* London: Collins.

Ardrey, R. 1976. *The Hunting Hypothesis: A Personal Conclusion Concerning the Evolutionary Nature of Man.* London: Collins.

Aristotle [350 BC] 2004. *Nicomachean Ethics* (tr. Ross, W. D.). Available at http:// www.etext.library.adelaide.edu.au/mirror/classics.mit.edu/Aristotle/nicomachaen.html

Aristotle 1996. *The Politics and the Constitution of Athens* (ed. Everson, S.). Cambridge: Cambridge University Press.

Aristotle [350 BC/1924/1953] 1994–2000. *Metaphysics* (tr. Ross, W. D). Available at: http://classics.mit.edu/Aristotle/metaphysics.4.iv.html

Armstrong, D. M. 1968. *A Materialist Theory of the Mind.* New York: Humanities Press.

Armstrong, D. M. 1978. *Universals and Scientific Realism.* Cambridge: Cambridge University Press.

Armstrong, D. M. 1989. *Universals: An Opinionated Introduction.* Boulder, CO: Westview Press.

Armstrong, D. M. 2000. "Universals as Attributes." In Kim, J. and Sosa, E. (eds.), *Metaphysics: An Anthology.* Oxford: Blackwell.

Armstrong, K. 2005. *A Short History of Myth.* Edinburgh, UK: Canongate.

Arneson, R. 1991. "Autonomy and Preference Formation." In Coleman, J. and Buchanan, A. (eds.), *In Harm's Way: Essays in Honor of Joel Feinberg.* Cambridge: Cambridge University Press.

Arnold, M. B. 1960. *Emotion and Personality* (Vol. 1: *Psychological Aspects*). New York: Columbia University Press.

Aronson, E. 1969. "The theory of Cognitive Dissonance: A Current Perspective." In Berkowitz, L. (ed.), *Advances in Experimental Social Psychology* (Vol. 4). New York: Academic Press.

Arnhart, L. 1998. *Darwinian Natural Right: The Biological Ethics of Human Nature.* Albany, NY: State University of New York Press.

Arrow, K. J. 1954. *Social Choice and Individual Values.* New York: Wiley.

Arrow, K. J. 1984. *Individual Choice under Certainty and Uncertainty.* Oxford: Blackwell.

Asch, S. E. 1951. "Effects of Group Pressure upon the Modification and Distortion of Judgement." In Guetzkow, H. (ed.), *Groups, Leadership and Men.* Pittsburgh, PA: Carnegie Press

Asch, S. E. 1956. "Studies on Independence and Conformity: A Minority of One against an Unanimous Majority." *Psychological Monographs* 70.

Atherton, J. S. 2003. *Learning and Teaching: Cognitive Dissonance*. Available at *http://www.-dmu.ac.uk/~jamesa/learning/dissonance.htm.*

Atherton, M. (ed.) 1999. *The Empiricists: Critical Essays on Locke, Berkeley, and Hume*. Blue Ridge Summit, PA: Rowman & Littlefield.

Audi, R. 1993. *Action, Intention, and Reason.* Ithaca, NY: Cornell University Press.

Aurelius, M. [c.167] 1974. *Meditations* (tr. Staniford, M.). Harmondsworth, Gt. Lon., UK: Penguin.

Austin, J. [1832] 1995. *The Province of Jurisprudence Determined.* Cambridge: Cambridge University Press.

Austin, J. L. 1962. *How to Do Things with Words*. Cambridge, MA: Harvard University Press.

Axelrod, R. 1984. *The Evolution of Cooperation.* New York: Basic Books.

Ayer, A. J. [1936] 1975. *Language, Truth and Logic.* Harmondsworth, Gt. Lon., UK: Penguin.

Ayer, A. J. 1953. *The Foundations of Empirical Knowledge*. London: Macmillan.

Ayer, A. J. (ed.) 1959. *Logical Positivism.* New York: Free Press.

Bacharach, M. & Gambetta, D. 1997. "Trust in Signs." In Cook, K. S. (ed.), *Trust in Society*. Russell Sage Foundation. New York.

Bacharach, M. and Gambetta, D. 2001. "Trust as Type Detection." In Castelfranchi, C. and Tan, Y - H. (eds.), *Trust and Deception in Virtual Societies*. Kluwer Academic.

Bacon, F. ([1597–1625] 1972. "Essays or Counsels Civil and Moral." In Elliot, C. W. (ed.), *The Harvard Classics*. New York: Collier.

Bacon, F. [1623] 1997. *The Great Instauration: The Novum Organum*. Whitefish, MT: Kessinger.

Baehr, J. S. 2006. "*A priori* and *A posteriori*." *The Internet Encyclopedia of Philosophy*. Available at http://www.iep.utm.edu/a/apriori.htm.

Baert, P. 1998. *Social Theory in the Twentieth Century*. Cambridge: Polity Press.

Baggini, J. 2002. *Making Sense: Philosophy behind the Headlines*. Oxford: Oxford

Baghramian, M. 2004. *Relativism*. London: Routledge

Bakhtin, M. [1930s] 1981. *The Dialogic Imagination: Four Essays* (ed. Holquist, M., trs. Emerson, C. and Holquist, M.). Austin, TX: University of Texas Press.

Baier, K. 1958. *The Moral Point of View*. Ithaca, NY: Cornell University Press.

Baker, K. 1992. "Defining the Public Sphere in Eighteenth Century France: Variations on a Theme by Habermas." In Calhoun, C. (ed.), *Habermas and the Public Sphere*. Cambridge, MA: MIT Press.

Bakhtin, M. [1975] 1981. *The Dialogic Imagination: Four Essays* (ed. Holquist, M.). Austin, TX: University of Texas Press.
Bambrough, R. 1979. *Moral Scepticism and Moral Knowledge.* London: Routledge and Kegan Paul.
Bandura A. 1977. *Social Learning Theory*. Englewood Cliffs, NJ: Prentice Hall.
Bandura, A. 1986. *Social Foundations of Thought and Action: A Social Cognition Theory*. Englewood Cliffs, NJ: Prentice-Hall
Banfield, E. C. 1958. *The Moral Basis of a Backward Society*. New York: Free Press.
Bannister, R. C. 1987. *Sociology and Scientism: The American Quest for Objectivity, 1980–1940.* Chapel Hill, NC and London: The University of North Carolina Press
Barbalet, J. M. 1998. *Emotion, Social Theory, and Social Structure*. Cambridge: Cambridge University Press.
Barkow, J. H., Cosmides, L. and Tooby, J. (eds.) 1992. *The Adapted Mind: Evolutionary Psychology and the Generation of Cultures*. New York: Oxford University Press.
Barnard, A. 2003. *History and Theory in Anthropology*. Cambridge: Cambridge University Press.
Barnard, C. 1938. *The Functions of the Executive*. Cambridge, MA: Harvard University Press.
Barnard, L. L. 1934. "Crowds". In Seligman, E. R. A. (ed.), *Encyclopaedia of Social Sciences* (Vol. IV). New York: Macmillan.
Barnard, L. L. 1934. "Mobs". In Seligman, E. R. A. (ed.), *Encyclopaedia of Social Sciences* (Vol. X). New York: Macmillan.
Barnes, B. 1974. *Scientific Knowledge and Sociological Theory*. London: Routledge and Kegan.
Barrett, W. 1958 *Irrational Man: A Study in Existential Philosophy*. Westport, CT: Greenwood.
Barry, N. 2000. *An Introduction to Modern Political Theory* (4th. ed.). Basingstoke Hamp., UK: Macmillan Press.
Barthes, R. [1975] 1977. *Roland Barthes by Roland Barthes* (tr. Howard, R.). New York: Hill & Wang.
Barthes, R. 1972. To Write: An Intransitive Verb." In Macksey, R, and Donato, E. (eds.), *The Language of Criticism and the Science of Man: The Structuralist Controversy*. Baltimore, MD: John Hopkins University Press.
Bartlett, S. J. and P. Suber (eds.). 1987. *Self-Reference: Reflections on Reflexivity*. Dordrecht, NL: Martinus Nijhoff.
Batton, A. de 2004. *Status Anxiety*. New York: Pantheon Books.

Baumeister, R. 1993. *Self-E*steem. New York: Plenum Press.
Bayle, P. [1606] 1965. *Historical and Critical Dictionary* (trs. Popkin, R. and Brush, C.). Indianapolis, IN: Boobs-Merrel
Beck, U. 1998. *Democracy without Enemies*. Cambridge: Polity Press.
Becker, G. S. 1996. *Accounting for Tastes*. Cambridge, MA: Harvard University Press.
Becker, G. S. [1964] 1975. *Human Capital* (2nd ed.). Washington, DC: National Bureau of Economic Research
Becker, G. S. 1976. *The Economic Approach to Human Behavior*. Chicago, IL: University of Chicago Press.
Beiser, F. 2005. *Schiller as Philosopher: A Re-examination*. Oxford: Oxford University Press.
Beiser, F. 2005. *Hegel*. New York: Routledge
Belsey, C. 2002, *Poststructuralism: A Very Short Introduction*. Oxford: Oxford University Press.
Bendix, E. 1989. *Embattled Reason: Essays on Social Knowledge*. Edison, NJ: Transaction Publishers.
Benedict, R. [1934] 1959. "Anthropology and the Abnormal." In Mead, M. (ed.), *An Anthropologist at Work: Writings of Ruth Benedict*. Boston, MA: Haughton Miffin.
Benedict, R. [1934] 1989. *Patterns of Culture*. New York: Houghton Mifflin.
Benedict, R. [1946] 1989. *The Chrysanthemum and the Sword: Patterns of Japanese Culture* (for. Vogel E. F.). Boston, MA: Haughton Miffin.
Bengtsson, J. O. 2006. *The Worldview of Personalism: Origins and Early Development*. New York: Oxford University Press.
Benson, P. 1987. "Freedom and Value." *Journal of Philosophy* 84: 465–86.
Bentham, J. [1789] 1970. *An Introduction to the Principles of Morals and Legislation* (eds. Burns, J. H. and Hart, H. L. A.). London: Athlone Press.
Benton, T. and Craib, I. 2001. *Philosophy of Social Science: The Philosophical Foundations of Social Thought*. Basingstoke Hamp., UK: Palgrave.
Bem, D. J. 1965. "An Experimental Analysis of Self-Persuasion." *Journal of Experimental Social Psychology* 1: 199–218
Bem, D. J. 1967. "Self-Perception: An Alternative Interpretation of Cognitive Dissonance Phenomena." *Psychological Review* 74: 183–200.
Beran, H. 1987. *The Consent Theory of Political Obligation*. London: Croom Helm.
Berenson,m M. 1976. "Freedom." In Lloyd, D. T. (ed.), *Philosopher and the Teacher*. London and New York: Routledge.

Berger, P. L. and Luckmann, T. 1966. *The Social Construction of Reality: A Treatise in the Sociology of Knowledge*. Harmondworth, Gt. Lon., UK: Penguin.

Bergson, A. J. 2004. "Durkheim's Theory of Mental Categories: A Review of the Evidence." *Annual Review of Sociology* 30: 395–408.

Berkeley, G [1734] 2004. *The Analyst: A Discourse Addressed to an Infidel Mathematician*. Available at http://www.maths.tcd.ie/pub/HistMath/People/Berkeley/.

Berkeley, G. [1710] 1962. *The Principles of Knowledge* (ed. Warnock, G. J.). London: Fontana.

Berkeley, G. [1713] 1948. "Three Dialogues between Hylas and Philonous." In Berkeley, G. *The Works of George Berkeley, Bishop of Clyne* (eds. Luse, A. A. and Jessop, T. E.). Edinburgh, UK: Thomas Nelson.

Berlin, I. 1969. *Four Essays on Liberty*. London: Oxford University Press.

Berlin, I. 1976. *Vico and Herder*. New York: Viking.

Bermúdez, J. L., Marcel, A. and Eilan, N. (eds.) 1995. *The Body and the Self*. Cambridge, MA and London: MIT Press.

Bernard, L. L. 1926. *An Introduction to Social Psychology*. New York: Henry Holt.

Berne, E. [1964] 1992. *Games People Play: The Psychology of Human Relationships*. New York: Balantine.

Bernoulli [1738] 1954. "Specimen Theoriae Novac de Mensura Sortis [Exposition of a New Theory of the Measurement of Risk]" (tr. Sommer, L.). *Econometrica* 22(1): 23–36.

Bernstein, P. L. 1996. *Against the Gods: The Remarkable Story of Risk*. New York: John Wiley.

Berofsky, B. 1995. *Liberation from Self*. New York: Cambridge University Press.

Bertens, *H. 2001. Literary Theory: The Basics.* London and New York: Routledge.

Bhaskar, R. 1975. *A Realist Theory of Science*. Leeds, UK: Leeds Books.

Bhaskar, R. [1975] 1997 *A Realist Theory of Science* (2nd ed.). New York and London: Verso.

Bhaskar, R. 1979. *The Possibility of Naturalism: A Philosophical Critique of the Contemporary Human Sciences*. London and New York: Routledge.

Bhaskar, R. [1979] 1998. *The Possibility of Naturalism: A Philosophical Critique of the Contemporary Human Sciences* (3rd ed.). London and New York: Routledge.

Bhaskar, R., 1993. *Dialectic: The Pulse of Freedom*. London: Verso.

Billig, M. 1976. *Social Psychology and Group Relations*. New York: Academic Press.

Bilton, T., Bonnett, K., Jones, P., Lawson, T., Skinner, D., Stanworth, M. and Webster, A. 1996. *Introductory Sociology* (3rd ed.). London: Macmillan.

Blackburn, S. 1993. *Essays in Quasi-Realism*. Oxford: Oxford University Press.

Blackburn, S. 1994. *Oxford Dictionary of Philosophy*. Oxford: Oxford University Press.

Blackburn, S. 2001. *Being Good*. Oxford: Oxford University Press.

Blackburn, S. 2003. *Ethics: A Very Short Introduction*. Oxford: Oxford University Press:

Blackburn, S. 2005. *Truth: A Guide for the Perplexed*. New York: Oxford University Press.

Blackmore, S. 2003. *Consciousness: An Introduction*. Oxford: Oxford University Press.

Blaikie, N. 1993. *Approaches to Social Enquiry*. Cambridge: Polity Press.

Blanchard, E. B. and Scarboro, M. E 1972. "Locus of Control, Political Attitudes, and Voting Behavior in a College Age Population." *Psychology Reports* 30: 529–30.

Blaise, P. [1670] 1966. *Pensées* (tr. Krasilsheimer, A. J.). Harmondworth, Gt. Lon., UK: Penguin.

Blass, T. 2004. *The Man Who Shocked the World: The Life and Legacy of Stanley Milgram*. New York: Basic Books.

Blau, P. M. 1964. *Exchange and Power in Social Life*. New York: Wiley.

Blauner, R. 1964. *Alienation and Freedom*. Chicago, IL: University of Chicago Press.

Block, N. 1980. "Introduction: What is Functionalism?" In Block, N. (ed.), *Readings in Philosophy of Psychology*. Cambridge, MA: Harvard University Press.

Bloomfield, L. 1933. *Language*. New York: Henry Holt.

Blumer, H. 1969. *Symbolism Interactionism: Perspective and Method*. Englewood Cliff, NJ: Prentice Hall.

Boeree, C. G. 2003. *Trait Theories of Personality*. Available at http://webspace.s-hip.edu/~cgboeree/-genp-sytraits.html.

Boeree, C. G. [1998] 2006. *Abraham Maslow, 1908–1970*. Available at http://webspace.-ship.edu/cgboeree/maslow.html.

Bohman, J. 1991. *New Philosophy of Social Science: Problems of Indeterminacy*. Cambridge: Polity Press.

Bohner, G., Moskowitz, G. and Chaiken, S. 1995. "The Interplay of Heuristic and Systematic Processing of Social Information." *European Review of Social Psychology* 6: 33–68.

Bond, R., and Smith, P. 1996. "Culture and Conformity: A Meta-Analysis of Studies using Asch's (1952b, 1956) Line Judgment Task." *Psychological Bulletin* 119: 111–37.

BonJour, L. 1985. *The Structure of Empirical Knowledge*. Cambridge, MA: Harvard University Press.

BonJour, L. 2002. *Epistemology: Classic Problems and Contemporary Responses*. Blue Ridge Summit, PA: Rowman & Littlefield.

Borges, J. L. 1964. "The Lottery in Babylon." In *Labyrinths: Selected Stories and Other Writings*. New York: New Directions.

Borman, E. G. 1975. *Discussion and Group Methods: Theory and Practice* (2nd ed.). New York: Harper and Row.

Bossuet, J. [1679] 1906. "Political Treatise." In Robinson, J. H. (ed.), *Readings in European History* (vol 2). Boston, MA: Ginn.

Bott, E. 1957. *Family and Social Network: Roles, Norms, and External Relationships in Ordinary Urban Families*. London: Tavistock.

Boulder, K. 1990. *Three Faces of Power*. Newbury Park, CA: Sage.

Bourdieu, P. 1973. "Cultural Reproduction and Social Reproduction." In Brown, R. (ed.), *Knowledge, Education and Social Change*. London: Tavistock.

Bourdieu, P. 1976. *Outline of a Theory of Practice* (tr. Nice. R.). Cambridge: Cambridge University Press.

Bourdieu, P. 1990. *The Logic of Practice* (tr. Nice. R.). Cambridge: Polity Press.

Bourdieu, P. 1998. *Acts of Resistance: Against the New Myths of our Time*. Cambridge: Polity Press.

Bourdieu, P. and Passeron, J.–C. [1970] 1990. *Reproduction in Education, Society and Culture* (tr. Wacquant L.) (2nd ed.). London: Sage

Bourdieu, P. and Wacquant L. 1992. *An Invitation to Reflexive Sociology*. Chicago, IL: University of Chicago Press, 1992.

Bourdieu, P., 1986. "The Forms of Capital." In Richardson, J. G. (ed.), *Handbook of Theory and Research for the Sociology of Education* (2nd ed.). New York: Greenwood.

Bowie, A. 1967. *From Romanticism to Critical Theory*. London: Routledge.

Bowie, M. 1979. "Jacques Lacan." In Sturrock, J. (ed.), *Structuralism and Since: From Lévi-Strauss to Derrida*. Oxford: Oxford University Press.

Bradley, F. H. [1893] 2005. *Appearances and Reality: A Metaphysical Essay*. Boston, MA: Adamant Media.

Bradley, F. H. [1876] 1988. *Ethical Studies* (2nd ed.). Oxford: Oxford University Press

Bramly, S. 1992. *Leonardo: the Artist and the Man* (trs. Reynolds, S.). London: Michael Joseph.

Brand, M. and Walton, D. (eds.) 1976. *Action Theory*. Dordrecht, NL: Reidel.

Branden, N. 2001. *The Psychology of Self-Esteem*. New York: Wiley.

Brandon, S. F. G. 1962. *Man and his Destiny in the Great Religions*. Manchester, UK: Manchester University Press.

Braybrooke, D. 1987. *Philosophy of Social Science*. Englewood Cliffs, NJ: Prentice Hall.

Brehm, J. and Cohen, A. 1962. *Explorations in Cognitive Dissonance*. New York: Wiley.

Brehm, J. W. 1976. "Responses to Loss of Freedom: A Theory of Psychological Reactance." In Thibaut, J. W., Spence, J. T. and Carson, R. C. (eds.), *Contemporary Topics in Social Psychology*. Morristown, NJ: General Learning Press.

Brehm, S. S. and Brehm, J. W. 1981. *Psychological Reactance: A Theory of Freedom and Control*. New York: Academic Press.

Brennan, J. F. 1969. "Autoeroticism or Social Feeling as Basic Human Development." *Journal of Individual Psychology* 25: 3–18.

Brennan, T. 2003. *The Transmission of Affect*. Ithaca, NY: Cornell University Press.

Brentano, F. [1874] 1995. *Psychology from an Empirical Point of View* (ed. McAlister, L. L., trs. Rancurello, A. C., Terrell, D. B., and McAlister, L. L.). London: Routledge.

Brink, D. 1989. *Moral Realism and the Foundations of Ethics*. Cambridge: Cambridge University Press.

Brooks, I. 1999. *Individuals, Groups and the Organisation*. London: Financial Times Management.

Brown, L. S. 1988. "Anarchism, Existentialism and Human Nature: A Critique." *The Raven* 2 (1): 49–60.

Bryant, C.G.A. 1985. *Positivism in Social Theory and Research*. Basingstoke Hamp., UK: Macmillan.

Buber, M. [1923] 1958. *I and Thou* (tr. Smith, R. G.). New York: Charles Scribner's Sons.

Buchanan, J. M., and Tullock, G. 1962. *The Calculus of Consent*. Ann Arbor, MI: University of Michigan Press.

Buckley, W. 1967. *Sociology and Modern Systems Theory*. Englewood Cliffs, NJ: Prentice Hall.

Bunge, M. 1996. *Finding Philosophy in Social Science.* New Haven, CT: Yale University.

Bunge, M. 1998. *Social Science under Debate: A Philosophical Perspective.* Toronto, Ont., CA: University of Toronto.

Burge, T. 1979. "Individualism and the Mental." *Midwest Studies in Philosophy* 4: 73–121.

Burge, T. 1986. "Individualism and Psychology." *Philosophical Review* 95: 3–45.

Burge, T. 1988. "Individualism and Self-Knowledge." *Journal of Philosophy* 85: 649–65.

Burge, T. 1989. "Individuation and Causation in Psychology." *Pacific Philosophical Quarterly* 70: 303–22.

Burke, T. E. 1983. *The Philosophy of Popper.* Manchester, UK: Manchester University Press

Burke, E. [1756] 1987. *A Philosophical Enquiry into the Origin of our Ideas of the Sublime and Beautiful* (2nd ed.). Oxford: Blackwell.

Burke, E. [1790] 1993. *Reflections on the Revolution in France.* Oxford: Oxford University Press.

Burrow, R., Jr, von 1999. *Personalism: A Critical Introduction.* Atlanta, GA: Chalice Press

Burton, R. [1621] 2001. *The Anatomy of Melancholy* (ed. Jackson, H.). New York: New York Review Books Classics.

Bushman, B. and Baumeister, R. 1998. "Threatened Egoism, Narcissism, Self-esteem, and Direct and Displaced Aggression: Does Self-love and Self-hate Lead to Violence." *Journal of Personality and Social Psychology* 75: 219–29.

Buss, D. M. 1999. *Evolutionary Psychology: The New Science of the Mind.* Needham Heights, MA: Allyn and Bacon.

Butler-Bowden, T. 2007. *50 Psychology Classics.* London and Boston, MA: Nicholas Brealey.

Butterfield, J. 1998. "Determinism and Indeterminism." In Craig, E.(ed.), *Routledge Encyclopedia of Philosophy.* London: Routledge.

Byatt, A. S. and Wood, H. H. (eds.) 2007. *Memory.* London: Chatto.

Byron, M. (ed.) 2004. *Satisficing and Maximising: Moral Theory's Practical Reason.* Cambridge: Cambridge University Press.

Calhoun, C. and Solomon, R. (eds.) 1984. *What is an Emotion?* New York: Oxford University Press.

Callinicos, A. 1999. *Social Theory: A Historical Introduction.* Cambridge: Polity Press.

Cameron, S. 2002. *The Economics of Sin: Rational Choice or no Choice at all.* Cheltenham, Glos., UK: Edward Elgar.

Campbell, C. 1996. *The Myth of Social Action*. Cambridge: Cambridge University Press.

Campbell, J. K., O'Rourke, M. and Silverstein, H. S. (eds.) 2007. *Causation and Explanation*. Cambridge, MA: MIT Press.

Campbell, K. 1989. *Abstract Particulars*. Oxford: Blackwell.

Camus, A. [1942] 1982. *The Outsider* (tr. Laredo, J.). Harmondworth, Gt. Lon., UK: Penguin.

Camus, A. [1942] 2005. *The Myth of Sisyphus* (tr. O'Brien, J.). Harmondworth, Gt. Lon., UK: Penguin.

Caplan, A. L. (ed.) 1978. *The Sociobiology Debate: Readings on Ethical and Scientific Issues*. New York: Harper and Row.

Capozza, D. and Brown, R. 2000. *Social Identity Processes*. Beverley Hills, CA: Sage

Carey, D. 2000. "Introduction." In Hutcheson, F. [1755], *A System of Moral Philosophy*. Bristol, UK: Thoemmes Press.

Carnap, R. [1928] 1969. *The Logical Structure of the World and Pseudoproblems in Philosophy* (tr.George, R. A.). Berkeley and Los Angeles, CA: University of California Press.

Cassam, Q. 1997. *Self and World*. Oxford: Oxford University Press.

Cassidy, D. 1991. *Uncertainty: The Life and Science of Werner Heisenberg*. New York: W. H. Freeman.

Caston, V. 1997. "Epiphenomenalisms, Ancient and Modern." *The Philosophical Review* 106: 309–63.

Cattell, R. B. 1965. *The Scientific Analysis of Personality*. Baltimore, MD: Penguin.

Cattel, R. B. 1980. *Personality and Learning Theory*. New York: Springer.

Caws, P. 1988. *Structuralism: The Art of the Intelligible*. Atlantic Highlands, NJ: Humanities Press.

Chaiken, S., Liberman, A. and Eagly, A. H. 1989. "Heuristic and Systematic Information Processing within and beyond Persuasion Context." In Uleman, J. S. and Bargh, J. A. (eds.), *Unintended Thought*. New York: Guilford.

Chalmers, D. 1996. *The Conscious Mind: In Search of a Theory of Conscious Experience*. New York: Oxford University Press.

Chan, W. – T. 1963. *A Source Book for Chinese Philosophy*. Princeton, NJ: Princeton University Press.

Charles, D. and Lennon, K. (eds.) 1992. *Reduction, Explanation and Realism*. Oxford: Clarendon.

Chen, S. and Chaiken, S. 1999. "The Heuristic-Systematic Model in its Broader Context." In Chaiken, S. and Trope, Y. (eds.), *Dual-Process Theories in Social Psychology*. New York: Guilford.

Chesterton, G. K. [1908] 2007. *Orthodoxy*. New York: Filiquarian. Available at http://books.google.co.uk/books?id=W6j4Qx2UF2AC&pg=PA97&lpg=PA97&dq=chesterton+%22the+real+trouble+with+this+world+of+ours+is%22&source=web&ots=yunxnJFil&sig=0zbAi2pTbtupcCvt9JjErodLw2Y&hl=en.

Chisholm, R. [1964] 2002. "Human Freedom and Self." In Kane, R. (ed.), *Free Will*. Malden, MA: Blackwell.

Chisholm, R. M. 1989. *Theory of Knowledge* (3rd ed.). Englewood Cliffs, NJ: Prentice Hall.

Chomsky, N. [1955] 1975. *The Logical Structure of Linguistic Theory*. New York: Springer.

Chomsky, N. 1965. *Aspects of the Theory of Syntax*. Cambridge, MA: MIT Press..

Chomsky, N. 1989. *Necessary Illusions: Thought Control in Democratic Societies*. Boston; MA: South End Press.

Christman, J. (ed.) 1989. *The Inner Citadel: Essays on Individual Autonomy*. Oxford and New York: Oxford University Press.

Christman, J. 1991. "Autonomy and Personal History." *Canadian Journal of Philosophy* 21 (1): 1–24.

Cicero [44 BC] 1971. *De Fato* [*On Fate*] (tr. Sharples, R. W.). Warminister, Wilts., UK: Aris & Phillips.

Clark, M. S. and Mills, J. 1993. "The Difference between Communal and Exchange Relationships: What it is and What it is not." *Personality and Social Psychology Bulletin* 19: 684–91.

Clarke R. [2000] 2004. "Incompatibilist (Nondeterministic) Theories of Free Will." In Zelta, E. N. (ed.) *The Stanford Encyclopedia of Philosophy*. Available at http://plato.stanford.edu/entries/incompatibilism-theories/.

Clarke, R. 2005. *Libertarian Accounts of Free Will*. New York: Oxford University Press.

Coady, C. A. J. 1992. *Testimony: A Philosophical Study*. Oxford: Oxford University Press.

Coelho, P. [1988] 1995. *The Alchemist*. London: HarperCollins.

Cohen, G. A. 2001. *Karl Marx's Theory of History: A Defence* (2nd ed.). Oxford: Oxford University Press.

Cohen, G. A. 1988. *History, Labour and Freedom*. Oxford: Oxford University Press..

Cohen, M., March, J. and Olsen, J. 1972. "A Garbage Can Model of Organizational Choice." *Administrative Science Quarterly* 17 (1): 1–23.

Coleman, J. S. 1990. *Foundations of Social Theory*. Cambridge, MA: Harvard University Press.

Collier, A. 1994. *Critical Realism: An Introduction to Roy Bhaskar's Philosophy*. New York and London: Verso.

Collins, H. and Kusch, M. 1998. *The Shape of Actions*. Cambridge, MA: MIT Press.

Collins, P. H. 2000. *Black Feminist Thought: Knowledge, Consciousness, and the Politics of Empowerment* (2nd ed.). New York and London: Routledge.

Collins, R. 1981. "On the Micro Foundations of Macrosociology." *American Journal of Sociology* 86 (4): 938–65.

Comte, A. [1830–42] 1896. *The Positive Philosophy* (tr. Martineau, H.) (3 vols.). London: Bell.

Condorcet, M. J. A. N. [1795] 1955. *Sketch for a Historical Picture of the Progress of the Human Mind* (tr.Barraclough, J.). New York: Noonday

Confucius [Kongfuzi] [5th century BC] 1992. *Lanyo* [*Analects*] (tr. Lau, D. C.). Hong Kong: Chinese University Press

Coniam, M. 2001. "The Forgotten Existentialist." *Philosophy Now* 32 (June/July): 20.

Cook, G. A. 1977. "G. H. Mead's Social Behaviorism." *Journal of the History of Behavioral Science* 13 (4): 307–16.

Cook, K. S. 1977a. "Exchange and Power in Networks of Interorganizational Relations." *The Sociological Quarterly* 18 (1): 62–82.

Cook, K. S. (ed.) 1987. *Social Exchange Theory*. Beverley Hills, CA: Sage.

Cooley, C. H. [1902]1983. *Human Nature and the Social Order*. New York: Scribner's.

Cooper, J. and Brehm, J. W. 1971. "Prechoice Awareness of Relative Deprivation as a Determinant of Cognitive Dissonance." *Journal of Experimental Social Psychology* 7: 571–81.

Cooper, J. and Fazio, R. H. 1984. "A New Look at Dissonance Theory." In Berkowitz, L. (ed.), *Advances in Experimental Social Psychology* (Vol. 17). New York: Academic Press.

Cornett, L. and Caporaso, J. A. 1992. "'And Still it Moves!' State Interests and Social Forces in the European Community." In Rosenau, J. N. and Czempiel, E.–O. (eds.), *Governance Without Government Order and Change in World Politics*. Cambridge: Cambridge University Press.

Coughlan, R. P. B. 1994. "Conceptualizing and Operationalizing Cultural Theory." In Coyle, D. J. and Ellis, R. J. (eds.), *Politics, Policy and Culture*. Boulder, CO: Westview.

Cournot, A. A. [1838] 1927. *Researches into the Mathematical Principles of the Theory of Wealth* (tr. Bacon, N. T.). New York: Macmillan.

Craig, E. (ed.) 2005. *The Shorter Routledge Encyclopedia of Philosophy*. London: Routledge.

Cramer, P. 1991. *The Development of Defense Mechanisms: Theory, Research and Assessment.* New York: Springer-Verlag.

Cressey, D. R. 1953. *Other People's Money: A Study of the Social Psychology of Embezzlement.* Glenco, IL: The Free Press.

Cresswell, M. J. 1985, *Structured Meanings. The Semantics of Propositional Attitudes*. Cambridge, MA and London: MIT Press.

Crisp, R. and Slote, M. 1997. *Virtue Ethics*. Oxford: Oxford University Press.

Crosbie-Brunett M and Lewis EA. (1993) "Theoretical Contributions from Social and Cognitive Behavioral Psychology." In Boss P. G., Dohetry W. J., LaRossa R., Schumm W. R. and Streinmetz S. K. (eds.), *Sourcebook of Family Theories and Methods: A Contextual Approach*. New York: Plenum Press.

Crosby, D. A. 1988. *The Specter of the Absurd: Sources and Criticisms of Modern Nihilism*. Albany, NY: State University of New York Press.

Crossley, N. 1996. *Intersubjectivity: The Fabric of Social Becoming*. London: Sage

Crunbaugh, J. C. 1973. "The Validation of Logotheropy." In Jurjrvich, R. M. (ed.), *Direct Psychotheropy*. Coral Gables, FL: University of Miami Press.

Culler, J 1976. *Saussure*. Glasgow, UK: Fontana/Collins.

Cunning, D. 1999. "Agency and Consciousness." *Synthese* 120: 271–94.

Cutting, B. and Kouzmin, A. 2002. "Evaluating Corporate Board Culture and Decision Making." *Corporate Governance: The International Journal of Effective Board Performance* 2 (2): 27–45.

D'Andrade, R. G. 1984. "Cultural Meaning Systems." In Shweder, R. A. and LeVine, R. A. (eds.), *Culture Theory: Essays on Mind, Self, and Emotion.* New York: Cambridge University Press.

Dahl, R. A. 1999. "The Anti-reflexive Revolution: On the Affirmation of the New Right." In Featherstone, M. and Lash, S. E. (eds.), *Spaces of Culture: City, Nation, World*. London: Sage.

Dahrendorf, R. 1968. "Homo Sociologicus." In Dahrendorf, R. (ed.), *Essays in the Theory of Society*. Stanford, CA: Stanford University Press.

Dale, J. 2002. *Ontology*. Montreal and Kingston, Ont., CA: McGill-Queen's University Press.

Danermark, B. 2003, *Explaining Society: An Introduction to Critical Realism in the Social Sciences*. London: Routledge.

Darwin, C. [1859] 2006. *On the Origin of Species by Means of Natural Selection, or the Preservation of Favored Races in the Struggle for Life*. Philadelphia, PA: University of Philadelphia Press.

Darwin, C. [1871] 2004. *The Descent of Man, and Selection in Relation to Sex*. Whitefish, MT: Kessinger.

Darwin, C. [1872] 1965. *Expressions of the Emotions in Man and Animals*. London: John Murray.

d' Ascoli, C. [Francesco degli Stabili] 1487. *Cecho Asculana* [*Acerba*]. Venice, IT: Per Bernardinum de Niouraria. Available at: http://www.esnips.com/doc/87671831e7c3-4e45-862d-ed3035ff942a/cecco%20d'Ascoli%20%20l'acerba%20(incompiuto%2013 27).

Davidson, D. 1980. "Mental Events." In Davidson, D. (ed.) *Essays on Actions and Events*. Oxford: Oxford University Press.

Davidson, D. 1984. *Inquiries into Truth and Interpretation*. Oxford: Oxford University Press.

Davies, M. F. 2006. "Irrational Beliefs and Unconditional Self-Acceptance. I. Correlational Evidence Linking Two Key Features of REBT." *Journal of Rational-Emotive & Cognitive-Behavior Therapy* 24 (2). Available at http://eprints.goldsmiths.ac.uk/archive-/00000059/02/JRECBT_1_GRO.pdf.

Davies, P. 1992. *The Mind of God: Science and the Search for Ultimate Meaning*. Ringwood, Vic., AU: Penguin.

Davis, J. 2003. *The Theory of the Individual in Economics: Identity and Value*. New York: Routledge.

Davis, M. H. 1994. *Empathy: A Social Psychological Approach*. Boulder, CO: Westview Press.

Dawkins, R. 1976. *The Selfish Gene*. Oxford: Oxford University Press.

Dawes, R. 1988 *Rational Choice in an Uncertain World*. New York: Harcourt Brace Jovanovich College Publishers.

Day, R. J. F. 2005. *Gramsci is Dead: Anarchist Currents in the Newest Social Movements*. London: Pluto Press.

Deaux, K. 1996. "Social Identification." In Tory Higgins, E. and Kruglanski, A. W. (eds.), *Social Psychology: Handbook of Basic Principles*. New York: Guilford.

de Beauvoir, S. [1949] 1972. *The Second Sex* (tr. Parshley, H. M.). Available at http://www.marxists.org/reference/subject/ethics/de-beauvoir/2nd-sex/index.-htm.

de Board, R. 1978. *The Psychoanalysis of Organizations: A Psychoanalytic Approach to Behavior in Groups and Organizations*. London: Tavistock.

de Botton, A. 2000. *The Consolations of Philosophy*. London: Hamish Hamilton.

de Haven-Smith, L. 1988. *Philosophical Critiques of Policy Analysis*. Gainesville, FL: University of Florida Press.

Deighton, L. 1992. *City of Gold*. Sydney: Random House.

Delanty, G. 2000. *Modernity and Postmodernity: Knowledge, Power and Self*. London: Sage.

Delger, C. N. 1991. *In Search of Human Nature: The Decline and Revival of Darwinism in American Social Thought*. New York: Oxford University Press.

Dennett, D. 1993. *Consciousness Explained*. Harmondworth, Gt. Lon., UK: Penguin.

Dennett, D. 2002. *Freedom Evolves*. London: Allen Lane.

Dennett, D. C. 1984. *Elbow Room*. Cambridge, MA: MIT Press.

Dennett, D. C. 2004. *Freedom Evolves*. New York: Penguin.

DePaul, M (ed.) 2000. *Resurrecting Old-Fashioned Foundationalism*. Blue Ridge Summit, PA: Rowman & Littlefield.

Derrida, J. 1976. *Of Grammatology* (tr. Spivak, G. C.). Baltimore and London: John Hopkins University Press.

Derrida, J. 1978. Writings and Differences (tr. Bass, A.). London and New York: Routledge:

Descartes, R. [1628] 1961. "Rules for the Direction of the Mind" (tr. Lafleur, L.) In Lafleur, L (ed. and tr.), *Philosophical Essays*. Indianapolis: Bobbs-Merrill.

Descartes, R. [1637] 1951. "A Discourse on Methods." In Descartes. R. *A., Discourse on Methods and Selected Writings* (tr. Veitich, J.). London: Dent & Sons.

Descartes, R. [1641] 1961. "Second Mediation: of the Nature of the Human Mind, and that it is More Easily Known than the Body." In Lafleur, L (ed. and tr.), *Philosophical Essays*. Indianapolis: Bobbs-Merrill.

Descartes, R. [1641] 1975. "Discourse on Method and Meditations on First Philosophy." In Cottingham, J., Stoothoff, R. and Dugald Murdoch, M. (eds.), *The Philosophical Writings of Descartes* (Vol. 2). Cambridge: Cambridge University Press.

Descartes, R. [1644] 1983. *Principia Philosophiae* [*Principles of Philosophy*] (trs. Miller, V. R. and Miller, R. P.). Dordrecht, NL: Reidel

Deutsch, M. and Gerard, G. B. 1955. "A Study of Normative and Informational Social Influences upon Individual Judgement." *Journal of Abnormal and Social Psychology* 51: 629–36.

Devitt, M. 1984. *Realism and Truth.* Princeton, NJ: Princeton University Press.

Devitt, M. and Sterelny, K. [1987] 1998. *Language and Reality: An Introduction to the Philosophy of Language* (2nd ed.). Oxford: Blackwell.

de Waal, F. 2006. *Primates and Philosophy: How Morality Evolved* (eds. Macedo, S. and Ober, J.). Princeton, NJ: Princeton University Press.

Dewey, J. [1932] 1985. *The Collected Works of John Dewey* (Vol. 7). Carbondale, IL: Southern Illinois University Press.

Dewey, J. [1895–98] 1972. *The Collected Works of John Dewey* (Vol. 5). Carbondale, IL: Southern Illinois University Press.

Dewey, J. 1933. *How We Think: A Restatement of the Relations of Reflective Thinking to the Education Process.* Lexington, MA: Heath.

Dewey, J. 1933. *Logic: Theory of Inquiry.* Troy, MO: Holt, Rinehart & Winston.

Diderot, D. [1771–73] 1999 *Jacques le Fataliste et son Maître* [*Jacques the Fatalist*]. (tr. Coward, D.). Oxford: Oxford University Press.

Dihle, A. 1982. *The Theory of Will in Classical Antiquity* (Sather 48). Berkeley, CA: University of California, Berkeley, Department of Classics.

Dilthey, W. [1883] 1988. *Introduction to the human sciences* (tr. Bentanzos, R. J.). Detroit, MI: Wayne State University Press.

Dilthey, W. [1910] 2000. "The Formation of the Historical World in the Human Sciences" (tr. Makkreel, R. A. and Rodi, F.). In Makkreel, R. A. and Rodi, F. (eds.), *Selected Works* (Vol. 3). Princeton, NJ: Princeton University Press.

Dixon, J. 2003. *Responses to Governance: The Governing of Corporations, Societies and the World.* Westport, CT: Praeger.

Dixon, J. and Dogan, R. 2002. "Hierarchies, Networks and Markets: Responses to Societal Governance Failures." *Administration Theory and Praxis* 24 (1): 175–196.

Dixon, J. and Dogan, R. 2003a "Analysing Global Governance Failure: A Philosophical Framework." *Journal of Comparative Policy Analysis* 5 (1): 20–24.

Dixon, J. and Dogan, R. 2003b. "Corporate Decision Making: Contending Perspectives and their Governance Implications." *Corporate Governance: International Journal of Business in Society* 3 (1): 39–57.

Dixon, J. and Dogan, R. 2003c. "A Philosophical Analysis of Management: Improving Praxis." *Journal of Management Development* 22 (6): 458–82.

Dixon, J. and Dogan, R. 2003d. "Towards Constructive Corporate Governance: From 'Certainties' to a Plurality Principle." *Reason in Practice: The Journal of the Philosophy of Management* 2 (3): 51–72.

Dixon, J. and Dogan, R. 2004. "The Conduct of Policy Analysis: Philosophical Points of Reference." *Review of Policy Research*, 21 (2 & 3): 559–80.

Dixon, J. and Dogan, R. 2005. "The Contending Perspectives on Public Management: A Philosophical Investigation." *International Public Management Journal* 8 (1): 1–22.

Dixon, J., Dogan, R. and Carrier, K. 2005. "On Investigating the 'Underclass': Contending Philosophical Perspectives." *Social Policy & Society* 4 (1): 21–30.

Dixon, J., Dogan, R. and Kouzmin, A. 2004. "The Dilemma of Privatised Public Services: Philosophical Frames in Understanding Failure and Managing Partnership Terminations." *Public Organization Review* 4 (1): 25–46.

Dixon, J. and Hyde, M. 2003. "Public Pension Privatization, Neo-Classical Economics, Decision Risks and Welfare Ideology." *International Journal of Social Economics* 30 (5): 633–50.

Dixon, J. and Newman, D. 1998. *Entering the Chinese Market: Risks and Discounted Rewards*. Westport, CT: Quorum Books.

Dixon, J., Sanderson, A. and Dogan, R. 2005. "Community and Communitarianism: A Philosophical Investigation." *Community Development Journal*, 40 (1): 4–16.

Dixon, J., Sanderson, A. and Tripathi, S. 2006. "Ethics, Trust and the Public Interest: The Contending Modes of Societal Governance." In Korac-Kakabadse, N. and Kakabadse, A. (eds.) *Governance, Strategy and Policy: Seven Critical Essays*. Basingstoke Hamp., UK: Palgrave Macmillan.

Dixon, J., Sanderson, A. and Tripathi, S. 2007. Sanderson, A. and Tripathi, S. "Governance and the Public Interest: The Challenges for Public Sector Leaders." In Koch, R. and Dixon, J. (eds.), *Public Governance and Leadership*. Weisbaden, DM: Gabler-Verlag.

Donagan, A. 1987. *Choice: The Essential Element of Human Action*. London: Routledge & Kegan Paul.

Dor, J. 2001. *Introduction to the Reading of Lacan: The Unconscious Structured Like a Language*. New York: Other Press.

Dostoevesky, F. [1880] 1948, *The Brothers Karamazov* (tr.Garnett, C. B.). New York: Macmillan.

Douglas, J. and Johnson, J. M. (eds.) 1977. *Existential Sociology*. New York: Cambridge University Press.

Douglas, M. 1970. *Natural Symbols: Explorations in Cosmology*. London: Barry and Rockliff.

Douglas, M. 1978. *Cultural Bias* (Occasional Paper 35). London: Royal Anthropological Institute of Great Britain and Ireland.

Douglas, M. 1982. "Cultural Bias." In Douglas, M. (ed.), *In the Active Voice*. London: Routledge and Kegan Paul.

Douglas, M. 1994. *Risk and Blame: Essays in Culture Theory*. London: Routledge.

Douglas, M. 1999. "Four Cultures: The Evolution of a Parsimonious Model." *GeoJournal* 47 (3): 411–15.

Douglas, M. and Isherwood, B. 1979. *The World of Goods: Towards an Anthropology of Consumption*. London: Allen Lane.

Douglas, M. and Ney, S. 1998. *Missing Persons: A Critique of the Social Sciences*. Berkeley and Los Angeles, CA: University of California Press.

Douglas, M., Gasper, D., Ney, S. and Thompson, M. 1997. "Human Needs and Wants." In Rayner, S. and Malone, E. L. (eds.), *Human Choice and Climate Change, 1: The Societal Framework*. Columbus, OH: Battelle Press.

Downs, A. 1957. *The Economic Theory of Democracy*. New York: Harper & Row

Draaisma, D. 2000. *Metaphors and Memory: A History of Ideas about the Mind*. Cambridge: Cambridge University Press.

Drake, D., Lovejoy, A. O. Pratt, J. B., Rogers, A. K. Santayana, G. Sellars, R. W. and Strong, C. A. 1920. *Essays in Critical Realism: a Co-operative Study of the Problem of Knowledge*. London: Macmillan.

Dryzek, J. S. (1987), "Complexity and Rationality in Public Life." *Political Studies* 35 (4): 424–42.

Dubin, R 1978. *Theory Building*. Free Press, New York.

Dulles, A. 1983. *Models of Revelation*. Garden City, NY: Doubleday.

Dummett, M. A. E. 1963. "Realism." In Dummett, M. A. E. (ed.), *Truth and Other Enigmas*. London: Duckworth.

Dumont, L. 1970 *Homo Hierarchus*. Chicago, IL: University of Chicago Press.

Dunn, T. 2008. *Loneliness as a Way of Life*. Cambridgre, MA: Harvard University Press.

Dupré, L. 1966 *The Philosophical Foundations of Marxism*. New York: Harcourt, Brace & World.

Duran, J. 1991. *Towards a Feminist Epistemology*. Savage, MD: Rowman & Littlefield.

Durkheim, E. [1895] 1962. *The Rules of Sociological Method*. Glencoe IL.: Free Press.

Durkheim, E. [1895] 1982. *The Rules of Sociological Method and Selected Texts on Sociology and Its Metho*d (ed. Lukes, S., tr. Halls, W. D). London: Macmillan.

Durkheim, E. [1897] 1952. *Suicide: A Study in Sociology*. London: Routledge and Kegan Paul.

Durkheim, E. [1912] 2001. *The Elementary Forms of Religious Life* (tr. Cosman, C.). Oxford: Oxford University Press.

Durkin, K. 1995. *Developmental Social Psychology: From Infancy to Old Age*. Oxford: Blackwell.

Dworkin, G. 1988. *The Theory and Practice of Autonomy*. Cambridge: Cambridge University Press.

Eagly, A. H. and Chaiken, S. 1993. *The Psychology of Attitudes*. Fort Worth, TX: Harcourt Brace Jovanovich.

Eagly, A. H. and Chaiken, S. 1998. "Attitude Structure and Function." In Gilbert, D. T., Fiske, S. T. and Lindzey, G. (eds.), *The Handbook of Social Psychology* (4th ed.). New York: McGraw-Hill.

Eagly, A. H., Chen, S., Chaiken, S. abed Shaw-Barnes K. 1999. "The Impact of Attitudes on Memory: An Affair to Remember." *Psychological Bulletin* 125: 64–89.

Earman, J. 1986. *A Primer on Determinism*. Dordrecht, NL: Reidel.

Eccles, J. C. 1994. *How the Self Controls its Brain*. Berlin: Springer-Verlag.

Edwards, P. (ed.) 1967. *The Encyclopedia of Philosophy*. New York:Macmillan.

Edwards, W. 1954. "The Theory of Decision-Making." *Psychological Bulletin* 51: 380–417.

Eilstein, H. 1995. "The Virus of Fatalism." In Gavrogulu, A., Stachel, J. and Wartofsky, M. (eds.), *Science, Mind and Art*. Dordrecht, NL: Kluwer.

Ekah, P. 1974. *Social Exchange Theory—The Two Traditions*. Cambridge, MA: Harvard University Press.

Elkin, R. A. and Leippe, M. R. 1986. "Physiological Arousal, Dissonance, and Attitude Change." *Journal of Personality and Social Psychology* 51: 55–65.

Ellis. A. 2005. *The Myth of Self-esteem: How Rational Emotive Behavior Therapy Can Change Your Life Forever*. Buffalo, NY: Prometheus.

Elster, J. 1979. *Ulysses and the Sirens*. Cambridge: Cambridge University Press.

Elster, J. 1982. "The Case for Methodological Individualism." *Theory and Society* 11: 453–82.

Elster, J. 1985a. *Making Sense of Marx*. Cambridge: Cambridge University Press.

Elster, J. 1985b. *Sour Grapes: Studies in the Subversion of Rationality*. Cambridge: Cambridge University Press.

Elster, J. 1986a. "Introduction". In Elster, J. (ed.), *Rational Choice*. Oxford: Basil Blackwell.
Elster, J. 1986b. *Rational Choice*. Oxford: Basil Blackwell.
Elster, J. 1988. *Multiple Self.* Cambridge: Cambridge University Press.
Elster, J. 1989a. *Nuts and Bolts for the Social Sciences*. Cambridge: Cambridge University Press.
Elster, J. 1989b. *Solomonic Judgements*. Cambridge: Cambridge University Press.
Elster, J. 1999a. *Alchemies of the Mind.* Cambridge: Cambridge University Press.
Elster, J. 1999b. *Strong Feelings*. Cambridge, MA: MIT Press.
Embree, L., Behnke, E.A., Carr, D., Evans, J. C., Huertas-Jourda, J., Kockelmans, J. J., Mckenna, W., Mickunas, A., Mohanty, J. N., Nenon, T., Seebohm, T. M., and Zaner, R. M. 1996. *The Encyclopedia of Phenomenology*. Dordrecht, NL: Kluwer.
Erikson, E, H, 1963. *Childhood and Society* (2nd ed.). New York: Norton.
Erikson, E, H, 1964. *Insight and Responsibility*. New York: Norton.
Etzioni, A. 1961. *A Comparative Analysis of Complex Organizations*. New York: Free Press.
Etzioni, A. 1968. *The Active Society: A Theory of Societal and Political Processes*. New York: Free Press.
Etzioni, A. (ed.) 1998. *The Essential Communitarian Reader*. Lanham, MD: Rowman & Littlefield.
Evans, D. A. and Alexander, S. 1970. "Some Psychological Correlates of Civil Rights Activity." *Psychology Reports* 26: 899–906.
Evans, R. 1967. *Dialogue with Erik Erikson.* New York: Harper Row.
Esyenck, H. J. 1967. *The Biological Basis of Personality*. Sprinfield, IL: Charles C. Thomas.
Esyenck, H. J. 1970. *The Structure of Human Personality* (3rd ed.). London: Methuen.
Esyenck, H. J. and Esyenck, M. W. 1985. *Personality and Individual Differences: A Natural Science Approach.* New York: Plenum.
Fahkry, M. 1958. *Islamic Occasionalism and it Critique by Averroes and Aquinas*. London: Allan & Unwin.
Fama, F. and Jensen, M. 1983a. "Separation of Ownership and Control." *Journal of Law and Economics* 26: 301–26.
Fama, F. and Jensen, M. 1983b. "Agency Problems and Residual Claims." *Journal of Law and Economics* 26: 327–49.
Fanon, F. 1961. *Black Skin, White Masks* (tr. Markmann, C. L.). New York: Grove Press.
Fardon, R. 1999. *Mary Douglas: An Intellectual Biography*. London: Routledge.

Farr, R. M. 1996. *The Roots of Modern Social Psychology 1872–1954*. Oxford: Blackwell.

Farthing, G. W. 1992. *The Psychology of Consciousness*. Engelwood Cliffs, NJ: Prentice Hall.

Feldman, R. and Conee, E. 2004. *Evidentialism: Essays in Epistemology*. Oxford: Oxford University Press.

Fest, J. 2003. *Inside Hitler's Bunker*. London and New York: Macmillan

Festinger, L. 1950. "Informal Social Communication." *Psychological Review* 57: 271–82.

Festinger, L. 1954. "A Theory of Social Comparison Processes." *Human Relations* 7: 117–40

Festinger, L. 1957. *A Theory of Cognitive Dissonance*. Evanston, IL: Row, Peterson.

Festinger, L. and Carlsmith, J. M. 1959. "Cognitive Consequences of Forced Compliance." *Journal of Abnormal and Social Psychology* 58: 203–10.

Feuerbach, L. A. [1841] 1893. *The Essence of Christianity* (tr. Evans. M.) (3rd ed.). London: Kegan Paul and Trench Trubner.

Feyerabend, P. 1963. "Mental Events and the Brain." *Journal of Philosophy* 60: 295–6.

Feyerabend, P. 1975. *Against Method,* London: Verso.

Fichte. J. G. [1794–95] 1970. "Foundations of the Entire Science of Knowledge (tr. Heath, P.)." In Heath, P. and Lachs, J. (eds.), *Science of Knowledge* (2nd ed.). New York: Appleton-Century-Croft.

Field, J. 2003. *Social Capital*. London: Routledge.

Figgis, J. N. [1896] 1965. *The Theory of the Divine Right of Kings*. Cambridge: Cambridge University Press.

Finch, H. L. 1995. *Wittgenstein*. Rockport, MA: Elements.

Fingerette, H. 1969. *Self-Deception*. London: Routledge & Kegan Paul

Fingarette, H. 1972. *Confucius—The Secular as Sacred*. New York: Harper.

Finley, N. and Norman, R. 1997. "The Concept of Social Parallax." *Women and Language* 20 (1): 43–46.

Firth, C. 2007. *Making up the Mind: How the Brain Creates Our Mental World*. Oxford: Blackwell.

Fischer, J. M. 1994. *The Metaphysics of Free Will*. Oxford: Blackwell.

Fischer, J. M. 1989. *God, Foreknowledge and Freedom*. Stanford, CA: Stanford University Press.

Fishbein, M. and Ajzen, I. 1975. *Belief, Attitude, Intention, and Behavior: An Introduction to Theory and Research*. Reading. MA: Addison-Wesley.

Fishburn, P. C. 1982 *The Foundations of Expected Utility*. Dordrecht, NL: D. Reidel.

Fisher, P. 2002. *The Vehement Passion*. Princeton, NJ: Princeton University Press.

Fiske, S. T. and Taylor, S. E. 1991. *Social Cognition* (2nd ed.). New York: McGraw Hill.

Flanagan, O. 1992. *Consciousness Reconsidered*. Cambridge, MA: MIT Press.

Flathman, R. E. 2002. *Thomas Hobbes: Skepticism, Individuality and Chastened Politics* (new ed.). Blue Ridge Summit, PA: Rowman & Littlefield.

Flaubert, G. [1856/1857] 2006. *Madam Bovary* (tr. Marx-Aveling, E.). Available at http://www.gutenberg.org/files/2413/2413-h/2413-h.htm.

Fletcher, J. 1966. *Situational Ethics*. Philadelphia, PA: Westminster Press.

Flewelling, R. T. 1915. *Personalism and the Problems of Philosophy*. New York: Methodist Book Concern

Flewelling, R. T. 1943 "Personalism." In Runes, D. D. (ed.), *Twentieth Century Philosophy*. New York: Philosophical Library

Foa, U. G. and Foa, E. B. 1971. "Resource Exchange: Towards a Structural Theory of Interpersonal Relations." In Seigman, A. Q. W. and Pope, B. (eds.), *Studies in Dydadic Communication*. New York: Pergamon.

Fodor, J. A. 1981. *Representations: Philosophical Essays on the Foundations of Cognitive Science*. Cambridge, MA: MIT Press.

Fodor, J. 1987. *Psychosemantics*. Cambridge, MA: MIT Press.

Fodor, J. 1991. "A Modal Argument for Narrow Content." *Journal of Philosophy* 88: 5–26.

Fodor, J. A. 1983. *Modularity of Mind: An Essay on Faculty Psychology*. Cambridge, MA: MIT Press.

Foot, P. [1978] 2002. *Virtues and Vices and Other Essays in Moral Philosophy*. Oxford: Clarendon.

Foot, P. 1978a. *Moral Relativism*. Lawrence, KS: University of Kansas Press.

Foot, P. 1978b. *Virtues and Vices*. Oxford: Basil Blackwell.

Foot, P. 2002. *Moral Delimmas and Other Topics in Moral Philosophy*. Oxford: Clarendon.

Forbes, G. 1989. *Language of Possibility*. Oxford: Oxford University Press.

Force, P. 2003. *Self–Interest before Adam Smith: A Genealogy of Economic Science*. Cambridge: Cambridge University Press.

Foucault, M. [1966] 1989. *The Order of Things. An Archaeology of the Human Sciences*. London and New York: Routledge. Available at http://booksgoogle.co.uk/books?id=7z0-

nXi4R8m4C&printsec=titlepage&vq=Foucault+1966+The+Order+of+Things &source=gbs_toc_s&cad=1#PPR12,M1.

Foucault, M. [1969] 2002. *The Archaeology of Knowledge* (tr. Sheriden Smith, A. M.). London and New York: Routledge. Available at http://books.google.co.uk/books?id=MA77jxOOmBcC&dq=foucault+1966+the+archeology+of+knowledge&pg=PP1&ots=YinxMcGXpJ&source=citation&sig=K4SU53_L2xDPWDnC7YA62Jkf6tE&hl=en&prev=http://www.google.co.uk/search?hl=en&q=Foucault+1966+The+Archeology+of+Knowledge &btnG=Google+Search&sa=X&oi=print&ct=result&cd=1&cad=bottom–3results

Foucault, M. 1978. *The History of Sexuality* (vol 1: *An Introduction*) (tr. Hurley, R.). New York: Pantheon.

Foucault 1983. "Discourse and Truth: the Problematization of Parrhesia: Six lectures given by Michel Foucault at the University of California at Berkeley, Oct–Nov. 1983" (ed. Pearson, J). Available at http://foucault.info/documents/parrhesia/.

Foucault, M. 1991. "Governmentality". In Burchell, G., Gordon, C. and Miller, P. (eds.), *The Foucault Effect: Studies in Governmentality*. Hemel Hempstead, Herts., UK: Harvester Wheatsheaf.

Frank, P. 1949. *Modern Science and it Philosophy*. Cambridge: MA: Harvard University Press.

Frankfurt, H. [1971] 2002. "Freedom of the Will and the Concept of a Person." In Kane, R. (ed.), *Free Will*. Malden, MA: Blackwell.

Frankl, V. E. [1946/1959] 1984. *Man's Search for Meaning*: An Introduction to Logotherapy (Pref. Allport, G. W.) (updated Touchstone ed.). New York: Washington Square Press.

Frankl, V. E. [1948/1976] 2000. *Man's Search for Ultimate Meaning* (for. Hunt, S.) (rev. paperback ed.). New York: Perseus Book Group.

Frankl, V. E. [1955] 1986. *The Doctor and the Soul: From Psychotherapy to Logotherapy*. London: Random House.

Frankl, V. E. [1969] 1988. *The Will to Meaning: Foundations and Applications of Logotherapy*. New York: New American Library.

Freeman, C. 2003. *The Closing of the Western Mind: The Rise of Faith and the Fall of Reason*. London: Pimlico.

Freeman, K. 1983 *Ancilla to the Pre–Socratic Philosophers* (reprint ed.). Cambridge: Harvard University Press.

Frege, G. [1884] 1980. *The Foundations of Arithmetic: A Logico–Mathematical Enquiry into the Concept of Numbers* (2nd ed.). Oxford: Blackwell.

Frege, G. [1918] 1997. "Thought." In Beany, M. (ed.) (1997) *The Frege Reader.* Oxford: Blackwell.

Freire, P. 1985. *The Politics of Education: Culture, Power and Liberation.* New York: Bergin and Garvey.

Freire, P. 1996. *Pedagogy of the Oppressed.* Harmondsworth, Gt. Lon., UK: Penguin.

French, J. R. P. and Raven, B. 1959. "The Bases of Social Power." In Cartwright, D. (ed.), *Studies in Social Power.* Ann Arbor, MI: University of Michigan Press.

Frese, M. and Sabini, J. 1985. *Goal Directed Behavior: The Concept of Action in Psychology.* Hillsdale, NJ: Lawrence Erlbaum.

Freud, A. [1936] 1948. *The Ego and the Mechanisms of Defense.* London: Horgarth and the Institute of Psychoanalysis.

Freud, S. [1912] 1959. "The Dynamics of the Transference." In Jones, E. (ed.) *Collected Papers of Sigmund Freud* (tr Riviere, J) (Vol. 2). New York: Basic Books.

Freud, S. 1922. *Group Psychology and the Analysis of the Ego.* London: Hogarth.

Freud, S [1923] 1927. *The Ego and the Id* (tr. Riviere, J.). London: Hogarth.

Freud, S. [1929] 1971. *The Complete Introductory Lectures on Psychoanalysis.* London: Allen & Unwin.

Freud, S. 1936. "Inhibitions, Symptoms and Anxiety." *Psychoanalytical Quarterly* 5: 415–43.

Freud, S. 1957. *A General Introduction to Psychoanalysis* (rev. ed.) (tr. Riviere, J.). New York: Permabooks.

Frey, D. 1986. "Recent Research on Selective Exposure to Information." In Berkowitz, L. (ed.), *Advances in Experimental Social Psychology* (Vol. 19). New York: Academic Press.

Fried, C. 1978. *Right and Wrong.* Cambridge, MA: Harvard University Press.

Friedman, M. 1955. "The Methodology of Positive Economics." In Freedman, M. (ed.), *Essays in Positive Economics.* Chicago: Chicago University Press.

Friedman, M. 1962. *Capitalism and Freedom.* Chicago: University of Chicago Press.

Friedman, M. and Friedman, R. 1980. *Free to Choose.* Harmondsworth, Gt. Lon., UK: Penguin.

Friedman, N. 1973. *The Machinery of Freedom: Guide to a Radical Capitalism.* New York: Harper and Row.

Friere, P. 1972. *Pedagogy of the Oppressed.* Harmondsworth, Gt. Lon., UK: Penguin.

Fukuyama, F. 1995. *Trust.* London: Hamish Hamilton.

Fumerton, R. 2002. *Realism and the Correspondence Theory of Truth*. Blue Ridge Summit, PA: Rowman & Littlefield.

Furnham, A. 1984. "Many Sides of the Coin: The Psychology of Money Usage." *Personality and Individual Differences* 5: 501–9.

Fuss, D. 1989. *Essentially Speaking: Feminism, Nature and Difference*. New York: Routledge.

Gac Sanit. [online]. 2006, Vol. 20, no. 4. Available at: http://scielo.isciii.es/scielo.php?sc–ript=sciarttext&pid=S021391112006000400015&lng=en&nrm=iso.

Gaede, E.A. 1983. *Politics and Ethics: Machiavelli to Niebuhr*. London: University Press of America.

Gambetta, D, 1988. "Can We Trust?" In Gambetta, D. (ed.), *Trust: Making and Breaking*. Oxford: Oxford University Press.

Garfinkel, H. [1967] 1984. *Studies in Ethnomethodology*. Oxford: Blackwell.

Garver, N. 1994. *This Complicated Form of Life*. Chicago, IL: University of Chicago Press.

Gauthier, D. 1986. *Morals by Agreement*. Oxford: Oxford University Press.

Gauthier, D. 1990. *Moral Dealing: Contract, Ethics, and Reason*. Ithaca, NY: Cornell University Press.

Gazzaniga, M. S., Ivry, R. B. and Mangun, G. R. 2002. *Cognitive Neuroscience: The Biology of the Mind* (2nd ed.). New York: W. W. Norton.

Geertz, C. 1973. *The Interpretation of Culture*. New York: Basic Books.

Geertz, C. 1983. "The Way We Think Now: Towards an Ethnography of Modern Thought." In Geertz, C. (ed.), *Local Knowledge*. New York: Basic Books.

Gerard, H. B. 1963. "Emotional Uncertainty and Social Comparison." *Journal of Abnormal and Social Psychology* 63: 568–73.

Gerard, H. B. and Rabbie, J. M. 1961. "Fear and Social Comparison." *Journal of Abnormal and Social Psychology* 61: 586–92.

Gergen, K. J. 1999. *An Introduction to Social Construction*. London: Sage.

Gergen, K. J. 2001. *Social Construction in Context*. London: Sage.

Gergen, K. J. and Thatchenkey, T. J. 1998. "Organizational Science in Postmodern Context." In Chia, R. C. H. (ed.), *In the Realm of Organization: Essays for Robert Cooper*. London: Routledge.

Gewirtz, J. L. 1969. "Mechanisms of social learning: Some roles of stimulation and behavior in early human development." In Goslin, D. A. (ed.), *Handbook of Socialization Theory and Research*. Chicago, IL: Rand McNally.

Gewirth, A. 1978. *Reason and Morality*. Chicago: University of Chicago Press.

Gibbard, A. 1990. *Wise Choice, Apt Feelings: A Theory of Normative Judgment*. Cambridge, MA: Harvard University Press.

Giddens, A. 1984. *The Constitution of Society*. Cambridge: Polity Press.

Giddens, A. 1990. *The Consequences of Modernity*. Cambridge: Polity Press.

Giddens, A. 1991. *Modernity and Self–Identity: Self and Society*. Cambridge: Polity Press.

Giddens, A. 1993. *New Rules of Sociological Method: A Positive Critique of Interpretative Sociologies* (2nd ed.). Palo Alto, CA: Stanford University Press.

Giddens, A. 1995. *The Constitution of Society: Outline of the Theory of Structuration*. Cambridge: Polity Press.

Giddens, A. 2001. *Sociology* (4th ed.). Cambridge: Polity Press.

Gigerenzer, G. 1991. "How to Make Cognitive Illusions Disappear: Beyond 'Heuristics and Biases'." In Stroebe, W. and Heewstone, M. (eds.), European Review of Social Psychology (Vol. 2). Chichester, ESuss, UK: Wiley.

Gigerenzer, G. 2007. *Gut Feelings: The Intelligence of the Unconscious*. New York: Viking.

Gigerenzer, G. and Goldstein, D. G. 1996. "Reasoning the Fast and Frugal Way: Models of Boounded Rationality." *Psychological Review* 103: 650–69.

Gilbert, D. T. and Malone, P. S. 1995. "The Correspondence Bias." *Psychological Bulletin* 117: 21–38.

Gini, A. 2006. *Why it is Hard to be Good*. New York and London: Routledge.

Glasersfeld, E. von 1995. *Radical Constructivism: A Way of Knowing and Learning*. London: Falmer Press.

Glasser, B. G. and Strauss, A. L. 1967. *The Discovery of Grounded Theory: Strategies for Qualitative Research*. Chicago, IL: Aldine.

Goffman, E. 1959. *The Presentation of Self in Everyday Life*. New York: Doubleday.

Goffman, E. 1961. *Encounters: Two Studies in the Sociology of Interaction*. Indianapolis, IN: Bobbs–Merrill.

Goffman, E. 1963. *Behavior in Public Places*. New York: Free Press.

Goffman, E. 1974. *Frame Analysis*. Cambridge, MA: Harvard University Press.

Goldie, P. 2004. *On Personality*. London: Routledge.

Goldstein, J. 1999. "Emergence as a Construct: History and Issues." *Emergence: Complexity and Organization 1: 49–72.*

Goodman, N. [1954] 1965. *Fact, Fiction and Forecast* (2nd ed.). New York: Bobbs–Merrill.

Gootnick, A. T. 1974. "Locus of Control and Political Participation of College Students: A Comparison of Unidimensional and Multidimensional Approaches." *Journal of Consulting and Clinical Psychology* 42: 54–8.

Gordon, H. and Gordon, R. 1995. *Sartre and Evil: Guidelines for a Struggle.* Westport, CT: Greenwood Press.

Gordon, S. 1991. *The History and Philosophy of Social Science*. London: Routledge.

Gore, P. S. and Rotter, J. B. 1963. "A Personality Correlate of Social Action." *Journal of Personality* 31: 58–64.

Gouinlock, J. 1972. *John Dewey's Philosophy of Value*. New York: Humanities Press.

Gould, S. J. 2002. *The Structure of Evolutionary Theory*. Cambridge MA: Harvard University Press.

Graham, G. 2007. "Behaviorism." Available at http://plato.stanford.edu/entries/behaviorism/.

Gramsci, A. 1971. *Selections from the Prison Notebooks* (eds. Hoare, Q. and Nowell Smith, G.). London: Lawrence and Wishart.

Gramsci, A. 1985. *Selections from Cultural Writings*. London: Lawrence and Wishart.

Grave, S. A. 1960. *The Scottish Philosophy of Common Sense*. Oxford: Clarendon.

Gray, J. 2002. *Straw Dogs: Thoughts on Humans and Other Animals*. London: Granta.

Gray, J. 2004. *Al Qaerda and What it Means to be Modern*. New York: Faber.

Graziano, W. G. and Eisenberg, N. 1997. "Agreeableness: A Dimension of Personality." In Hogan, J., Johnson, J. and Briggs, S. (eds.), *Handbook of Personality Psychology*. San Diego, CA: Academic Press.

Greach, P. 2001. *Truth and Hope*. Notre Dame, IN: University of Notre Dame Press.

Greene, B. 1999. *The Elegant Universe: Superstrings, Hidden Dimensions, and the Quest for the Ultimate Theory*. New York: Vintage

Grendstad, G. and Selle, P. 1999. "The Formation and Transformation of Preferences: Cultural Theory and Postmaterialism Compared." In Thompson, M., Grendstat, G. and Selle, P. (eds.), *Cultural Theory as Political Science*. London: Routledge.

Gribbin, J. 2005. *The Fellowship: The Story of a Revolution*. London: Allen Lane.

Griffin, J. P. 1964. *Wittgenstein's Logical Atomism*. Oxford: Clarendon.

Griffin, J. P. 1986. *Well–Being*. Oxford: Clarendon.

Gross, J. and Rayner, S. 1985. *Measuring Culture: A Paradigm for the Analysis of Social Organizations*. New York: Colombia University Press.

Grote, J. 1876. *A Treatise on the Moral Ideals*. Cambridge: Deighton, Bell. Available at: http://books.google.co.uk/books?id=4wHvCeDg02EC&dq=John

+Grote++A+Treatise+on+Moral+Ideals&pg=PR2&ots=a–abIRmDGt&sig=n SzcBRJ2eGqAHwXEdZ2Dd8zP3pr-ev=http://www.google.co.uk/search %3Fhl%3Den%26q%3DJohn%2BGrote%2B%2BA-%2BTreatise%2Bon %2BMoral%2BIdeals%26btnG%3DSearch%26meta%3Dcr%253D-countryUK%257CcountryGB&sa=X&oi=print&ct=title#PPR3,M1

Grünbaum, A. 1984. *The Foundations of Psychoanalysis: A Philosophical Critique*. Berkeley and Los Angeles, CA: University of California Press.

Guba, E. G. and Lincoln, Y. S. (1994), "Competing Paradigms in Qualitative Research." In Denzin, N. K. and Lincoln, Y. S. (eds.) *Handbook of Qualitative Research*. Newbury Park, CA: Sage.

Gui, B. and Sugden, R. (eds.) 2005. *Economics and Social Interaction*. Cambridge: Cambridge University Press

Guignon., C. B. 1993. "Authenticity, Moral Values and Psychotheopy." In Guignon., C. B. (ed.), *The Cambridge Companion to Heidegger*. Cambridge: Cambridge University Press.

Guignon., C. B. and Hiley, D. R. 1996. "Biting the Bullet: Rorty on Private and Public Morality." In Malachowski, A. (ed.), *Reading Rorty*. Oxford: Blackwell.

Guignon, C. B. 2004. *On Being Authentic*. New York: Routledge.

Guyer, P. 2006. *Kant*. New York: Routledge.

Gyatso, T. 2001. *Ancient Wisdom, Modern World: Ethics for the New Millennium* (2nd ed.). London: Abacus.

Haas, E. B. 1990. *When Knowledge is Power: Three Models of Change in International Organizations*. Berkeley and Los Angeles, CA: University of California Press.

Habermas, J.1968, *Knowledge and Human Interest*. Boston, MA: Beacon Press.

Habermas, J. 1971. *Towards a Rational Society*. Boston, MA: Beacon Press.

Habermas, J. 1975. *Legitimation Crisis*. Boston. MA: Beacon Press.

Habermas, J. [1981] 1985. *The Theory of Communicative Action* (Vol. 1: *Reason and the Rationalization of Society*). Boston, MA: Beacon Press.

Habermas, J. 1986, "Hannah Arnedt's Communications Concept of Power." In Lukes, S. (ed.), *Power*. New York: New York University Press.

Habermas, J. 1987. *The Theory of Communicative Action* (vol 2: *Lifeworld and Systems: A Critique of Functionalist Reason*) (tr. McCarthy, T.). Boston, MA: Beacon Press.

Habermas, J. 1996. *Between Facts and Norms: Contributions to a Discourse Theory of Law and Democracy*. Cambridge: Polity Press.

Habermas, J. 2003. *Truth and Justification*. Cambridge: Polity Press.

Hägerström, A. 1964. *Philosophy and Religion* (tr Sandin, R. T.). London: Allen and Unwin.
Haidt, J. 2003. "The Moral Emotions." In Davidson, R. J. (ed.), *Handbook of Affective Sciences*. New York: Oxford University Press.
Hajer, M. A. 1993. "Discourse Coalitions and the Institutionalization of Practice." In Fischer, F. and Forester, J. (eds.), *The Argumentative Turn in Policy Analysis and Planning*. London: UCL Press.
Hales, C. 2001. *Managing through Organization: The Management Process, Forms of Organisation and the Work of Managers*. London: Business Press.
Hall, R. A. Jr. 1987. *Leonard Bloomfield: Essays on his Life and Work*. Amsterdam, NL: Benjamins.
Hall, A. D. and Hogan, R. E. 1969. "Definition of System." In Litterer, J. A. (ed.), *Organizations, Systems. Control and Adaption* (Vol. II). New York: Wiley.
Hall, C. S. and Nordby, V. J. 1973. *A Primer of Jungian Psychology*. New York: New American Library.
Hallett, G. L. 1991. *Essentialism: A Wittgensteinian Critique*. New York: SUNY Press.
Hammond, M., Howarth, J. and Keat, R. 1991. *Understanding Phenomenology*. Oxford: Blackwell.
Hampshire, S. 2005. *Spinoza and Spinozism*. Oxford: Clarendon.
Hampton, J. 1986. *Hobbes and the Social Contract Tradition*. Cambridge: Cambridge University Press.
Hankinson, R. J. 1995. *The Sceptics*. London: Routledge.
Hanson, N. R. 1958. *Patterns of Discovery*. Cambridge: Cambridge University Press.
Harding, S. 1986. *The Science Question in Feminism*. New York: Cornell University.
Harding, S. 1991. *Whose Science? Whose Knowledge? Thinking from Women's Lives*. Ithica, NY: Cornell University Press.
Hare, R. M. 1952. *The Language of Morals*. Oxford: Clarendon.
Hare, R. M. 1963. *Freedon and Reason*. Oxford: Oxford University Press.
Hare, R. M. 1997. *Sorting out Ethics*. Oxford: Oxford University Press.
Harman, G. 2000. "Moral Philosophy meets Social Psychology: Virtue Ethics and the Fundamental Attribution Error." In: Harman, G (ed.), *Explaining Value and Other Essays in Moral Philosophy*. New York: Oxford University Press.
Harmon, G. H. 1965. "The Inference to the Best Explanation." *Philosophical Review* 74 (1): 88–95.
Harré, R. 1970. *The Principles of Scientific Thinking*. London: Macmillan.
Harré, R. 1972. *The Philosophies of Science*. Oxford: Oxford University Press.

Harré, R. 1980. "Social Being and Social Change." In Brenner, M. (ed.), *The Structure of Action*. Oxford: Blackwell.

Harré, R. 1983. *Personal Being*. Oxford: Basil Blackwell.

Harré, R. 1986. *Varieties of Realism*, Oxford: Blackwell.

Harré, R. 1988. *The Singular Self: An Introduction to the Psychology of Self*. London: Sage.

Harré, R. and Gillett, G. 1994. *The Discursive Mind*. London: Sage.

Harris, M. 1979. *Cultural Materialism: The Struggle for a Science of Culture*. New York, Random House.

Harris, T. [1967] 1996. *I'm OK–You're OK*. New York: Avon.

Hart, H. L. A. [1961] 1994. *The Concept of Law* (eds. Bullock, P. and Raz, J.) (2nd ed.). Oxford: Clarendon.

Harvey, D. 1992. *The Condition of Postmodernism: An Enquiry*. Oxford: Oxford University Press.

Harvey, J. B. (1999). *How Come Every Time I Get Stabbed in the Back, My Fingerprints are on the Knife?* San Francisco, CA: Jossey-Bass.

Haselbach, A. 1994. "On Ways and Patterns of Thinking 'Identity'" In Novak-Lukanovic, S. (ed.), *The Multiple Identity: What is it and How does it Work*. Ljubljana, SL: Slovenian National Commission for Unesco and Institute for Ethnic Studies (European project: Overlapping Cultures and Plural Identities/Cultures Partielles et Identités Multiple).

Hasker, W. 1999. *The Emergent Self*. Ithaca, NY: Cornell University Press.

Harford, T. 2007. *The Logic of Life: Uncovering the New Economics of Everything*. New York: Little, Brown.

Hauser, M. D. 2006. *Moral Minds: How Nature Designed Our Universal Sense of Right and Wrong*. New York: Little, Brown.

Haworth, L. 1986. *Autonomy: An Essay in Philosophical Psychology and Ethics*. New Haven: Yale University Press.

Hayek, F. A. 1942. "Scientism and the Study of Man I." *Economica* 9: 267–91.

Hayek, F. A. 1943. "Scientism and the Study of Man II." *Economica* 10: 34–63.

Hayek, F. A. 1942. "Scientism and the Study of Man III." *Economica* 11: 27–39.

Hayek, F. A. 1948. *Individualism and Economic Order*. Chicago, IL: University of Chicago Press.

Hayek, F. A. 1953. *The Counter-Revolution of Science*. New York: The Free Press.

Hayek, F. A. 1960. *The Constitution of Liberty*. London: Routledge & Kegan Paul.

Hayek, F. A. 1989. *The Fatal Conceit: The Errors of Socialism*. Chicago, IL: University of Chicago Press.

Hayek, F. A. 1973. *Law, Legislation and Liberty* (Vol. 1 *Rules and Order*). London: Routledge and Kegan Paul.

Hayek, F. A. 1976. *Law, Legislation and Liberty* (Vol. 2 *The Mirage of Social Justice*). London: Routledge and Kegan Paul.

Hayek, F. A. 1978. *New Studies in Philosophy, Politics, Economics and the History of Ideas*. London: Routledge and Kegan Paul.

Hayek, F. A. 1979. *Law, Legislation and Liberty* (Vol. 3 *The Political Order of a Free People*). London: Routledge and Kegan Paul.

Hayes, M. 1994. *The New Right in Britain: An Introduction to Theory and Practice.* London: Pluto Press.

Hayman, R. 1997. *Nietzsche: Nietzsch's Voices*. London: Pheonix.

Heath, J. 2001. *Communicative Action and Rational Choice*. Cambridge, MA: MIT Press.

Heclo, H. 1978. "Issue Networks and the Executive Establishment." In King, A. (ed.), *The New American Political System.* Washington, DC: American Enterprise Institute.

Hegel, G. W. F. [1806] 1998. "Independence and Dependence of Self-consciousness Lordship and Bondage." In Houlgate, S. (ed.), *Hegel Reader.* Oxford: Blackwell.

Hegel, G. W. F. [1807] 1977. *Phenomenology of Spirit* (tr. Miller, A. V.). Oxford: Oxford University Press).

Hegel, G. W. F. [1816] 1969. *Hegel's Science of Logic* (tr. Miller, A. V.). (London: Allen and Unwin.

Hegel, G. W. F. [1817] 1970. *Philosophy of Nature (Part Three of the Encyclopaedia of Philosophical Sciences*) (tr. Perry, M. J.) (3 vols.). London: George Allen and Unwin.

Hegel, G. W. F. [1817] 1991. *The Encyclopedia Logic: Part 1 of the Encyclopaedia of Philosophical Sciences* (trs. Geraets, T. F., Suchting, W. A. and Harris, H. S.). Indianapolis, IN: Hackett.

Hegel, G.F.W. [1821] 1991. *Elements of the Philosophy of Right* (ed. Wood, A. W., tr. Nisbet, H. B.). Cambridge: Cambridge University Press.

Heidegger, M. [1927] 1967. *Being and Time* (tr. Macquarrie, J. and Robinson, E.). Oxford: Basil Blackwell.

Heidegger, M. [1927] 1996. *Being and Time* (trs. Stanbaugh, J.). New York: New York State University Press.

Heider F. 1946. "Attitudes and Cognitive Organization." *The Journal of Psychology* 21: 107–112.

Heider, F. [1958] 1982. *The Psychology of Interpersonal Relations.* Hillsdale, NJ: Lawrence Erlbaum.

Hekman, S. 1983. *Weber, the Ideal Type, and Contemporary Social Theory.* Notre Dame, IN: University of Notre Dame Press.

Held, D. 1980. *Introduction to Critical Theory.* Berkeley and Los Angeles, CA: University of California Press.

Hempel, C. G. 1966. *Philosophy of Natural Science.* Englewood Cliffs, NJ: Prentice Hall.

Hempel, C. G. 1980. "The Logical Analysis of Psychology." In Block, N. (ed.), *Readings in the Philosophy of Psychology* (Vol. 1). Cambridge, MA: Harvard University Press.

Hendriks, F. and Zouridis, S. 1999. "Cultural Biases and New Media for the Public Domain: Cui Bono." In Thompson, M., Grendstat, G. and Selle, P. (eds.), *Cultural Theory as Political Science.* London: Routledge.

Hesse, M. 1966. *Models and Analogies in Science.* Notre Dame, IN: University of Notre Dame.

Hetcher, S. A. 2004. *Social Norms in a Wired World.* Cambridge: Cambridge University Press.

Heuer, R. J. Jr. 1999. *Psychology of Intelligence Analysis.* Washington, DC: Centre for the Study of Intelligence, Central Intelligence Agency. Available at http://www.au.af.mil/au/-awc/awcgate/psych-intel/art12.html

Hewstone, M. and Augoustinos, M. 1998. "Social Attributions and Social Representation." In Flick, U. (ed.), *The Psychology of the Social.* Cambridge: Cambridge University Press.

Heyd, D. 1982. *Supererogation: Its Status in Ethical Theory.* Cambridge: Cambridge University Press.

Higgins, K. and Solomon, R. 1993. *The Age of German Idealism.* London and New York: Routledge.

Higgins, T. E. 1990. "Personality, Social Psychology, and Person-Situation Relations: Standards and Knowledge Activation as a Common Language." In Pervin, L. A. (ed.), *Handbook of Personality: Theory and Research.* New York: Guilford.

Hinde, R. 2002. *Why Good is Good: The Sources of Morality.* London: Routledge.

Hirschman, A. O. 1991. *The Rhetoric of Reaction: Perversity, Futility, Jeopardy.* Cambridge, MA: Harvard University Press.

Hischkop, K. 2003. "Tragedy in an Untragic Culture." Unpublished paper, Department of English and American Studies, University of Manchester, Manchester, United Kingdom.

Hitchcock, C. [1997] 2002. "Probabilistic Causation." In Zelta, E. N. (ed.), *The Stanford Encyclopedia of Philosophy.* Available at http://plato.stanford.edu/entries/causation-p-robabilistic/.

Ho, D. Y. F. 1995. "Selfhood and Identity in Confucianism, Taoism, Buddhism and Hinduism: Contrasts with the West." *Journal of the Theory of Social Behavior* 25 (2): 115–39.

Ho, D. Y. F. 1998. "Social relationships and Relationship Dominance: An Analysis based on Methodological relationalism." *Asian Journal of Social Psychology* 1 (1): 1–16.

Ho, D. Y. F. and Peng, S. Q. [1998] 1999. "Methodological Relationalism and it Application in Eastern and Western Cultures." *Sociological Research* 4: 34–43 (in Chinese), translated in *Sociology* 1: 9–18.

Ho, D. Y. F., Chan, S. F. F., Peng, S. Q. and Ng, A. K. 2001. "The Dialogical Self: Converging East-West Constructions." *Culture & Psychology* 7 (1): 393–408.

Ho, D. Y. F., .Chan, S. F. and Zhang, Z. X. 2001. "Metarelational analysis: An Answer to 'What's Asian about Asian Social Psychology'." *Journal of Psychology in Chinese Societies* 2 (1): 7–26.

Ho, D. Y. F., Peng, S. Q. Lai, A. C. and Chan, S. F. 2001. "Indigenization and Beyond: Methodological Relationalism in the Study of Personality across Cultural traditions." *Journal of Personality* 69 (6): 925–53.

Hobbes, T. [1642] 1949. *De Cive, or On the Citizen.* New York: Appelton-Century-Crofts.

Hobbes, T, [1651] 1962. *Leviathan* (ed. Oakeshott, M.). New York: Collier.

Hobbes, T. [1651] 1996. *Leviathan* (ed. Tuck, R.). Cambridge: Cambridge University Press.

Hobsbawm, E. 1997. *On History.* London: Weidenfeld & Nicolson.

Hoefer, C. 2003. Causal Determinism." In Zalta, E. N. (ed.), *The Stanford Encyclopedia of Philosophy.* Available at: http://plato.stanford.edu/entries/determinism-causal/.

Hoernlé, R. F. A. 1927. *Idealism as a Philosophy.* New York: George H. Doran.

Hoffer, E. [1951] 1989. *The True Believer: Thoughts on the Nature of Mass Movements* (Perennial Library ed.). New York: Harper & Row.

Hofstede, G. 1991. *Cultures and Organizations: Software of the Mind.* New York: McGraw-Hill.

Hogarth, R. 1980. *Judgement and Choice.* New York: John Wiley.

Holling, C. S. 1986. "The Resilience and Vulnerability of Eco-systems." In Clark, W. C. and Munn, R. E. (eds.), *The Sustainable Development of the Biosphere.* Cambridge: Cambridge University Press.

Hollingdale, R. J. 1970. "Introduction." In Schopenhauer, A. [1851], *Essays and Aphorisms* (tr. Hollingdale, R. J.). Harmondsworth, Gt. Lon., UK: Penguin.

Hollis, M. 1977. *Models of Man: Philosophical Thoughts on Social Action.* Cambridge: Cambridge University Press.

Hollis, M. 1989. "Honour among Thieves." *Proceedings of the British Academy* 175: 165–87.

Hollis, M. 1994. *The Philosophy of Social Science.* Cambridge: Cambridge University Press.

Hollis, M. and Lukes, S (eds.) 1982. *Rationality and Relativism.* Cambridge, MA: MIT Press.

Holmstrom-Hintikka, G. and Tuomela, R. (eds.) 1997. *Contemporary Action Theory* (2 vols.). Dordrecht, NL: Kluwer.

Holt, T. 2005–6. *Fallacy of Composition.* Available at: http://logicalfallacies.info/fallacy-ofcomposition.html.

Homans, G. C. (1958). "Social Behavior as Exchange." *American Journal of Sociology* 63: 597–606.

Homans, G. C. 1951. *The Human Group*, London: Routledge and Kegan Paul.

Homans, G. C. 1974. *Social Behavior: Its Elementary Forms,* New York: Harcourt Brace Jovanovich.

Hood, C. 1998. *The Art of the State: Culture, Rhetoric, and Public Management.* Oxford: Clarendon.

Hoose, B. 1987. *Proportionalism.* Washington DC: Georgetown University Press.

Hoppe, R. 2000. "Grid-Group Culture Theory and the Politics of Problem Definition." A paper presented at the 8th Biennial Jerusalem Conference in Canadian Studies (Israel).

Horney, K. 1937. *The Neurotic Personality of our Times.* New York: Norton.

Horney, K. 1945. *Our Inner Conflicts.* New York: Norton.

Hospers, J. 1966. "What Means this Freeedom." In Berofsky, B. (ed.), *Free Will and Determinism.* New York: Harper & Row.

How, A. 2003. *Critical Theory.* Basingstoke, Hamp., UK: Palgrave Macmillan.

Howard, N. 1971. *Paradoxes of Rationality: Games, Metagames, and Political Behavior.* Cambridge, MA: MIT Press.

Howard, N. 1999. *Confrontational Analysis: How to Win Operations other than War.* Washington, DC: The Command and Control Research Programme, US Department of Defence.

Hsu, F. L. K. (ed.) 1961. *Psychological Anthropology. Approaches to Culture and Personality.* Homewood, IL: The Dorsey Press.

Hughes, M. 1973. "Our Concern with Others." In Montefiore, A. (ed.), *Philosophy and Personal Relations.* London: Routledge & Kegan Paul.

Humbolt, W. von [1791] 1969. *The Limits of State Action* (ed. and tr. Burrow, J. W.). Cambridge: Cambridge University Press

Hume, D. [1739–40] 1978. *A Treatise of Human Nature* (orig. ed. Selby-Biggs, L. A., rev. ed. Nidditch, P. P.). Oxford: Clarendon.

Hume, D. [1748] 1975. *An Enquiry Concerning Human Understanding* (orig. ed. Selby-Bigge, L.A., rev. ed. Nidditch, P.H.) (3rd ed.). Oxford: Clarendon.

Hume, D. [1751] 1998. *An Enquiry Concerning the Principles of Morals* (ed. Beauchamp, T. L.). Oxford: Oxford University Press

Hume, D. [1777] 1902. *An Enquiry Concerning the Human Understanding* [1748] *and Concerning the Principles of Morals* [1751] (ed. Selby-Biggs, L. A.) (2nd ed.). Oxford: Clarendon.

Humphrey, N. 2006. *Seeing Red: A Study in Consciousness*. Harvard: Harvard University Press.

Hurka, T. 1993. *Perfectionism*. New York: Oxford University Press.

Hurley, S. 1998. *Consciousness in Action*. Cambridge, MA: Harvard University Press.

Husserl, E. [1907] 1966. *The Idea of Phenomenology*. (tr. Alston, W.P. and Nakhnikian, G.). The Hague, NL: Martinus Nijhoff.

Husserl, E. [1928] (1964), *On the Phenomenology of the Consciousness of Internal Time* (tr. Churchill, J. S., ed. Heidegger, M.). Bloomington: Indiana University Press.

Husserl, E. [1928] 1931. *Ideas* (tr. Gibson, W. R. B.) (3rd ed.). London: Allen and Unwin.

Husserl, E. [1929] 1981. *Husserl: Shorter Work* (eds. McCormick, P. and Elliston, F. A.). Notre Dame, IN: University of Notre Dame Press.

Husserl, E. [1931] 1960. *Cartesian Meditations: An Introduction to Phenomenology*. (tr. Cairns, D.). The Hague, NL: Martinus Nijhoff.

Hutcheson, F. [1755] 2000. *A System of Moral Philosophy*. Bristol, UK: Thoemmes Press.

Hyslop, A. (1998) "Methodological Epiphenomenalism." *Australasian Journal of Philosophy* 76: 61–70.

Ivanhoe, P. J. 1993. *Confucian Moral Self-Cultivation*. New York: Peter Lang.

Ives, P. 2003. *Language and Hegemony in Gramsci*. London: Pluto Press.

Jackson, F. 1996. "Mental Causation." *Mind* 105: 377–413.

Jackson, R. 2001. *Nietzsche: A Beginner's Guide*. London: Hodder & Straughton.

Jacobi, J. 1962. *The Psychology of C. G. Jung*. New Haven, CT: Yale University Press.

Jacquette, D. J. 2002. *Ontology*. Montreal & Kingston, Ont., CA: McGill-Queen's University Press.

Jagger, R. 1972. *The Development of Bertrand Russell's Philosophy*. London: Allen & Unwin.

James, W. 1884. "What is an Emotion?" *Mind* 9: 188–205. Available at http://psychclassics.yorku.ca/James/emotion.htm.

James, W. 1890a. *The Principles of Psychology.* Available at http://psychclassics.yorku.-ca/James/Principles/prin9.htm

James, W. 1890b. "The Stream of Consciousness." Available at http://pchchclassics.york-u.ca/ James/jimmy11.htm.

James, W. 1896. *The Will to Believe*: *An Address to the Philosophical Clubs of Yale and Brown Universities.* Available at http://falcon.jmu.edu/~omearawm/ph101willto-believe.html

James, W. [1897] 1979. *The Will to Believe and Other Essays in Popular Philosophy*. Cambridge, MA and London: Harvard University Press

James, W. [1907] 1995. *Pragmatism* [*a New Name for Some Old Ways of Thinking*]. Toronto, ONT, CA: General Publishing

James, W. [1909] 1979. *The Meaning of Truth.* Cambridge, MA and London: Harvard University Press.

James, W. 1912. *Essays in Radical Empiricism* (ed. Perry, R. B.). New York: Longman Green. Available at: http://spartan.ac.-brocku.ca/~lward/James/James_1912/ James_191-2_toc.html.

Janicaud, D. 2005. *The Human Condition* (tr. Brennan, E., intro. Critchley, S). London: Routledge.

Janis, I. L. 1972. *Groupthink: Psychological Policy Decisions and Fiascoes.* Boston, MA: Houghton Mifflin.

Jarvie, I. C. 1998. "Situational Logic and its Reception." *Philosophy of the Social Sciences* 28 (3): 365–80.

Jensen, L. 1998. "Cultural Theory and Democratizing Functional Domains." *Public Administration* 76 (1): 117–39.

Jensen, L. 1999. "Images of Democracy in Danish Social Housing." In Thompson, M., Grendstat, G. and Selle, P. (eds.), *Cultural Theory as Political Science*. London: Routledge.

Johnson, A. G. [1995] 2000. *The Blackwell Dictionary of Sociology: A User's Guide to Sociological Language* (2nd ed.). Oxford: Blackwell.

Johnson, L. E. 1992. *Focusing on Truth.* New York and London: Routledge.

Johnson, R. 2000. "Scientific Explanations of Social Phenomena: Overcoming the Positivist-Interpretivist Divide." A paper presented at the 41st Annual Convention of the International Studies Organization (Los Angeles, CA). Available at http://www.ci-aonet.org/isa/jor01/.

Johnston, H. and Klandermans, B. 1995. "The Cultural Analysis of Social Movements." In Johnston, H. and Klandermans, B. (eds.), *Social Movements and Culture*. London: UCL Press.

Johnston, I. 1997. "Lecture on Aristotle's Nicomachaean Ehics," Available at http://www.-mala.bc.ca/~johnstoi/introser/aristot.htm.

Johnston, P. 1989. *Wittgenstein and Moral Philosophy*. London: Routledge.

Jolley, N. 2005. *Leibniz*. New York: Routledge.

Jones, E. E., Kanouse, D. E., Kelley, H. H., Nisbet, R. E., Valins, S. and Weiner, B. (eds.) 1972. *Attribution: Perceiving the Causes of Behavior*. Morristown, NJ: General Learning Press.

Jordan, G. 1990. "Sub-governments, Policy Communities and Network Labels." *Journal of Theoretical Politics* 2 (3): 319–38.

Jouanna, J. [1992] 1999. *Hippocrates* (tr. DeBevoise, M. B.). Baltimore, MD: Johns Hopkins University Press

Joule, R. V. and Beauvois, J.–L. 1998. "Cognitive Dissonance Theory: A Radical View." *European Review of Social Psychology* 8: 1–32.

Journard, S. 1971. *Self-disclosure*. New York: Wiley.

Jung, C. G. [1921] 1923. *Psychological Types* (tr. Godwyn-Baynes, H.). Available at: http://psychclassics.yorku.ca/Jung/types.htm.

Jung, C. G. [1934] 1981. *The Archetypes and The Collective Unconscious*. (2nd ed.) (tr. Hull, R. F. C.) (Collected Works, Vol. 9, Pt. 1). Princeton, NJ: Bollingen.

Jung, C. G. 1934. "The Concept of the Collective Unconscious." Available at http://www.ti-mestar.org.

Jung, C. G. 1969. *The Structure and Dynamics of the Psyche* (2nd ed.) (tr. Hull, R. F. C.) (Collected Works, Vol. 8). Princeton, NJ: Bollingen.

Kahneman, D. and Tversky, A. 1972. "Judgement of Representativeness." *Cognitive Psychology* 3: 430–54.

Kohneman, D. and Tversky, A. 1979. "Prospect Theory: An Analysis of Decision Theory Under Risk." *Econometrica* 47: 263–91.

Kahneman, D. and Tversky, A. 1984. "Choices, Values and Frames." *American Psychologist* 39 (4): 342–47.

Kahneman, D., Slovic, P. and Tversky, A. (eds.) 1982. *Judgement under Uncertainty: Heuristics and Biases*. Cambridge: Cambridge University Press.

Kahneman, D. (2003). "Maps of Bounded Rationality: A Perspective on Intuitive Judgment and Choice." In Frangsmyr, T. (ed.), *Les Prix Nobel 2002* [Nobel Prizes 2002]. Stockholm, SE: Almquist & Wiksell International.

Kahoe, K. 2003. "The Praxis Prism—The Epistemology of Antonio Gremsci." *Cork On-line Law Review*: ix

Kane, R. 1996. *The Significance of Free Will.* New York: Oxford University Press.

Kane, R. (ed.) 2002a. *Free Will.* Malden, MA: Blackwell.

Kane, R. 2002b. "Introduction." In Kane, R. (ed.), *Free Will.* Malden, MA: Blackwell.

Kane, R. [2001] 2002c. "Free Will: New Directions for an Ancient Problem." In Kane, R. (ed.), *Free Will.* Malden, MA: Blackwell.

Kant, I. [1781–87] 1956. *Critique of Pure Reason* (tr. Beck, L.W.). Indianapolis, IN: Bobbs-Merrill.

Kant, I. [1785] 2003. *Fundamental Principles of the Metaphysic of Morals: Second Section, Transition from Popular Moral Philosophy to the Metaphysic of Morals,* (tr. Abbott, T. K.). Available at http://www.msu.org/ethics/contenteythics/text/kant/-kanttxt2.html.

Kant, I. [1788] 1906, *Critique of Practical Reason* (tr. Abbott, T. K.). London: Longmans.

Kapitan' T. (1992), "Peirce and the Autonomy of Abductive Reasoning." *Erkenntnis* (*Historical Archive*) 37 (1): 1–26.

Kardiner, A., Du Bois, C., Linton, R. and James Wes, J. 1945. *The PsychologicalFrontiers of Society***.** New York: Columbia University Press.

Karpf, F. B. 1932. *American Social Psychology—its Origins, Development and European Background.* New York: Macmillan.

Kassin, S. 2003. *Psychology*. Englewood Cliff, NJ: Prentice Hall.

Kateb, G. 1963. *Utopia and Its Enemies*. New York: Free Press.

Katz, D. 1960 "The Functional Approach to the Study of Attitudes." *The Public Opinion Quarterly* 24 (2): 163–204

Katzenstein, P. J. 1996. "Introduction: Alternative Perspectives on National Security." In Katzenstein, P. J. (ed.), *The Culture of National Security: Norms and Identity in World Politics*. New York: Columbia University Press.

Kegan, J. 2007. *What is Emotion? History, Measures and Meaning*. New Haven, CT: Yale University Press.

Kelly, G. A. 1955. *The Psychology of Personal Constructs*. New York: Norton.

Kelley, H. H. 1967. Attribution Theory in Social Psychology." In Levine, D. (ed.), *Nebraska Symposium on Motivation* (Vol. 15). Lincoln, NE: University of Nebraska Press

Kelley, H. H.1972. "Causal Schema and the Attribution Process." In Jones, E. E., Kanouse, D. E., Kelley, H. H., Nisbet, R. E., Valins, S. and Weiner, B. (eds.), *Attribution: Perceiving the Causes of Behavior.* Morristown, NJ: General Learning Press.

Kelley, H. H. 1973. "The Processes of Causal Attribution." *American Psychologist* 28: 107–28.

Kelley, H. H. 1979. *Personal Relationships: Their Structures and Processes.* Hillsdale, NJ: Erlbaum.

Kelley, H. H. and Thibaut, J. W. 1978. *Interpersonal Relations: A Theory of Interdependence.* New York: Wiley.

Kenny, A. 1963. *Action, Emotion and Will.* London: Routledge & Kegan Paul.

Kierkegaard, S. [1843] 1941. *Repetition: A Venture in Experimenting Psychology* (tr. Lowrie, W.). Princeton, NJ: Princeton University Press.

Kierkegaard S. [1844] 1980. *The Concept of Anxiety* (tr. Thomte R.). Princeton, NJ: Princeton University Press.

Kierkegaard, S. [1845] 1940. *Stages on Life's Way* (tr. Lowrie, W.). Princeton, NJ: Princeton University Press.

Kierkegaard, S. [1846] (1941), *Concluding Unscientific Postscript* (trs. Swenson, D. F. and Lowrie, W.). Princeton, NJ: Princeton University Press.

Kierkegaard, S. [Anti-Climacus] [1849] 1980. *The Sickness unto Death: A Christian Psychological Exposition for Upbuilding and Awakening* (trs. Hong, H. and Hong, E.). Princeton, NJ: Princeton University Press.

Kim, J. 1993. *Supervenience and Mind.* Cambridge: Cambridge University Press.

Kim, J. 1998. *Mind in a Physical World.* Cambridge, MA: MIT Press.

Kincaid, H. 1996. *Philosophical Foundations of the Social Sciences: Analysing Controversies in Social Research.* Cambridge: Cambridge University Press.

King, A. 1999 "Against Structure: a Critique of Morphogenetic Social Theory." *The Sociological Review* 47 (2): 199–227.

King, A. 2005. "The Habitus Process: A Sociological Process." *Journal of the Theory of Social Behavior* 35 (4): 463–68.

King, G., Keohane, R. O. and Verba, S. 1994. *Designing Social Inquiry: Scientific Inference in Qualitative Research.* Princeton, NJ: Princeton University Press.

Kirk, R. 1999. *Relativism and Reality: A Contemporary Introduction.* London: Routledge.

Kirkham, R. L. 1992. *Theories of Truth: A Critical Introduction.* Cambridge, MA: MIT Press.

Kiser, E. 2005. "The Microfoundations of Social Action: Toward an Analytical Weberianism." A paper presented at the annual meeting of the American Sociological Association (Philadelphia, PA). Available at http://www.allacademic. com/met/p2140-3_i-ndex.httm

Kitcher, P. 1985. *Vaulting Ambition: Sociobology and the Quest for Human Nature.* Cambridge, MA: MIT Press.

Kitcher, P. 1998. *Kant's Critique of Pure reason: Critical Essays*. Blue Ridge Summit, PA: Rowman & Littlefield.

Knapp, P. 1994. *One World – Many Worlds: Contemporary Sociological Theory*. New York: Harper-Collins.

Knorr-Cetina, K. D. 1981. *The Manufacture of Knowledge: An Essay on the Constructivist and Contextual Nature of Science*. Oxford: Pergamon.

Koffka, K. 1935. *The Principles of Gestalt Psychology*. New York: Harcourt Brace and World.

Kohut, H. 1971. *The Analysis of Self*. New York: International University Press.

Kohut, H. and Wolf, E. S. 1978. "The Disorders of Self and their Treatment." *International Journal of Psychoanalysis* 59: 413–26.

Komorita, S. S. and Parks, C. D. 1995. "Interpersonal Relations: Mixed-Motive Interaction." *Annual Review of Psychology* 46: 183–207.

Kotarba, J. A. 1984. "A Synthesis: The Existential Self in Society." In Kotarba, J. A. and Fontana, A. (eds.), *The Existential Self in Society*. Chicago, IL: University of Chicago Press.

Kotarba, J. A. and Fontana, A. (eds.) 1984. *The Existential Self in Society*. Chicago: University of Chicago Press

Kotarba, J. A. and Johnson, J. M. 2002. *Postmodern Existential Sociology*. Walnut Creek, CA: AltaMira Press.

Kozulin, A. 1990. *Vygotsky's Psychology: A Biography of Ideas*. Cambridge, MA: Harvard University Press.

Kraut, R. 2007. *What is Good and Why: The Ethics of Well-Being*. Cambridge, MA: Harvard University Press.

Kretzmann, N. and Stump, E. (eds.). 1993. *The Cambridge Companion to Aquinas*. Cambridge: Cambridge University Press.

Kripke, S. A. 1979. "A Puzzle About Belief." In Margalit, A. (ed.), *Meaning and Use*. Dordrecht, NL: Reidel.

Kripke, S. A. 1982. *Wittgenstein on Rules and Private Language*. Oxford: Blackwell.

Kropotkin, P. 1987. *The State: Its Historic Role*. London: Freedom Press.

Kropotkin, P. 1995. *The Conquest of Bread and Other Writings*. Cambridge: Cambridge University Press.

Kruglanski, A. W. and Ajzen, I. 1983. "Bias and Error in Human Judgment." *European Journal of Social Psychology* 13: 1–44.

Krull, D. S. and Erickson, D. J. 1995. "On Judging Situations: The Effortful Process of Taking Dispositional Information into Account." *Social Cognition* 13: 417–38.

Kuhn, T. 1970. *The Structure of Scientific Revolutions*. Chicago, IL: University of Chicago Press.

Kukathas, C. 1989. *Hayek and Modern Liberalism*, Oxford: Clarendon.

Labriola, A. [1896] 1908. *Essays on the Materialist Conception of History* (tr. Kerr, C. H.). Available at: http://socserv.mcmaster.ca/econ/ugcm/3ll3/marx/labriola.html.

Lacan, J. 1968. *Speech and Language in Psychoanalysis* (tr. Wilden, A.). Baltimore, MD: John Hopkins University Press.

Laing, R. D. 1960. *The Divided Self: An Existential Study in Sanity and Madness*. Harmondsworth, Gt. Lon., UK: Penguin.

Lakoff, G. and Johnston, M. 1980. *Metaphors We Live By*. Chicago, IL: University of Chicago Press.

Lakoff, G. and Johnston, M. 1999. *Philosophy in the Flesh*. New York: Basic Books.

La Mettrie, J. O. de 1748. *L'Homme Machine* [Man a Machine]. Available at http://www. cscs.umich.edu/~crshalizi/LaMettrie/Machine/

Lang, G. 2002. "Moral Relativism and Cultural Chauvinism." *Philosophy Now* 36 (June/July): 24–7.

Lasch, C. 1979. *The Culture of Narcissism: American Life in an Age of Diminishing Expectations*. New York: Norton.

Lasswell, H.D. 1948. *Power and Personality*. New York: The Viking Press.

Latour, B. and Woolgar, S. 1979. *Laboratory Life*. Princeton: Princeton University.

Laver, M. 1997. *Private Desires, Political Action*. Thousand Oaks, CA: Sage.

Lazarus, R. S. 1966. *Psychological Stress and the Coping Process*. New York: McGraw-Hill.

Leadbeater, C. 2000. *Living on Thin Air: The New Economy*. Harmondsworth, Gt. Lon., UK: Penguin.

Leader, DE. 2007. *The New Black: Mourning, Melancholia and Depression*. London: Hamish Hamilton.

Leal, F. and Saran, R. 1998. "A Dialogue on the Socratic Dialogue." In *Occasional Working Papers in Ethics and the Critical Philosophy* (Vol. 2). London: Society for the Furtherance of the Critical Philosophy.

Leach, E. 1970. *Lévi-Strauss*. London: Fontana.

Lehrer, K. 1991. *Metamind*. Oxford: Oxford University Press.

Leibenstein, H. 1976. *Beyond Economic Man*. Cambridge, MA: Harvard University Press.

Leibniz, G. W. [1714] 1973. "The Monadology." In Parkinson, G. H. R. (ed.), *Leibniz: Philosophical Writings* (tr. Morris, M. and Parkinson, G. H. R.). London: Dent.

Leibniz, G. W. [1716–17] 1956. *The Correspondence with Clarke* (ed. Alexander, H. G.). Manchester: Manchester University Press.

Leibniz, G. W. [1704, 1764] 1996. *New Essays on Human Understanding* (trs. Remnant, P. and Bennet, J.) (2nd ed.). New York: Cambridge University Press.

Lerner, M. J. 1980. *A Belief in a Just World: A Fundamental Delusion*. New York: Plenum.

Levenson, H. 1981. "Differentiating among Internality, Powerful Others, and Chance." In Lefcourt, H. M. (ed.), *Research with the Locus of Control Construct, 1: Assessment Methods*. Orlando, FL: Academic Press.

Levine, J. M. and Murphy, G. 1943. "The Learning and Forgetting of Controversial Material." *Journal of Abnormal and Social Psychology* 38: 507–17.

Lévinas, E. [1961] 1969. *Totality and Infinity* (tr. Lingis, A.). Pittsburg, PA: Duquesne University Press.

Lévinas, E. 1985. *Ethics and Infinity: Conversations with Philippe Nemo* (tr. Cohen, R. A.). Pittsburgh, PA: Duquesne University Press.

Lévinas, E. 1998. *Of God who Comes to Mind* (tr. Bergo, B.). Stanford, CA: Stanford University Press.

Levine, A. 1993. *The General Will: Rousseau, Marx, Communism*. Cambridge: Cambridge University Press.

LeVine, R. A. 1984. "Properties of Culture: An Ethnographic View." In Shweder, R. A. and LeVine, R. A. (eds.), *Culture Theory: Essays on Mind, Self, and Emotion*. New York: Cambridge University Press

Levi-Strauss, C. [1958/1963] 1974. *Structural Anthropology* (Vol. 1) (tr. Jacobson, C. and Schoepf, B.). London: Allen Lane/ Penguin.

Lévi-Strauss, C. [1962] 1963. *Totemism* (tr. Needham, R.). Boston, MA: Beacon Books.

Lewin, K. 1948. "Experimenting in Social Space." In Lewin, G. W. (ed.), *Resolving Social Conflicts*. New York: Harper and Row.

Lewin, K. 1952. "Defining the Field at a Given Time." In Cartwright, D. (ed.), *Field Theory in Social Sciences: Selected Theoretical Papers*. London: Tavistock.

Lewin, K. 1972. "Needs, Force and Violence in Psychological Fields." In Hollander, E. P. and Hunt, R. G. (eds.), *Classic Contributions to Social Psychology*. London: Oxford University Press.

Lewis, C. I. [1929] 1956. *Mind and the World Order*. New York: Charles Scribner's Sons.

Lewis, C. I. 1946. *An Analysis of Knowledge and Valuation*. La Salle, IL: Open Court.

Lewis, C. S. 1944. *The Inner Ring* (the Memorial Lecture at King's College, University of London). Available at: http://homepages.which.net/~radical.faith/misc/lewis.htm.

Lewontin, R. C., Rose, S. and Kamin, L. J. 1984. *Not in Our Genes: Biology, Ideology, and Human Nature*. New York: Pantheon.

Libet, B. 1985. "Unconscious Cerebral Initiative and the Role of Conscious Will in Voluntary Action." *Behavioral and Brain Science* 8: 529–66.

Libet, B., Freeman, A. & Sutherland, J. K. B. (eds.) 1999. *The Volitional Brain: Towards a Neuroscience of Freewill*. Charlottesville, VA: Imprint Academic.

Libet, B., Gleason, C. A., Wright, E. W. and Pearl, D. K. 1983. "Time of Conscious Intention to Act in Relation to Onset of Cerebral Activity (Readiness-Potential)." *Brain* 106: 623–42.

Lin, N. 2001. *Social Capital: A Theory of Social Structure and Action*. Cambridge: Cambridge University Press.

Linder, D. E., Cooper, J. and Jones, E. E. 1967. "Decision Freedom as a Determinant of the Role of Incentive Magnitude in Attitudinal Change." *Journal of Personality and Social Psychology* 6: 245–54.

Linell, P. 2007. *Essentials of Dialogism: Aspects and Elements of a Dialogical Approach to Language, Communication and Cognition*. Linköping, SE: Department of Communication Studies, Linköping Universit. Available at http://www.liu.se/isk/rese-arch/per_li/ linell_-essentials-of-dialogism_050625.pdf.

Lipsey, R G. and Chrystal, K. A. [1953] 1995. *An Introduction to Positive Economics* (8th ed.). Oxford: Oxford University Press.

Lipton, P. [1991] 2004. *Inference to the Best Explanation* (2nd ed.). London: Routledge. Available at: http://books.google.co.uk/books?id=qs75dwpeVEEC&dq=lipton+infere-nce+best+explanation&pg=PP1&ots=0kMTzi3KH4&sig=rG28ZHZH53lYn0J3BZnHoBd9lDg&hl=en&prev=http://www.google.co.uk/search?hl=en&q=Lipton+Inference+Best+Explanation&btnG=Google+Search&sa=X&oi=print&ct=title&cad=one-book-with-thu-mbnail#PPP1,M1

Loar, B. 1988. "Social Content and Psychological Content." In Grimm, R. and Merrill, D. (eds.), *Contents of Thought*. Tucson, AR: University of Arizona Press.

Locke, J. [1688] 1960. "The First Treatise of Government." In Locke, J., *Two Treatises of Government* (ed. Laslett, P.). Cambridge: Cambridge University Press.

Locke, J. ([1689] 1960). "The Second Treatise of Government: An Essay Concerning the *True Original, Extent, and End* of Civil Government." In Locke, J., *Two Treatises of Government* (ed. Laslett, P.). Cambridge: Cambridge University Press.

Locke, J. [1690] 2004. *An Essay Concerning Human Understanding*. Available at http://www.arts.cuhk.edu.hk/Philosophy/Locke/echu/.

Lockwood, D. 1966. "Sources of Variation in Working Class Images of Society." *Sociological Review* 14: 249–67.

Lom, P. 1998. *Scepticism, Liberalism and Illiberalism: An Inquiry into the Implications of Doubt*. San Domenico, IT: European University Institute.

Lonergan, B. J. F. [1957] 1992. *Insight: A Study of Human Understanding*. Toronto, Ont., CA: Toronto University Press.

Lonergan, B. J. F. 1972. *Method in Theology*. New York: Herder & Herder, 1972.

Longford, M. J.1985. *The Good and the True—An Introduction to Christian Ethics*. Norwich: SCM-Canterbury Press.

Lossky, N. O. 1951. *History of Russian Philosophy*. New York: International Universities Press.

Loux, M. J. 2002. *Metaphysics: A Contemporary Introduction* (2nd ed.). London: Routledge.

Lowe, E. J. 2005. *Locke*. London: Routledge.

Lowell, J. R. 1884. *On Democracy*. Available at http://xroads.virginia.edu/~drbr/lowell2.html.

Lucas, J. R. 1993. *The Freedom of Will*. Oxford: Oxford University Press.

Lucas, J. R. 1993. *Responsibility*. Oxford: Oxford University Press.

Lucey, K. 1996. *On Knowing and the Know*. Buffalo, NY: Prometheus.

Luft, J. and Ingham, H. 1955. *The Johari Window, a Graphic Model of Interpersonal Awareness* (Western Training Laboratory in Group Development). Los Angeles, CA: University of California at Los Angeles Extension Office.

Luhmann, N. 1979. *Trust and Power*. New York: Wiley

Luhmann, N. 1988. "Familiarity, Confidence and Trust: Problems and Alternatives." In Gambetta, D. (ed.), *Trust: Making and Breaking*. Oxford: Oxford University Press.

Lukács, G. [1923] 1971. *History and Class Consciousness* (tr. Livingstone, R.). London: Merlin.

Lukes, S. 1968. "Methodological Individualism Reconsidered." *The British Journal of Sociology* 19 (2): 119–29.

Lukes, S. 1974. *Power: Radical View*. London: MacMillan.

Lumsden, C. J. and Wilson, E. O. 1981. *Genes, Mind and Culture: The Coevolutionary Process*. Cambridge, MA: Harvard University Press.

Luntly, M. 1995. *Reason, Truth and Self*. London: Routledge.

Lycan, W. (ed.) 1990. *Mind and Cognition*. Oxford: Blackwell.

Lyotard, J.–F. 1979. *The Postmodern Condition: A Report on Knowledge* (trs Bennington, G and Massumi, B.). Minneapolis, MN: University of Minnesota Press.

MacDonald, S. (ed.) 1991. *Being and Goodness*. Ithaca, NY: Cornell University Press.

Machiavelli, N. [1531] 1969. *The Discourses* (ed.Crick, B.). London: Pelican.

Machiavelli, N. [1532] 1977. *The Prince* (ed. and tr. Adams, R. M.). New York: W. W. Norton.

MacIntyre, A. 1985. *After Virtue* (2nd ed.). London: Duckworth.

Mackie, R. L. 1977. *Ethics*. New York: Penguin.

Magnusson, D. and Endler, N. S. 1976. *Personality at the Crossroads: Current Issues in Interactional Psychology*. Hillsdale, NJ: Erlbaum.

Maimonides, M. [c1190] 1969. *The Guide of the Perplexed* (tr. Pines, S.). Chicago, IL: University of Chicago Press.

Malebranche, N. [1774–75] 1980. *The Search after Truth* (tr. Lennon, T. and Olscamp, P. J.). Columbus, OH: Ohio State University Press.

Mamadouh, V. 1999. "National Political Cultures in the European Union." In Thompson, M., Grendstat, G. and Selle, P. (eds.), *Cultural Theory as Political Science*. London: Routledge.

Mandeville, B. [1714] 1988. *The Fable of the Bees: or, Private Vices, Publick Benefits* (2 vols.) (ed. Kaye, F. B.). Indianapolis, IN: The Liberty Fund.

Manning, P. K. 1973. "Existential Sociology." *Sociological Quarterly* 14 (2): 200–25.

Marcel, G. 1952. *Men against Humanity* (tr. Fraser, G. S.). London: Harvill.

March, J. G. 1999. *The Pursuit of Organizational Intelligence*. Malden, MA: Blackwell.

March, J. G. and Olsen, J. P. 1976. *Ambiguity and Change in Organizations*. Bergen, NO: Universitets Forlaget.

Markey, J. 1925–26. "A Redefinition of Social Phenomena: Giving a Basis for Comparative Sociology." *American Journal of Sociology* 31: 733–43. Available at: http://www.brocku.ca/MeadProject/Markey/Markey_1926.html.

Markova, I. 1983. "The Origin of the Social Psychology of Language in German Expressivism." *British Journal of Social Psychology* 22: 315–25.

Marks, J. (ed.) 1986. *The Way of Desire*. Chicago, IL: Precedent.

Marshall, G. (ed.) 1998. *A Dictionary of Sociology* (2nd ed.). Oxford: Oxford University Press.

Martin, R. and Barresi, J. (eds.) 2003. *Personal Identity*. Oxford: Blackwell.

Marx, K. [1844] 1963. "Estranged Labour." In *Early Writings* (tr. and ed. Bottomore, T. B.). London: Watts.

Marx, K. [1844] 1967. "Economic and Philosophical Manuscripts." In Easton, L. D. and Guddat, K. H. (eds.), *Writings of the Young Marx on Philosophy and Society*. New York: Doubleday.

Marx, K. [1845, 1924] 2002. *Theses on Feuerbach* (trs. Smith, C. and Cuckson, D.). Available at: http://www.marxists.org/archive/marx/works/1845/theses/index.htm

Marx, K. [1859] 1999. *A Contribution to the Critique of Political Economy* (tr. Ryazanskaya, S. W.). Available at http://marxists.org/archive/marx/works/1859/critique-pol-economy/htm.

Marx, K [1859] 2001. *Preface to a Critique of Political Economy.* London: The Electric *Book Company.* Available at: www. elecbook.com.

Marx, K. [1867] 1993. *Capital: A Critique of Political Economy*. Harmondworth, Gt. Lon., UK: Penguin.

Marx, K and Engels, F. [1845–46] 1932. *The German Ideology: Critique of Modern German Philosophy According to Its Representatives Feuerbach, B. Bauer and Stirner, and of German Socialism According to Its Various Prophets.* Available at http://www. marxists.org/archive/marx/works/1845/german-ideology/index.htm.

Marx, K and Engels, F. [1848/1969] 2002. *Manifesto of the Communist Party* (trs. Smith, C. and Engels, F.). Available at http://www.marxists.org/archive/marx/-works/1848/ communist-manifesto/index.htm.

Maslow, A. H. [1964] 1970. *Religions, Values, and Peak Experiences.* Available at http://www.druglibrary.org/schaffer/lsd/maslow.htm

Maslow, A. H. [1962] 1968. *Towards a Psychology of Being.* New York: Nostrand.

Maslow, A. H. 1970. *Motivation and Personality* (2nd ed.). New York: Harper Row.

Maslow, A. H. 1971. *The Further Reaches of Human Nature.* New York: The Viking Press.

Matheson, P. E. 1916. *Epictetus: The Discourses and Manual, together with Fragments of his Writings* (2 vols.). Oxford: Clarendon Press. Available at http://www archive. org/details/epictetus01epicuoft; http://www.archive.org/details/epictetus02epicuoft.

Mathews, K. A. 1997 *Hostility.* Available at http://www.macses.ucsf.edu/research-/Psychosocial/notebook/hostility.

Matthews, G., Deary, I. J. and Whiteman, M. C. 2003. *Personality Trai*ts (2nd ed.). Cambridge: Cambridge University Press.

Maturana, H. R. 1991. "Science and Daily Life: the Ontology of Scientific Explanations." In Steier, F. (ed.). *Research and Reflexivity.* London: Sage.

May, R. 1953. *Man's Search for Himself.* New York: W. W. Norton.

May, R. 1958. "The Origins and Significance of the Existential Movement in Psychology." In May, R., Angel, E. and Ellenberger (eds.), *Existence: A New Dimension in Psychiatry and Psychology.* New York: Basic Books.

May, R. 1967. *Psychology and the Human Dilemma.* New York: Van Norstrand.

May, R. 1983. *The Discovery of Being: Writings on Existentialist Psychology.* New York: Norton.

May, T. 1993. *Social Research: Issues, Methods and Process.* Buckingham, Bucks, UK: Open University.

Mayer, R. C., Davis, J. H. Schoorman, F. D. 1995. "An Integrative Model of Organizational Trust." *Academy of Management Review* 20 (3): 709–34.

Mazzini, J. [1860] 1907. *The Duties of Man and Other Essays.* London: Dent & Sons.

McAllister, D. J. 1995. "Affect- and Cognition-Based Trust as Foundations for Interpersonal Cooperation in Organizations." *Academy of Management Journal* 38:24–59.

McCann, C. R. Jr. 2004. *Individualism and the Social Order.* New York: Routledge

McCelland, D. C., Atkinson, J. W., Clark, R. A. and Lowell, E. L. 1953. *The Achievement Motive.* New York: Appleton-Century-Crofts.

McClelland, D. C. 1961. *The Achieving Society.* Princeton, NJ: Van Nostrand.

McCelland, K. A. and Fararo, T. (eds.) 2006. *Purpose, Meaning and Action.* Basingstoke Hamp., UK: Palgrave Macmillan.

McClintock, C. G. 1972. "Social Motivation—A Set of Propositions." *Behavioral Science* 17: 438–54.

McCloskey, D. N. 1998. *The Rhetoric of Economics* (2nd ed.). Madison, WI: University of Wisconsin Press.

McFarland, D. 2007. *Quality Robots, Happy Dogs: The Question of Alien Minds.* Oxford: Oxford University Press.

McGinn, C. 1982. *The Character of Mind*. Oxford: Oxford University Press.

McGinn, C. 1983. *The Subjective View*. Oxford: Oxford University Press.

McGinn, C. 1989. "Can We Solve the Mind-Body Problem?" *Mind* 98: 349–56.

McGuire, W., and McGuire, C. 1982. "Significant Others in Self-space. In Suls, J. (ed.), *Psychological Perspectives on the Self* (Vol. 1). Hillsdale, NJ: Erlbaum.

McKinney, J. C. 1966. *Constructive Typologies and Social Theory*. New York: Meredith.

McKinney, J. P. 1981. "The Construct of Engagement Style: Theory and Research." In Lefcourt, H. M. (ed.), *Research with the Locus of Control Construct, 1: Assessment Methods*. Orlando, FL: Academic Press.

McMahon, R. 1979. *Human Beings: The World of Jean-Paul Sartre*. Chicago, IL: Chicago University Press.

McTaggart, J. 1927. *The Nature of Existence* (Vol. 2) (ed. Broad, C. D). Cambridge: Cambridge University Press.

Mead, G. H. 1929. "A Pragmatic Theory of Truth." *Studies in the Nature of Truth, University of California Publications in Philosophy 11:* 65–88.

Mead, G. H. 1934. *Mind, Self, and Society*. Chicago, IL: University of Chicago Press.

Mead, G. H. 1938. *The Philosophy of the Act* (eds. Dunham, A. M. and Morris, C. W.). Chicago: University of Chicago Press.

Mead, M. [1935] 1963. *Sex and Temperament in Three Primitive Societies*. New York: Morrow Quill.

Mead, M. 1942. *And Keep Your Powder Dry: An Anthropologist Looks at America*. New York: William Morrow.

MedicineNet.com 2003. *Webster's New World Medical Dictionary* (2nd ed.). London: Wiley.

Meilaender, G. C. 1984. *The Theory and Practice of Virtue*. Notre Dame, IN: University of Notre Dame Press.

Melden, A. I. 1961. *Free Action*. London: Routledge & Keegan Paul.

Mele, A. (ed.) 1997. *The Philosophy of Action*. Oxford: Oxford University Press,

Mele, A. R. 2003. *Motivation and Agency*. New York: Oxford University Press.

Mènard, C. 2000. *Institutions, Contracts and Organizations: Perspectives from New Institutional Economics*. Cheltenham, Glos., UK: Edward Elgar.

Menger, C. [1883] 1963. *Problems of Economics and Sociology* (tr. Nock, F. J, ed. Schneider, L.). Urbana, IL: University of Illinois Press.

Messner, D. 1997. *The Network Society: Economic Development and International Competitiveness as Problems of Social Governance*. London: Frank Cass.

Meyers, D. T. 1989. *Self, Society, and Personal Choice*. New York: Columbia University Press.

Meyers, G. E. 1986. *William James: His Life and Thought*. New Haven, CT: Yale University Press.

Midgley, M. 2003. *The Myths We Live By*. London: Routledge

Milgram, S. 1963. "Behavioral Study of Obedience." *Journal of Abnormal and Social Psychology* 67: 371–78.

Milgram, S. 1974. *Obedience to Authority: An Experimental View*. New York: HarperCollins.

Miller N. and Dollard J. 1941. *Social Learning and Imitation*. New Haven, CT: Yale University Press.

Mills, C. W. [1959] 1970. *The Sociological Imagination*. Harmondsworth, Gt. Lon., UK: Penguin.

Mill, J. S. [1859] 1963. "On Liberty." In Robson, J. M. (ed.). *The Collected Works of John Stuart Mill*. Toronto, Ont., CA: University of Toronto Press.

Mill, J. S. [1861] 1968. "Utilitarianism." In Mill. J. S. *Utilitarianism, Liberty and Representative Government*. London and Toronto, Ont., CA: Denton.

Mill, J. S. [1843] 1988. *A System of Logic*. (ed. Ayer, A. J. London: Duckworth.

Miller, D. (ed.) 1991. *Liberty*. Oxford: Oxford University Press.

Miller, D. T., Norman, S. A. and Wright, E. 1978. "Distortion in Person Perception as a Consequence of the Need for Effective Control." *Journal of Personality and Social Psychology* 36: 598–607.

Miller N. and Dollard J. 1941. *Social Learning and Imitation*. New Haven, CT: Yale University Press.

Miller, S. I. and Fredericks, M. 1994. *Qualitative Research Methods: Social Epistemological and. Practical Inquiry*. New York: Peter Lang.

Mills, J. and Clark, M. S. 1982. "Communal and Exchange Relationships." In Wheeler, L. (ed.), *Review of Personality and Social Psychology* (Vol. 4). Beverley Hills, CA: Sage.

Milman, H. H. [1855] 2006. *History of Latin Christianity including that of the Popes to the Pontificate of Nicholas V*. London: John Murray. Available at http://books. google.com/books?id=58ICAAAAQAAJ&pg=PA469&lpg=PA469&dq=cecco+%22dF+ascoli%22&source=web&ots=53RNdnYjqj&sig=zjpXilp7pxMdm40z_M8K1GGGj-I.

Milton, J. [1644] 1949. "Aeropagitica: A Speech for the Liberty of Unlicensed Printing, to the Parliament of England." In Bush, D. (ed.), *The Portable Milton*. New York: The Viking Press.

Mirowski, P. 1991. When Game Theory Grows Deadly Serious: The Military Influence on the Evolution of Game Theory." *History of Political Economy* 24: 227–60.

Mischel, W. 1968. *Personality and Assessment*. NewYork: Wiley.

Mischel, W. 1973. "Towards a Cognitive Social Learning Theory Reconceptualization of Personality." *Psychological Review* 80: 252–83.

Mises, L. von [1949] 1996. *Human Action: Treatise on Economics* (tr. Greaves, B. B.) (4th ed.). Auburn, AL: Ludwig von Mises Institute. Available at: http://www.mises.org/humanaction/pdf/HumanActionScholars.pdf.

Mises, L. von [1962] 1978. *The Ultimate Foundation of Economic Science: An Essay in Method* (tr. Greaves, B. B.). Kansas City MO: Sheed, Andrew and McMeet. Available at http://mises.org/books/ufofes/default.aspx.

Mitchell, B. 1980. *Morality: Religious and Secular*. Oxford: Clarendon.

Mitsis, P. 1988. *Epicurus' Ethical Theory: The Pleasures of Invulnerability*. Ithaca, NY: Cornell University Press.

Moldt, D. and Scheve, C. von 2001. "Emotional Action for Emotional Agents." In *Proceedings of the AISB'01 Symposium on Emotion, Cognition, and Affective Computing* (21–24 March), York, UK, at http://www.informatik.uni-hamb urg.de/ TGI/forschung-/projekte/emotion/Moldt_vonScheve_AISB01.pdf.

Molenaers, N. and Thompson, M. 1999. "The Cultural Conditions for Democracy and Their Implications for Transitional Societies." In Thompson, M., Grendstat, G. and Selle, P. (eds.), *Cultural Theory as Political Science*. London: Routledge.

Molina, L. de [1588–89] 1988. *On Divine Foreknowledge* (*Pt. IV of the Concordia*) (tr. Freddoso, A. J.). Ithaca, NY: Cornell University Press.

Mollon, P. 2000 *The Unconscious*. Cambridge: Icon.

Monad, J. 1971. *Chance and Necessity*. London: Collins.

Montaigne, M. de [1563–92] 1957. *The Complete Works of Montaigne* (tr. Frame, D. R.). Stanford, CA: Stanford University Press.

Moore, G. E. 1903. *Principa Ethica*. Cambridge: Cambridge University Press.

Moore, G. E. 1959. *Philosophical Papers*. London: George Allen and Unwin.

Moran, D., 2000, *Introduction to Phenomenology*. London and New York: Routledge.

More, T. [1516] 1989. *Utopia* (eds. Logan, G. M. and Adams, R. M.). Cambridge: Cambridge University Press.

Moreland, J. P. 2001. *Universals*. Montreal & Kingston, Ont., CA: McGill-Queen's University Press.

Morgan, B. 2009. *Acquaintances: The Space Between Intimates and Strangers*. Maidenhead, Berks., UK: Open University Press, McGraw-Hill Education.

Morris, P. 1987. *Power: a Philosophical Analysis*. Manchester, UK: Manchester University Press.

Morton, A. D. 2007. *Unravelling Gramsci: Hegemony and Passive Revolution in the Global Political Economy*. London: Pluto Press.

Moser, P. K. 1989. *Knowledge and Evidence*. Cambridge: Cambridge University Press.

Moser, P. K. 2002. *The Oxford Handbook of Epistemology*. New York: Oxford University Press.

Mounce, H. O. 1997. *The Two Pragmatisms: From Peirce to Rorty*. London: Routledge.

Mozi [5th century BC] 1963. *Mo Tzu: Basic Writings* (tr. Watson, B.). New York: Columbia University Press.

Muirhead, J. H. 1932. *Rule and End in Morals*. Oxford: Oxford University Press.

Murphy, J. P. 1990. *Pragmatism: From Peirce to Davidson*. Boulder, CO: Westview Press.

Murphy, R. T. 1980. *Hume and Husserl: Towards Radical Subjectivism*. The Hague, NL: Martinus Nijhoff.

Murray, A. J. H. 1997. *Reconstructing Realism: Between Power Politics and Cosmopolitan Ethics*. Edinburgh: Edinburgh University Press. Available at http://books. google.com/books?id=UW0b6ABr9QEC&dq=bounded+realm+of+activi-ty.

Nadler, S. (ed.) 1993. *Causation in Early Modern Philosophy: Occasionalism and Preestablished Harmony*. University Park, PA: Pennsylvania State University Press.

Nagel, T. [1976] 1993. "Moral Luck." In Statman, D. (ed.). *Moral Luck*. Albany, NY: SUNY Press.

Nagel, T. 1979. "Subjective and Objective." In Nagel, T. (ed.). *Moral Questions*. Cambridge: Cambridge University Press.

Nagel, T. 1986. *The View from Nowhere*. New York: Oxford University Press.

Nash, O. [1935] 2000 "Kind of Ode to Duty." In Martin, T. H. W, Chamberlain, D. and Weiler, I. (eds.), *Man's Search for Values*. Crescent City, FL: Gage Publishing.

Natanson, M. (ed.) 1963. *Philosophy of the Social Sciences*. New York: Random House.

Navia, L. E. 2007. *Socrates: A Life Examined*. Amherst, NY: Prometheus Books.

Nesselroade, J. R. and Cattell, R. B. (eds.) 1988. *Handbook of Multivariate Experimental Psychology* (2nd ed.). New York: Plenum.

Neumann, J. von and O. Morgenstern, O. [1944] 1953. *Theory of Games and Economic Behavior* (2nd ed.). Princeton, NJ: Princeton University Press.

Newby, H. 1977. *The Deferential Worker: A Study of Farm Workers in East Anglia*. London: Allen Lane.

Newcombe, T. M. 1956. "The Prediction of Interpersonal Attraction." *American Psychologist* 11: 575–86.

Newsome, D. 1997. *The Victorian World Picture: Perceptions and Introspections in an Age of Change*. New Brunswick, NJ: Rutgers University Press.

Nielson, K. [1971] 2002a. "The Compatibility of Freedom and Determinism." In Kane, R. (ed.), *Free Will*. Malden, MA: Blackwell.

Nietzsche [1871] 1993. *The Birth of Tragedy* (tr. Hollingdale, R. J.). Harmondworth, Gt.Lon., UK: Penguin.

Nietzsche. F. [1878] 1994. *Human, All Too Human* (tr. Faber, M.). Harmondworth, Gt. Lon., UK: Penguin.

Nietzsche, F. [1879] 1974. *Gay Science, with a Prelude of Rhymes and an Appendix of Songs* (tr. Kaufmann, W.). New York: Random House.

Nietzsche, F. [1881] 1997. *Daybreak: Thoughts on the Prejudices of Morality* (eds. Clarke, M and Leiter, B.). Cambridge: Cambridge University Press.

Nietzsche. F. [1883] 1967. "Thus Spoke Zarathustra" (tr. Kaufmann, W.). In *The Portable Nietzsche*. New York: Viking.

Nietzche, F. [1886] 1998. *Beyond Good and Evil*, (tr. Faber, M, intro. Holub, R. C.) Oxford: Oxford University Press.

Nietzche, F. [1887] 2003. *Genealogy of Morals.* Available at http://www.mala.bc.ca~joh-nstoi/Nietzche/genealogytofc.htm.

Nietzsche, F. [1887] 1967. "On the Genealogy of Morals" (tr. Kaufmann, W.). In *On the Genealogy of Morals and Ecce Homo.* New York: Random House.

Nietzsche, F. [1888] 1969. *Twilight of the Idols and the Anti-Christ* (tr. Hollingdale, R. J.). Harmondworth, Gt. Lon., UK: Penguin.

Nietzsche, F. 1889. *Twilight of the Idols or How One Philosophizes with a Hammer* (tr. Kaufman, W). Available at http://www.geocities.com/ thenietzschannel/twi. httm#maxim.

Nietzsche, F. [1895] 1967. *The Will to Power: Attempt at a Revaluation of all Values* (tr. Kaufmann, W.). New York: Random House.

Nightingale, D. J. and Cromby, J. 1999. *Social Constructionist Psychology: A Critical Analysis of Theory and Practice*. Buckingham, Bucks., UK: Open University Press.

Nisbett, R. and Ross, L.1980. *Human Inference: Strategies and Shortcomings of Human Judgment.* Englewood Cliffs, NJ: Prentice-Hall.

Nock, A. J. [1924] 1991. "On Doing the Right Thing." In Hamilton, C. H. (ed.), *The State of the Union: Essays in Social Criticism by Albert Jay Nock.* Indianapolis, IN. Liberty Fund.

Noonan, H. W. 2003, *Personal Identity* (2nd ed.). London: Routledge
Nozick, R. 1974. *Anarchy, State and Utopia.* Oxford: Basil Blackwell.
Nozick, R. 1981. *Philosophical Explanations.* Oxford: Oxford University Press.
Nunn, C. 2005. *Del La Mettrie's Ghost: The Story of Decisions.* Basingstoke, Hamp., UK: Palgrave Macmillan.
O'Brien, G. E. 1984. "Locus of Control, Work, and Retirement." In Lefcourt, H. M. (ed.), *Research with the Locus of Control Construct* (Vol. 3: *Extensions and Limitations*). Orlando, FL: Academic Press.
O'Connor, T. [1998] 2002. "The Agent as Cause." In Kane, R. (ed.), *Free Will.* Malden, MA: Blackwell,
O'Neill, O. 1989. *Constructions of Reason: Explorations of Kant's Practical Philosophy.* Cambridge: Cambridge University Press.
Oaks, D. H. 1998. "Rights and Responsibilities" in Etzioni, A. (ed.) *The Essential Communitarian Reader.* Lanham, MD: Rowman & Littlefield.
Ockham, W. [c 1300–47] 1990. *Philosophical Writings, (*eds. and trs.Boehner, P. and Brown S. F.). Indianapolis, IN: Hackett Publishing.
Ockham, W. [c 1329] 1974. "*Summa Logicae.*" In Loux, M. J. (ed.), *Ockham's Theory of Terms.* Notre Dame, IL: Notre Dame University Press.
O'Connor, D. J. 1975. *The Correspondence Theory of Truth.* London: Hutchinson.
Offe, C. 1999. 'How We Can Trust our Fellow Citizens." In Warren, M. E. (ed.) *Democracy and Trust.* Cambridge: Cambridge University Press.
Olafson, F. 1967. *Principles and Individuals: An Ethical Interpretation of Existentialism.* Baltimore, MD: John Hopkins University Press.
Olli, E. 1995. *Cultural Theory Specified—the Coherent, Sequential and Synthetic Individual Approaches* (Paper 230). Bergen, NO: University of Bergen: Department of Comparative Politics.
Olli, E. 1999. "Rejection of Cultural Biases and Effects on Party Preferences." In Thompson, M., Grendstat, G. and Selle, P. (eds.), *Cultural Theory as Political Science.* London: Routledge.
Oliner, S. P. and Oliner, P. M. 1988. *The Altruistic Personality: Rescuers of Jews in Nazi Europe.* New York: Free Press.
Olson, M. 1965. *The Logic of Collective Action: Public Goods and the Theory of Groups.* Cambridge, MA: Harvard University Press.
Onuf, N. G. 1989. *World of Our Making: Rules and Rule in Social Theory and International Relations.* Columbia, SC: University of South Carolina Press.
Orlofsky. J. L. 1976. "Intimacy Status: Relationship to Interpersonal Perception." *Journal of Youth and Adolescence* 5 (1): 73–78.
Ortega y Gasset, J. [1929–31] 2002. *What is Knowledge?* (tr. García-Gómez, J.). Albany, NY: State University of New York Press.

Ortega y Gasset, J. [1935] 2001. *Towards a Philosophy of History*. Chicago, IL: University of Illinios Press.

Orwell, G. [1949] 1983. *1984*. New York: Harcourt Brace Jovanovich.

Osgood, C. E. and Tannenbaum, P. H. 1955. "The Principle of Congruity in the Prediction of Attitude Change." *Psychology Review* 62 (1): 42–55.

Ostrander, D. 1982. "One-and Two-dimensional Models of the Distribution of Beliefs." In Douglas, M. (ed.), *Essays in the Sociology of Perception*. London: Routledge and Kegan Paul.

Ouellette, J. A. and Wood, W. 1998. "Habit and Intention in Everyday Life: The Multiple Processes by which Past Behavior Predicts Future Behavior." *Psychological Review* 124: 54–74.

Owen, D. 2007. *The Hubris Syndrome: Bush, Blaire and the Intoxication of Power*. London: Methuen.

Packard, V. 1959. *The Status Seekers*. New York: David Mackay.

Palmer, R. 1969. *Hermeneutics: Interpretation Theory in Schleiermacher, Dilthey, Heidegger, and Gadamer*. Evanston, IL: Northwestern University Press.

Parducci, A. 1995. *Happiness, Pleasure, and Judgment: The Contextual Theory and Its Applications*. Hillsdale, NJ: Lawrence Erlbaum.

Pareto, V. [1902] 1966. *Sociological Writings* (ed. Finer, S. E.). Oxford: Basil Blackwell.

Parker, J. 2000. *Structuration*. Milton Keynes, UK: Open University.

Parkin, F. 1971. *Class Inequality and Political Order*. London: MacGibbon and Kee.

Parker, W. D. 2007. *Methodological Individualism vs Methodological Holism: Neoclassicism, Institutionalism and Socionomic Theory* (Discussion Paper). Gainsville, GA: Socionomic Foundation.

Parkinson, G. A. R. (ed.) [1934] 1973. *Leibnitz: Philosophical Writings*. London: Dent and Son.

Parry, G. 1972. "The Machiavellianism of the Machiavellians." In Parekh, B. and Berki, R. N. (eds.), *The Morality of Politics*. London: George Allen and Unwin.

Parsons, T. 1937. *The Structure of Social Action* (2 vols.). New York: Free Press.

Parsons, T. 1951. *The Social System*. London: Collier-Macmillan.

Parsons, W. 1995. *Public Policy: An Introduction to the Theory and Practice of Policy Analysis*. Cheltenham, Glos., UK: Edward Elgar.

Pascal, B. [1670] 1966. *Pensée*. Harmondsworth, Gt. Lon., UK: Penguin.

Passes, N. and Agnew, R. (eds.) 1997. *The Future of Anomie Theory*. Boston, MA: Northeastern University Press.

Pavlov, I. 1927. *Conditioned Reflexes: An Investigation of Physiological Activity of the Cerebral Cortex* (tr. Anrep, G. V.). Oxford: Oxford University Press. Available at http://psychclassics.yorku.ca/Pavlov/

Peel, J. D. Y. 1971. *Herbert Spencer: the Evolution of a Sociologist*. London: Heinemann.

Peikoff, L. 1993. *Objectivity: the Philosophy of Ayn Rand*. New York: Penguin.

Peirce, C. S. 1877. "The Fixation of Belief." *Popular Science Monthly* 12 (November): 1–15. Available at http://www.peirce.org/writings/p107.html.

Peirce, C. S. [1878] 1992. "How to Make our Ideas Clear." In Houser, N. and Kloesel, C (eds.), *The Essential Peirce* (Vol. 1). Bloomington IN: Indiana University Press.

Peirce, C. S. 1932a. *Collected Papers of Charles Sanders Peirce* (Vol. 1 *Principles of Philosophy*) (eds. Hartshorne, C and Wiess, P.). Cambridge, MA: Harvard University Press.

Peirce, C. S. 1932b. *Elements of Logic* (eds. Hartshorne, C and Wiess, P.). Cambridge, MA: Harvard University Press.

Peirce, C. S. 1984. *Writings of Charles S. Peirce: A Chronological Edition* (gen. ed. Eller, J. R.) (Vol. 2). Bloomington, IN: Indiana University Press.

Pejovich, S. (ed.) 2001. *The Economics of Property Rights* (2 vols.). Cheltenham, Glos., UK: Edward Elgar.

Penner, L. A., Fritzsche, B. A., Craiger, J. P. and Freifeld, T. S. 1995. "Measuring the Prosocial Personality." In Butcher, J. and Spielberger, C. D. (eds.), *Advances in Personality Assessment* (Vol. 10). Hillsdale, NJ: Lawrence Erlbaum.

Pepitone, A. and Wilpinski, C. 1960. "Some Consequences of Experimental Rejection." *Journal of Abnormal and Social Psychology* 60: 359–64.

Pereboom, D. (ed.) 1999. *The Rationalists: Critical Essays on Descartes, Spinoza, and Leibniz*. Blue Ridge Summit, PA: Rowman & Littlefield.

Perna, M. A. 2001. "Imagination & Creativity in Jean-Paul Sartre." *Philosophy Now* 32 (June/July): 15–17.

Perry, J., (ed.) 1975. *Personal Identity*. Berkeley and Los Angeles, CA: University of California Press

Peters, T. 1997. *Playing God?: Genetic Determinism and Human Freedom*. New York: Routledge.

Pettit, P. 2001. *A Theory of Freedom: From the Psychology to the Politics of Agency*. Cambridge: Polity Press.

Piaget, J. [1936] 1963 *The Origins of Intelligence in Children*. New York: W.W. Norton.

Piaget, J. [1946] 1969. *The Child's Conception of Time*. London: Routledge and Kegan Paul.

Piaget, J. 1955. *The Construction of Reality in the Child* (tr. Margaret Cook, M.). London: Routledge and Kegan Paul.

Piaget, J. [1963] 2001. *The Psychology of Intelligence*. New York: Routledge.

Piaget, J. 1968. *Genetic Epistemology* (tr. Duckworth, E.). New York: Columbia University Press.

Piaget, J. 1970. *Structuralism* (ed. and tr. Maschler, C.). New York: Basic Books.

Picken, L. E. R. 1960. *The Organization of Cells and other Organisms*. Oxford: Clarendon Press.

Pigliucci, M. 2001. "The Ethics of it for Tat." *Philosophy Now* 33 (September/October): 28–9.

Pinker, S. [1994] 1995. *The Language Instinct: How the Mind Creates Language*. New York: HarperCollins.

Pinker, S. 2002. *The Blank Slate: The Modern Denial of Human Nature*. London: Book Club Associates.

Pinker, S. 2007. *The Stuff of Thought: Language as a Window into Human Nature*. New York: Allan Lane/Penguin.

Pitt, J. 1989. *Theories of Explanation*. Oxford: Oxford University Press.

Pizzorno, A. 1966. "Amoral Familism and Historical Marginality." *International Review of Community Development* 15: 55–60.

Place, U. T. 1956. "Is Consciousness and Brain Process." *British Journal of Psychology* 41 (1): 44–50.

PlanetPsych 1999–2006. "Defense Mechanisms." Available at http://www.planetpsych. com.Psychology_101/defense_mechanisms.htm.

Plant, R. 1999. "The Moral Boundaries of Markets." In Norman, R. (ed.), *Ethics and the Market*. Aldershot, Hants., UK: Ashgate.

Plato [390s–347 BC] 1997. *Plato: Complete Works* (ed. Cooper, J. M.). Indianapolis, IN: Hackett.

Plato [c380s BC] 1952. *Phaedras* (tr. Hackforth, R.). Cambridge: Cambridge University Press.

Plato [c360 BC] 1955. *The Republic* (ed. Lee, H. P. D.). Harmondworth, Gt. Lon., UK: Penguin.

Plekhanov, G. V. [1897] 2004. *The Materialist Conception of History*. Available at http://www.marxists.org/archive/plekhanov/1897/history/part1.htm.

Pöggeler, O. 1987. *Martin Heidegger's Path of Thinking*. Atlantic Highlands, NJ: Humanities Press.

Poland, J. 1994. *Physicalism: The Philosophical Foundations.* New York: Oxford University Press.

Pope, A. [1720] 1895. *An Essay on Man: Moral Essays and Satires.* London: Cassell

Popkin, R. H. 1979. *The History of Scepticism from Erasmus to Spinoza.* Berkeley and Los Angeles, CA: University of California Press,

Popkin, S. 1979. *The Rational Peasant: The Political Economy of Rural Society in Vietnam.* Berkeley and Los Angeles, CA: University of California Press.

Popper, K. [1935/1959] 2000. *The Logic of Scientific Discovery* (2nd ed.). London: Routledge.

Popper, K .R. 1945. "The Poverty of Historicism III." *Economica* 11: 69–89.

Popper, K. [1957] 2004. *The Poverty of Historicism.* London: Routledge and Kegan Paul.

Popper, K. R. [1962] 1969. *Conjectures and Refutations: The Growth of Scientific Knowledge* (3rd ed.). London: Routledge.

Popper, K. R. 1974. "Intellectual Autobiography." In Schlipp, P. A. (ed.), *The Philosophy of Karl Popper.* La Salle, IL: Open Court.

Popper, K. R. [1974] 1992. *Unended Quest* (Routledge Classics). London: Routledge.

Popper, K. R. 1979. *Objective Knowledge.* Oxford: Clarendon.

Popper, K. R. and Eccles, J. C. 1977. *The Self and it Brain.* Berlin: Springer.

Porter, L. W. and Lawler, E. E. 1968. *Managerial Attitudes and Performance.* Homewood, IL: Dorsey Press.

Portes, A. 1972. "Rationality in the Slum: An Essay on Interpretive Sociology." *Comparative Studies in Sociology and History* 14: 668–86.

Posner, R. 1992. *Economic Analysis of Law* (4th ed.). New York: Aspen.

Price, H. H. 1932. *Perception.* London: Methuen.

Price, M. and Thompson, M. 1997. "The Complex Life: Human Land Uses in Mountain Ecosystems." *Global Ecology and Biogeography Letter* 6: 77–90.

Progoff, I. 1953. *Jung's Psychology and its Social Meaning.* London: Routledge & Kegan Paul.

Proust, M. [1913] 2002. *In Search of Lost Time* (Vol. 1 *Swann's Way*) (trs. Scott-Moncrieff, C. K. and Kilmartin, T., rev. Enright, D. J.). London: Vintage.

Pruitt, D. G. and Kimmel, M. J. 1977. "Twenty Years of Experimental Gaming: Critique, Synthesis, and Suggestions for the Future." *Annual Review of Psychology* 28: 363–92.

Psillos, S. 1999. *Scientific Realism: How Science Tracks Truth.* London: Routledge

Psillos, S. 2002. *Causation and Explanation*. Montreal, Ont., CA: McGill-Queens University Press.

Pugh, D. S and Hickson, D. J. 1996. *Writers on Organizations* (5th. ed.). Harmondworth, Gt. Lon., UK: Penguin.

Putnam, H. 1975. "The Meaning of 'Meaning'." In Gunderson, K. (ed.), *Language, Mind and Knowledge* (Minnesota Studies in the Philosophy of Science, VII). Minneapolis, MN: University of Minnesota Press.

Putman, H. 1980. "The Nature of Mental States." In Block, N. (ed.), *Readings in Philosophy of Psychology*. Cambridge, MA: Harvard University Press.

Putnam, H. 1987. *The Many Faces of Realism*. La Salle, IL: Open Court.

Putnam, H. 1988. *Representation and Reality*. Cambridge MA: MIT Press.

Putman, R. D. 2000. *Bowling Alone: The Collapse and Revival of American Community*. New York: Simon & Schuster.

Pye, L. 1968. "Political Culture." In Sillis, D. L. (ed.), *International Encyclopedia of the Social Sciences*. New York: Macmillan and the Free Press.

Pylyshyn, Z. W. 2007. *Things and Places: How the Mind Connects with the World*. Cambridge, MA: MIT Press.

Quinn, P. L. 1999. "Divine Command Theory." In LaFollette, H. (ed.), *The Blackwell Guide to Ethical Theory*. Oxford: Blackwell.

Quine, W. van. 1951 "Two Dogmas of Empiricism." *The Philosophical Review* 60 (1): 20–43. Available at http://www.ditext.com/quine/quine.html.

Rae, A. 1986. *Quantum Physics: Illusion or Reality*. Cambridge: Cambridge University Press.

Rahman, F. 1958. *Prophecy is Islam*. Chicago, IL: University of Chicago Press.

Ramachandran, V. S. and Blakeslee, S 1998. *Phantoms of the Brain: Probing the Mysteries of the Human Mind*. New York: HarperCollins.

Rand, A. 1957. *Atlas Shrugged*. New York: Random House.

Rand, A. 1965. *The Virtue of Selfishness: A New Concept of Egotism*. New York: American Library.

Rand, A. 1966. *Capitalism: The Unknown Ideal*. New York: New American Library.

Randall, J. H. [1926] 1949. *The Making of the Modern Mind* (rev. ed.). Boston, Houghton Mifflin.

Rashid, A. 2001. *Jihad: The Rise of Militant Islam in Central Asia*. New Haven, CT: Yale University Press.

Ravn, I. 1991. "What Should Guide Reality Construction?" In Steier, F. (ed.), *Research and Reflexivity*. Newbury Park, CA: Sage.

Rawls, J. A. 1971. *A Theory of Justice*. Oxford: Oxford University Press.

Rayner, S. 1982. "The Perceptions of Time and Space in Egalitarian Sects: A Millenarian Cosmology." In Douglas, M. (ed.), *Essays in the Sociology of Perception*. London: Routledge & Kegan Paul.

Rayner, S. 1988. "The Rules that Keep us Equal." In Flanagan, J. G. and Rayner, S. (eds.), *Rules, Decisions and Inequality*. Brookfield, VT: Avebury.

Rayner, S. 1991. "A Cultural Perspective on the Structure and Implementation of Global Environmental Agreements." *Evaluation Review* 15 (1): 75–102.

Raz, J. 1975. *Practical Reason and Norms*. London: Hutchinson.

Reber, A. S. 1995. *Dictionary of Psychology* (2nd ed.). Harmondsworth, Gt. Lon., UK: Penguin.

Reeve, A. 1996a "Alienation." In McLean, I. (ed.), *The Concise Oxford Dictionary of Politics*. Oxford: Oxford University Press.

Reeve, A. 1996b. "Millenarianism." In McLean, I. (ed.), *The Concise Oxford Dictionary of Politics*. Oxford: Oxford University Press.

Reiman, J. 1994. "Liberalism and Its Critics." In Delaney, C. F. (ed.) *The Liberalism-Communitarianism Debate*. Totowa, NJ: Rowman & Littlefield.

Rein, M. and Schön, D. A. 1993. "Reframing Policy Discourse." In Fischer, F. and Forester, J. (eds.), *The Argumentative Turn in Policy Analysis and Planning*. London: UCL Press.

Rescher, N. 1973. *The Coherence Theory of Truth*. Oxford: Oxford University Press.

Rescher, N. 1994. *Risk: A Philosophical Introduction*. Washington DC: University Press of America.

Rey, G. 1997. *Contemporary Philosophy of Mind*. Oxford: Blackwell.

Riasanovsky, N. V. 1995. *Emergence of Romanticism*. New York: Oxford University Press.

Rice, A. K. 1969. "Individual, Group and Intergroup Processes." *Human Relations* 22: 565–84.

Richards, R. J. 1987. *Darwin and the Emergence of Evolutionary Theories of Mind and Behavior*. Chicago, IL: University of Chicago Press.

Richardson, R. C. 2007. *Evolutionary Psychology as Maladapted Psychology*. Cambridge, MA: MIT Press.

Richardson, R. D. 1998. *Schleiermacher on Workings of the Knowing Mind*. Lewiston, NY: Edwin Mellon.

Ricoeur, P. 1981. *Hermeneutics and the Human Sciences: Essays on Language, Action and Interpretation* (ed. and tr. Thompson, J. B.). Cambridge: Cambridge University Press.

Ricoeur. P. [2000] 2005. *Memory, History, Forgetting* (tr. Blamey, K and Pellauer, D.). Chicago, IL: University of Chicago Press.

Ridley, M. 1997. *Origins of Virtue: Human Instincts and the Evolution of Cooperation*. Harmondsworth, Gt. Lon., UK: Penguin.

Ridley, M. 2003. *Nature versus Nurture: Genes, Experience, and What Makes Us Human*. New York: HarperCollins.

Riesman, D. 1950. *The Lonely Crowd*. New Haven, CT: Yale University Press.

Ring, P. and Van de Ven, A. 1994. "Developmental Processes of Cooperative Interorganizational Relationships." *Academy of Management Review* 19 (1): 90–118.

Rist, J. 1967. *Plotinus: The Road to Reality*. Cambridge: Cambridge University Press.

Ritter, A. 1980. *Anarchism: A Theoretical Analysis*. Cambridge: Cambridge University Press.

Rivas, T. and van Dongen, H. [2001] 2003. "Exit Epiphenomenalism: The Demolition of a Refuge." *Journal of Non-Locality and Remote Mental Interactions* 11 (1). Available at http://members.lycos.nl/Kritisch/index-23.html.

Robbins, J. 2001. *Is it Righteous to be? Interviews with Emmanuel Levinas*. Stanford, CA: Stanford University Press.

Robertson, B. A. 1996. "Islamic Fundamentalism." In McLean, I. (ed.), *The Concise Oxford Dictionary of Politics*. Oxford: Oxford University Press.

Robey, D. (ed.) 1973. *Structuralism: An Introduction*. Oxford: Oxford University Press.

Robinson, H. 2003. "Dualism." In Stich, S. and T. Warfield, T. (eds.), *The Blackwell Guide to Philosophy of Mind*. Oxford: Blackwell.

Robinson, T. M. 1995. *Plato's Psychology* (2nd ed.). Toronto: University of Toronto Press.

Rofe, A. 2001. "Revealed Wisdom: From the Bible to Qumran." A paper presented at the Sixth Orion International Symposium on "Sapiential Perspectives: Wisdom Literature in Light of the Dead Sea Scrolls," Hebrew University of Jerusalem. Available at http://orion.mscc.huji.ac.il/symposiums/6th/rofeFullPaper.html.

Rogers, C. R. 1961. *On Becoming a Person*. Boston, MA: Houghton Mifflin

Rokeach, M. 1968. *Beliefs, Attitudes, and Values: A Theory of Organization and Change*. San Francisco, CA: Jossey-Bass.

Rokeach, M. 1973. *The Nature of Human Values*. New York: Free Press.

Rolls, E. 2006. *Emotions Explained*. Oxford: Oxford University Press.

Rorty, A. (ed.) 1976. *The Identities of Persons*. Berkeley and Los Angeles, CA: University of California Press.

Rorty, R. 1971. "Mind–Body Identity, Privacy and Categories." In Rosenthal, D. (ed.), *Materialism and the Mind–Body Problem*. Englewood Cliffs, NJ: Prentice Hall

Rorty, R. 1984. "A Reply to Six Critics." *Analysis & Kritik* 6: 90–7.

Rorty, R. 1985. "Postmodern Bourgeois Liberalism." In Hollinger, R. (ed.), *Hermeneutics and Praxis*. Notre Dame, IL: Notre Dame University Press.

Rorty, R. 1986a. "Freud and the Moral Revolution." In Smith, J. H. and Kerrigan, W. (eds.), *Pragmatism's Freud: The Moral Disposition of Psychoanalysis*. Baltimore, MD: John Hopkins University Press.

Rorty, R. 1986b. "The Contingency of Selfhood." *London Review of Books*, 8 (May): 15–17.

Rorty, R. 1997. "Realism, Antirealism, and Pragmatism: Comments on Alston, Chisholm, Davidson, Harman, and Searle." In Kulp, C. B. (ed.), *Realism/Antirealism and Epistemology*. Totowa, NJ: Rowman & Littlefield.

Rosa, A. de la 1998. *Forest Gump*. Available at http://home.earthlink.net/~ajdlro/f
orrest.html.

Rosenberg, M. J. and Hovland, C. L. 1960. *Attitude Organization and Change: An Analysis of Consistency*. New Haven, CT: Yale University Press.

Rosenberg, M. 1979. *Conceiving the Self*. New York: Basic Books.

Rosenblum, N. L. 1998. *Membership and Morals*. Princeton, NJ: Princeton University Press.

Rosenkrantz, R. 1977. *Inference, Method, and Decision*. Boston, MA: Reidal.

Rosenthal, S. B. 1976. *The Pragmatic A priori: A Study in the Epistemology of C. I. Lewis*. St Louis, MO: W. H. Green.

Ross, L. and Nisbett, R. E. 1991. *The Person and the Situation*. Philadelphia: Temple University Press.

Ross, S. 1973. "The Economic Theory of Agency: The Principal's Problem." *American Economic Review* 65 (1): 134–39.

Ross, W. D. 1930. *The Right and the Good*. Oxford: Clarendon.

Rothbard, M. 1973. *For a New Liberty*. New York: MacMillan.

Rothstein, B. 2005. *Social Traps and the Problem of Trust*. Cambridge: Cambridge University Press.

Rotter, J. B. 1954. *Social Learning and Clinical Psychology*. Englewood Cliffs, NJ: Prentice-Hall

Rotter, J. B. 1966. "Generalized Expectancies of Internal Versus External Control of Reinforcement." *Psychology Monographs* 80 (609).

Rotter, J. B. 1981. "The Psychological Situation in Social Learning Theory." In Magnusson, D. (ed.), *Towards a Psychology of Situations: An Interactive Perspective*. Hillsdale, NJ: Laurance Erlbaum.

Rotter, J. B. 1982. "Social Learning Theory." In Feather, N. T. (ed.), *Expectations and Actions: Expectancy-value Models in Psychology*. Hillsdale, NJ: Laurance Erlbaum.

Rotter, J. B., Chance, J. E. and Phares, E. J. 1972. *Applications of a Social Learning Theory of Personality*. New York: Holt, Rinehart and Winston.

Rousseau, J. [1755] 1993. "A Discourse on a Subject Proposed by the Academy of Dijon: What is the Origin of Inequality amongst Men, and is it Authorised by Natural Law?" (tr. Cole, G. D. H.). In Rousseau, J., *The Social Contract and Discourses,* London: Everyman.

Rousseau, J. [1755] 1994. *Discourse upon the Origin of Inequality amongst Mankind*. New York: Oxford University Press.

Rovane, C. 1998. *The Bounds of Agency: An Essay in Revisionary Metaphysics*. Princeton, NJ: Princeton University Press.

Ruben, D. - H. 1998. "The Philosophy of Social Science." In Grayling, A. (ed.), *Philosophy 2: Further Thought on the Subject*. Oxford: Oxford University Press.

Rubin, D. - H. 1994. *Explanation*. Oxford: Oxford University Press.

Rumi, J. 1956. *Rumi, Poet and Mystic* (tr and ed. Nicholson, R. A.). London: George, Allen and Unwin.

Rummell, R. J. 1976. *The Conflict Helix* (Vol. 2). Beverly Hills, CA: Sage. Available at http://www.hawaii.edu/powerkills/NOTE11.HTM.

Rusbult, C. E. and Van Lange, P. A. M. 1996. "Interdependence Processes." In Higgins, E. T. and Kruglanski, A. W. (eds.), *Social Psychology Handbook of Basic Principles*. New York: Guildford.

Russell, B. [1912] 1997. *The Problems of Philosophy*. New York: Oxford University Press.

Russell, B. 1917. "Knowledge by Acquaintance and Knowledge by Description." In *Mysticism and Logic*. London: George Allen and Unwin.

Russell, B. 1927. *An Outline of Philosophy*. London: George Allen & Unwin.

Russell, B. 1940. *An Inquiry into Meaning and Truth*. London: George Allen & Unwin.

Russell, B. 1946. *A History of Western Philosophy*. London: George Allen & Unwin.

Russell, B. 1948. *Human Knowledge: Its Scope and Its Limitations*. London: George Allan & Unwin.

Ruthven, M. 1997. *Fundamentalism: the Search for Meaning*. Oxford: Oxford University Press.

Ruthven, M. 1997. *Islam: A Very Short Introduction*. Oxford: Oxford University Press.

Rutter, M. 2006. *Genes and Behavior: Nature-Nurture Interplay Explained*. Oxford: Blackwell.

Ryan, A. 1970. *The Philosophy of Social Explanation*. London: Macmillan.

Ryckman, R. M. 2000. *Theories of Personality* (7th ed.). Belmont, CA: Wadsworth.

Ryle, G. 1949. *The Concept of Mind*. London: Hutchinson

Ryn, C. 1978. *Democracy and the Ethical Life*. Baton Rouge, LO: Louisiana State University Press.

Sabatier, P. A. 1986. "Top-down and Bottom-up Approaches to Implementation Research: A Critical Analysis and Suggested Synthesis." *Journal of Public Policy* 6: 21–48.

Sabatier, P. A. 1987. "Knowledge, Policy-oriented Learning, and Policy Change: An Advocacy Coalition Framework." *Knowledge: Creation, Diffusion, Utilization* 8 (4): 649–92

Sabatier, P. A. 1988. "An Advocacy Coalition Framework of Policy Change and the Role of the Policy-oriented Learning Therein." *Policy Sciences* 24: 129–68.

Sabatier, P. A. 1991. "Towards Better Theories of the Policy Process." *PS: Political Science and Politics* 24: 147–56.

Sabatier, P. A. 1993. "Policy Change Over a Decade or More." In Sabatier, P. A. and Jenkins-Smith, H. C. (eds.), *Policy Change and Learning: An Advocacy Coalition Approach*. Boulder, CO: Westview.

Sabatier, P. A. and Jenkins-Smith H. C. (eds.) 1993. *Policy Change and Learning: An Advocacy Coalition Approac*. Boulder, CO: Westview.

Sacks, O. 1985. *The Man who Mistook his Wife for a Hat: And Other Clinical Tales*. London: Pan Macmillan.

Sacks, S. (ed.) 1979. *On Metaphor*. Chicago, IL: University of Chicago Press.

Sagan, C. 1996. *The Demon-Haunted World*. London: Headline.

Sambursky, S. 1956. "On the Possible and Probable in Ancient Greece." In Kendall, M. G. and Plackett, R. L. (eds.), *Studies in the History of Statistics and Probability* (Vol. 2). New York: Macmillan.

Sampson, E. E. 1993. *Celebrating the Other: A Dialogic Account of Human Nature*. New York: Harvester Wheatsheaf.

Sandbach, F. H. 1975. *The Stoics*. London: Chatto & Windus.

Sandel, M. 1992. "The Procedural Republic and the Unencumbered Self." In Avineri, S. and de-Shalit, A. (eds.), *Communitarianism and Individualism.* Oxford: Oxford University Press.

Santayana, G. 1905–1906. *The Life of Reason: Or, The Phases of Human Progress* (5 vols.). Available at http://www.Gutenberg.Org/Etext/15000.

Sapir, E. 1958. *Selected Wrting of Edward Sapir in Language, Culture and Personality* (ed. Mandelbaum, D. G.). Berkeley and Los Angeles, CA: University of California Press.

Sartre, J.–P. [1938] 1948. *The Emotions: Sketch of a Theory* (tr. Frechtman, B.). New York: Philosophical Library.

Sartre, J.–P. [1943] 1957. *Being and Nothingness: An Essay of Phenomenological Ontology* (tr. Barnes, H. E.). London: Methuen.

Sartre, J.–P. [1946] 1973. *Existentialism and Humanism* (tr. Mairet, P.). London, Methuen.

Sartre, J.–P. [1960] 1976. *Critique of Dialectical Reason.* London: New Left Books.

Sartre, J.–P. 1971. *Sketch for a Theory of the Emotions* (trs. Mairet, P.). London: Methuen.

Saussure, F. de [1916/1959] 1974. *Course in General Linguistics* (tr. Baskin, W, intro. J. Culler. J.). London: Peter Own.

Savage, L. J. 1954. *The Foundations of Statistics.* New York, NY: Wiley.

Scarre, G. 1996. *Utilitarianism.* London: Routledge.

Schacht, R. 1983. *Nietzsche.* London: Routledge.

Schachter, S. 1959. *The Psychology of Affiliation.* Palo Alto, CA: Stanford University Press.

Schachter, S. and Singer, J. E. 1962. "Cognitive, Social and Physiological Determinants of Emotional States." *Psychological Review* 69: 379–99.

Schaffer, J. [2003] 2007. "The Metaphysics of Causation." In Zelta, E. N. (ed.), *The Stanford Encyclopedia of Philosophy.* Available at: http://plato.stanford.edu/entries/causattion-metaphysics/.

Scharpf, F. W. 1991. *Crisis and Choice in European Social Democracy* (trs. Crowley, R. and Thompson, F). Ithaca, NY: Cornell University Press.

Schatzki, T. R. 2002. *The Site of the Social: A Philosophical Account of the Constitution of Social Life and Change.* University Park, PA: Penn State University Press.

Scheffler, S. 1974. *Four Pragmatists: A Critical Introduction to Peirce, James, Mead and Dewey.* London: Routledge & Kegan Paul.

Scheffler, S. 1988. *Consequentialism and its Critics.* Oxford: Oxford University Press.

Scheffler, S. 1992. *Human Morality*. Oxford: Oxford University Press.
Schein, E. H. 1991. "What is Culture?" In Frost, P. J., Moore, L. F., Louis, M. R., Lundberg, C. C., and Martin, J. (eds.), *Reframing Organizational Culture*. Newbury Park, CA: Sage.
Scheler, M. 1987. *Person and Self-Value: Three Essays* (tr. Fringes, F. S.). The Hague, NL: Martinus Nijhoff.
Schiller, F. C. S. [1903] 1912. *Humanism: Philosophical Essays (*2nd ed.). London and New York: Macmillan.
Schiller, F. C. S. [1907] 1912. *Studies in Humanism* (2nd ed.). London and New York: Macmillan.
Schiller, J. C. F. von [1793] 2005. "On Grace and Dignity" (tr. Curren, J. V.). In Curren, J. V. and Fricher, C. (eds.), *Schiller's "On Grace and Dignity" in its Cultural Context*. Rochester, NY: Camden House.
Schlegel, A. W. von 1847. *The Philosophy of Life and Philosophy of Language in a Course of Lectures* (tr. Morrison, A. J. W.). London: Henry G. Bohn. Available at http://books.google.co.uk/books?id=jWf83ij_bjQC&vq=Von+Schlegel+1847+1998&source=gbs_summary_s&cad=0.
Schleiermacher, F. D. E. [1799] 1988. *On Religion: Speeches to Its Cultured Despisers* (ed. Crouter, R.). Cambridge: Cambridge University Press
Schleiermacher, F. D. E. [1805–1810] 1977. *Hermeneutics: The Handwritten Manuscripts* (trs. Duke, J. and Forstman, J.). Missoula, MT: Scholars Press.
Schopenhauer, A. [1813] 1974. *The Fourfold Root of the Principle of Sufficient Reason* (tr. Payne, E. F. J.). Chicago, IL: Open Court.
Schopenhauer, A. [1818 and 1844] 1969. *The World as Will and Representation* (tr. Payne, E. F. J.) (2 vols.). New York: Dover.
Schopenhauer, A. [1839] 1985. *On the Freedom of the Will* (tr. Kolenda, K.). Oxford: Basil Blackwell.
Schopenhauer, A. [1839] 1999. *Prize Essay on the Freedom of the Will* (ed. Zöller, G.). Available at http://books.google.com/books?hl=en&id=fW5Dl-tUSoC&dq=schopenhau-er+prize+essay+on+the+freedom+of+the+will&printsec=frontcover&source=web&ots=fmABtQGWKF&sig=CNmDOSDs2RGPSkECKZu63umGCvk.
Schopenhauer, A. [1851] 1970. *Essays and Aphorisms* (tr. Hollingdale, R. J.). London: Penguin.
Schumpter, J. A. 1909. "On the Concept of Social Value." *Quarterly Journal of Economics* 23: 213–32.
Schumpter, J. A. 1976. *Capitalism, Socialism and Democracy* (5th ed.). London: Counterpoint.

Schutz, A. [1932] 1967. *The Phenomenology of the Social World* (trs. Walsh, G. and Lehnert, F.). Evanston, IL: Northwestern University Press.

Schutz, A. and Luckmann, T. 1973. *The Structures of the Social World* (Vol. 1) (trs. Zaner, R. M. and Engelhardt, H. T. Jr.). Evanston, IL: Northwestern University Press.

Schutz, A. and Luckmann, T. 1983. *The Structures of the Life-World* (Vol. II) (trs. Zaner, R. M. and Parent, D. J.). Evanston, IL: Northwestern University Press.

Schutz, W. C. 1958. *FIRO: A Three-dimensional Theory of Interpersonal Behavior*. New York: Rinehart.

Schwartz, B. 2004. *The Paradox of Choice: Why More is Less*. New York: HarperCollins.

Schwarz, M. and Thompson, M. 1990. *Divided We Stand: Redefining Politics, Technology and Social Choice*. Philadelphia, PA: University of Pennsylvania Press.

Scruton, R. 1984. *A Short History of Modern Philosophy: From Descartes to Wittgenstein*. London: Routledge & Kegan Paul.

Scruton, R. 2002. *The Meaning of Conservatism* (3rd ed.). Basingstoke Hamp., UK: Palgrave.

Scruton, R. 2007. *Culture Counts: Faith and Feeling in a World Besieged*. New York: Encounters Books.

Searle, J. R. 1969. *Speech Acts: An Essay in the Philosophy of Language*. Cambridge: Cambridge University Press.

Searle, J. R. 1983. *Intentionality*. Cambridge: Cambridge University Press.

Searle, J. R. 1995. *The Construction of Social Reality*. New York: Free Press.

Searle, J. R. 2001. *Rationality in Action*. Cambridge MA: MIT Press.

Searle, J. R. 2004. *Mind: A Brief Introduction*. New York: Oxford University Press.

Searle, J. R. 2006. *Freedom and Neurobiology: Reflections on Free Will, Language, and Political Power*. New York: Columbia University Press.

Seigel, J. 2004. *The Idea of Self: Thought and Experience in Western Europe since the Seventeenth Century*. Cambridge: Cambridge University Press.

Seligman, A. B. 1997. *The Problem of Trust*. Princeton: Princeton University Press.

Seligman, M. 2003. *Authentic Happiness: Using the New Positive Psychology to Realize Your Potential for Lasting Fulfilment*. New York: Free Press.

Sellars, R. W. 1916. *Critical Realism: A Study of the Nature and Conditions of Knowledge*. Chicago: Rand-Mcnally.

Sen, A. 1987. "Rational Behavior." In Eatwell, J., Millgate, M. and Newman, P. (eds.), *The New Palgrave: A Dictionary of Economics*. London: Macmillan.

Sen, A. K. 2001. *Development as Freedom*. Oxford: Oxford University Press.

Sebeok, T. A. 1989. *The Sign and its Masters*. Lantham, MD: University Press of America.

Sergeev, M. 1999. "Orthodoxy and Democracy: Sociological Themes in the Philosophy of Nikolai Losskii." A paper presented at the Annual Meeting of the American Academy of Religion in Boston, November. Available at http://www.Georgefox.Edu/Academics/-Undergrad/Departments/Soc-Swk/Ree/Sergeev_Oad01.Doc.

Sewell, W. H. 1992. "A Theory of Structure: Duality, Agency and Transformation." *American Journal of Sociology* 98 (1): 1–29

Sextus Empricus [c200] 1994. *Outlines of [Pyrrhonism] Sceptisism* (trs. Annas, J. and Barnes, J.). Cambridge: Cambridge University Press.

Shaftsbury, A. A. Cooper, Third Earl of [1711] 1978. *Characteristics of Men, Manners, Opinions and Times*. Hildescheim, DM: Georg Olms.

Shand, J. 2002. *Philosophy and Philosophers: An Introduction to Western Philosophy*. Stocksfield, Nthumb., UK: Acumen.

Shavitt, S. 1989. "Operationalizing Functional Theories of Attitude." In Anthony R. Pratkanis, A. R., Steven J. Breckler, S. J. and Anthony G. Greenwald, A. G. (eds.), *Attitude Structure and Function*. Hillsdale, NJ: Laurance Erlbaum.

Shepherd, L. J. 1993. *Lifting the Veil: The Feminine Face of Science*. Boston: Shambala.

Sher, G. 1987. *Desert*. Princeton, NJ: Princeton University Press.

Sherif, M., Harvey, O. J., White, B. J., Hood, W. R. and Sherif, C. W. 1961. *Intergroup Conflict and Cooperation: The Robert Cave Experiment*. Noeman, OK: Institute of Group Relations.

Sherrington, C. S. [1937–38] 1978. *Man on His Nature* (ed. Denny-Brown, D. E.). New York: Macmillan.

Shoemaker, S. 1963. *Self-Knowledge and Self-Identity*. Ithaca, NY: Cornell University Press.

Shope, R. K. 1983. *The Analysis of Knowing: A Decade of Research*. Princeton, NJ: Princeton University Press.

Shrader-Frechette, K. 1985. *Risk Analysis and Scientific Method*. Boston, MA: Kluwer.

Shrauger, J. S. 1975. "Responses to Evaluation as a Function of Initial Self-perception." *Psychology Bulletin* 82: 581–96.

Shun, K. – l. and Wong, D. 2004. *Confucian Ethics: A Comparative Study of Self, Autonomy and Community*. Cambridge: Cambridge University Press.

Shusterman, R. 1988. "Postmodern Aestheticism: New Moral Philosophy." *Theory, Culture and Society* 5 (2–3) 345–66.

Shweder, R. A. 1984. "Preview: A Colloquy of Culture Theorists." In Shweder, R. A. and LeVine, R. A. (eds.), *Culture Theory: Essays on Mind, Self, and Emotion*. New York: Cambridge University Press

Shweder, R. A. and Bourne, E. J. 1984. "Does the Concept of Person Vary Cross-culturally?" In Shweder, R. A. and LeVine, R. A. (eds.), *Culture Theory: Essays on Mind, Self, and Emotion*. New York: Cambridge University Press.

Sibeon, R. 2004. *Rethinking Social Theory*. London: Sage.

Sidgwick, H. [1874] 1907. *The Methods of Ethics* (7th ed.). London: Macmillan.

Sieber, S. 1981. *Fatal Remedies*. New York: Plenum.

Silver, A. 1989. "Friendship and Ttrust as Moral Ideals: An Historical Approach. *European Journal of Sociology* 30: 274–97.

Silz, W. 1929. *Early German Romanticism*. Cambridge, MA: Harvard University Press.

Simmel, G. [1908] 1950. *Soziologie. Untersuchungen über die Formen der Vergesellschaftung* [*Sociology: Studies on the Forms of Association*]. Leipzig-München: Duncker & Humblot, partially reproduced in Wolff, K. H. (ed. and tr.) 1950. *The Sociology of Georg Simmel*, Glencoe, IL: Free Press.

Simmel, G. 1910–11. "How is Society Possible?" *American Journal of Sociology* 16: 372–91.

Simmel, G. [1922] 1955. "The Web of Group Affiliations." In Simmel, G. *Conflict and The Web of Group Affiliations* (trs. Wolff, K. H. and Bendix, R.). Glencoe, IL: Free Press.

Simon, H. A. 1956. "Rational Choice and the Structure of the Environment." *Psychological Review* 63: 129–38.

Simon, H. A. 1957 *Models of Man: Social and Rational*. New York: Wiley.

Simon, H. A. [1947] 1960. *Administrative Behavior* (2nd ed.). New York: Macmillan.

Simon, H. A. [1947] 1976. *Administrative Behavior* (3rd ed.). New York: Macmillan.

Simon, H. A. 1982. *Models of Bounded Rationality*. Cambridge, MA: MIT Press

Singer, P. 1983. *Hegel: A Very Short Introduction*. Oxford: Oxford University Press.

Singer, P. (ed.) 1991. *A Companion to Ethics*. Oxford: Blackwell.

Singer, P. 1993. *Practical Ethics*. Cambridge: Cambridge University Press.

Singer, P. 1997. *How are We to Live?* Oxford: Oxford University Press.

Singer, S. J. 2001. *The Splendid Feast of Reason*. Berkeley and Los Angeles, CA: University of California Press.

Skinner, B. F. 1938. *The Behavior of Organisms*. New York: Appleton-Century-Crofts.

Skinner, B. F. 1953. *Science and Human Behavior*. New York: Macmillan.

Skinner, B. F. 1971. *Beyond Freedom and Dignity*. New York: Knopf.

Skinner, B. F. 1973. *About Behaviorism: Radical Behaviorism for the Intillegent Layperson*. New York: Kopf.

Skinner, B. F. 1969. *Contingencies of Reinforcement*. New York: Appelton-Century-Crofts.

Skinner, B. F. [1977]. 2002a. "Walden Two: Freedom and the Behavioral Sciences." In Kane, R. (ed.), *Free Will*. Malden, MA: Blackwell.

Skirbekk, G. (ed.) 1983. *Praxiology: An Anthology*. Oslo, NO: Universitetsforlaget.

Slimansky, S. 2002. *Free Will and Illusion*. Oxford: Oxford University Press.

Smart, J. J. C. 1963. *Philosophy and Scientific Realism*. London: Routledge & Kegan Paul.

Smart, J. J. C. and Williams, B. 1973. *Utilitarianism For and Against*. Cambridge: Cambridge University Press.

Smircich, L. 1983. "Concepts of Culture and Organizational Analysis." *Administrative Science Quarterly* 28: 339–58.

Smith, A. [1759] 1976. *A Theory of the Moral Sentiments*. Oxford: Oxford University Press.

Smith, A. [1776] 1977. *The Wealth of Nations*. New York: Penguin.

Smith, D. 1990. "Women's Experience as a Radical Critique of Sociology." In Farganis, J. (ed.), *Readings in Social Theory: the Classic Tradition to Post-Modernism* (3rd ed.). Boston, MA: McGraw-Hill.

Smith, D. W. 1982 *Helvetius: A Study in Persecution*. Westport, CT: Greenwood.

Smith D. W. 2006. *Husserl*. New York: Routledge.

Smith, M. B., Bruner, J. SW. and White, R. W. 1956. *Opinions and Personality*. New York: Wiley

Snowden, D. J. 2005. "Multi-ontology Sense Making: A New Simplicity in Decision Making." *Management Today* (South Africa) (Vol. 20). Available at http://www.kwork.-org/Stars/Snowden/Snowden.pdf.

Snyder, M., and DeBono, K. G. 1987. "A Functional Approach to Attitudes and Persuasion." In Zenna, M. P., Olson, J. M. and Herman, C. P. (eds.), *Social Influence: The Ontario Symposium* (Vol. 5). Hillsdale, NJ: Lawrence Erlbaum

Sorrentino, E. (ed.) 1992. *Schleiermacher's Philosophy and the Philosophical Tradition*. Lewiston, NY: Edwin Mellon.

Sosa, E. (ed.) 1994. *Knowledge and Justification* (2 vols). Brookfield, VT: Ashgate.

Spencer, W. [1851] 1995. *Social Statics*. New York: Robert Schalkenback Foundation.

Spiker, C. C. 1989. "Cognitive Psychology: Mentalistic or Behavioristic?" *Advanced Child Development Behavior* 21: 73–90.

Spinoza, B. de [1677] 1985. *Ethics Demonstrated in a Geometrical Manner*. In *The Collected Works of Spinoza* (Vol. 1) (ed. and tr. Curley, E.). Princeton, NJ: Princeton University Press.

Spiro, M. E. 1984. "Some Reflections on Cultural Determinism and Relativism with Special Reference to Emotion and Reason." In Shweder, R. A. and LeVine, R. A. (eds.), *Culture Theory: Essays on Mind, Self, and Emotion*. New York: Cambridge University Press.

Stack, G. J. 1977. *Kierkegaard's Existential Ethics* (Studies in the Humanities, 16 Philosophy). Montgomery, AL: Alabama University Press.

Stalnaker, R. 1989. "On What's in the Head." *Philosophical Perspectives* 3: 287–316.

Staub, E. 1974. "Helping a Distressed Person: Social, Personality, and Stimulus Determinants." In Berkowitz, L. (ed.). *Advances in Experimental Social Psychology* (Vol. 7). New York: Academic Press.

Stewart, D. [1828] 2005a. *The Philosophy of the Active and Moral Powers of Man* (Pt. One). Whitefish, MT: Kessinger.

Stewart, D. [1828] 2005b. *The Philosophy of the Active and Moral Powers of Man* (Pt. Two). Whitefish, MT: Kessinger.

Stevenson, C. L. 1944. *Ethics and Language*. New Haven, CT: Yale University Press.

Stevenson, C. L. 1963. *Facts and Values: Studies in Ethical Analysis*. New Haven, CT: Yale University Press.

Stevenson, J. L. 1879. *Truth of Intercourse*. Available at http://www.grtbooks.com/-exitfram.asp?idx=3&yr=1886&aa=ST&at=DO&ref=stevenson&URL=http://www.bartleby.com/28/11.html.

Stich, S. 1990. *The Fragmentation of Reason*. Cambridge, MA: MIT Press.

Stingl, M. 1997. "Ethics 1." In Canfield, J. V. (ed.), *Philosophy of Meaning: Knowledge and Value in the Twentieth Century*. London: Routledge.

Stokes, G. 1998. *Popper. Philosophy, Politics and Scientific Method*. Cambridge: Polity Press

Stoljar, N. 2000. "Autonomy and the Feminist Intuition." In Mackenzie, C. and Stoljar, N. (eds.), *Relational Autonomy: Feminist Perspectives on Autonomy, Agency, and the Social Self*. New York: Oxford University Press.

Stolle, D. 1998 "Bowling Together, Bowling Alone: The Development of Generalized Trust in Voluntary Associations." *Political Psychology* 19 (3): 497–525.

Stonequist, E. V. 1937. *The Marginal Man: A Study in Personality and Culture Conflict*. New York: Charles Scribner's Sons.

Stones, R. 2005. *Structuration Theory*. Basingstoke, Hamp., UK: Palgrave Macmillan.

Storey, J. 1993. *An Introductory Guide to Cultural Theory and Popular Culture*. Hemel Hempstead, Herts., UK: Harvester Wheatsheaf.

Stratham, A., Gleicher, F., Boninger, D. S. and Edwards, C. S. 1994. "The Consideration of Future Consequences: Weighing Immediate and Distant Outcomes of Behavior." *Journal of Personality and Social Psychology* 66: 742–52.

Strauss, A. L. 1959. *Mirrors and Masks: The Search for Identity*. Glencoe, IL: Free Press.

Strauss, A. L. 1978. *Negotiations: Varieties, Contexts, Processes and Social Arrangement*. San Francisco, CA: Jossey-Bass.

Strawson, G. 1986. *Freedom and Belief*. Oxford: Clarendon.

Streng, F. 1967. *Emptiness: A Study in Religious Meaning*. Nashville TN and New York: Abingdon.

Strickland, B. R. 1965. "The Prediction of Social Action from a Dimension of Internal-External Control." *Journal of Social Psychology* 66: 353–58.

Stroll A. 2002. *Wittgenstein*. Oxford: Oneworld.

Stroll, A. 2006. *Did My Genes Make Me Do It and Other Philosophical Dilemmas*. Oxford: Oneworld.

Swartz, R. J. (ed.) 1965. *Perceiving, Sensing, and Knowing*. New York: Doubleday.

Sztompka, P. 1996. "Trust and Emerging Democracy: Lessons from Poland." *International Sociology* 11 (1): 37–62.

Taleb, N. N. 2007. *The Black Swan: The Impact of the Highly Improbable*. London: Allen Lane

Tajfel, H. 1969. "Cognitive Aspects of Prejudice." *Journal of Social Issues* 25 (4): 79–97.

Tajfel, H. 1981. *Human Groups and Social Categories*. Cambridge: Cambridge University Press.

Tajfel, H. (ed.) 1982. *Social Identity and Intergroup Relations*. Cambridge: Cambridge University Press.

Tajfel, H. and Turner, J. C. 1979. "An Integrative Theory of Intergroup Conflict." In Austin, W. G. and Worchel, S. (eds.), *The Social Psychology of Intergroup Relations*. Monterey, CA: Brooks-Cole.

Tajfel, H. and Turner, J. C. 1986. "The Social Identity Theory of Inter-group Behavior." In Worchel, S. and Austin, L. W. (eds.), *Psychology of Intergroup Relations*. Chicago, IL: Nelson-Hall.

Taylor, C. 1979. *Hegel and Modern Society*. Cambridge: Cambridge University Press.

Taylor, C. 1985. *Philosophy and the Human Sciences*. Cambridge: Cambridge University Press.

Taylor, C. 1989. *Sources of the Self*. Cambridge; MA: Harvard University Press.

Taylor, C. 1991. *The Ethics of Authenticity*. Cambridge; MA: Harvard University Press.

Taylor, C. C. W. (ed. and tr) 1999. *The Atomists: Leucippus and Democritus Fragment*s. Toronto: University of Toronto Press.

Taylor, G. 1985. *Pride, Shame and Guilt: Emotions of Self-Assessment*. Oxford: Clarendon.

Taylor, K. 1982. *The Political Ideals of the Utopian Socialists*. London: Frank Cass.

Taylor, P. W. 1975. *Principles of Ethics*. Belmont, CA: Wadsworth.

Terence [Publius Terentius Afer] [166 BC/1974] 1992. *The Girl from Andros* [*Andria*] (tr. Bovie, P.). In Bovie, P., Carrier, C. and Parker, D. (eds.), *Terence: The Comedies* (Great Roman Drama in Translation Series). New Brunswick, NJ: Rutgers University Press.

Teresa, Mother and Kolodieichuk, B. 2007. *Mother Theresa: Come Be My Light*. New York: Doubleday.

Tetlock, P. E. and Manstead, A. S. R. 1985. "Impression Management versus Intrapsychic Explanations in Social Psychology: A Useful Dichotomy?" *Psychological Review* 92: 59–77.

Thayer, R. 1996. *The Origins of Origins of Everyday Moods*. Oxford: Oxford University Press.

Thévenaz, P. 1962. *What Is Phenomenology? and Other Essays* (trs. Courtney, C. and Edie, J. M., ed. Edie, J. M.). Chicago, IL: Quadrangle Books.

Thibaut, J. W. and Kelley, H. H. 1959. *The Social Psychology of Groups*. New York: Wiley.

Thibaut, J. W. and Walker, L. 1975. *Procedural Justice: A Psychological Analysis*. New York: Wiley.

Thomas, W. I. and Znaniecki, F. 1918–20. *The Polish Peasant in Europe and America* (2 vols.) (2nd ed.). New York: Dover.

Thompson, J. D. 1967. *Organizations in Action*. New York: McGraw-Hill.

Thompson, J. B. 1990. *Ideology and Modern Culture,* Cambridge: Polity Press.

Thompson, M. 1996. *Inherent Relationality: An Anti-dualist Approach to Institutions* (LOS Center Report). Bergen, NO: University of Bergen, LOS Center.

Thompson, M. and Ellis, R. J. 1997. "Introduction." In Ellis, R. J. and Thompson, M. (eds.), *Culture Matters: Essays in Honor of Aaron Wildavsky*. Boulder, CO: Westview.

Thompson, M. and Taylor, P. 1986. *The Surprise Game: An Exploration of Constrained Relativism* (Warwick Papers in Management 1). London: University of Warwick, Institute for Management Research and Development.

Thompson, M. and Wildavsky, A. 1986. "A Poverty of Distinction: From Economic Homogeneity to Cultural Heterogeneity in the Classification of Poor People." *Policy Sciences* 19: 163–99.

Thompson, M., Ellis, R. J. and Wildavsky, A. 1990. *Culture Theory*. Boulder, CO: Westview.

Thompson, M., Ellis, R. J. and Wildavsky, A. 1992. "Political Cultures." In Hawkesworth, M. and Kogan, M. (eds.), *Encyclopaedia of Government and Politics*. London: Routledge.

Thompson. N. 1992. *Existentialism and Social Work*. London: Avebury.

Thorn, A. 2001. "The Issue of Metaphysical Primacy." Available at http://www.geocities.
com/Athens/Spar4ta/1019/AFE/Metaphysical_Primacy.htm

Thorngate, W. 2001. "The Social Psychology of Policy Analysis." *Journal of Comparative Policy Analysis* 3 (1): 85–112.

Thorpe, W. H. 1962. *Biology and the Nature of Man*. London and New York: Oxford University Press.

Thucydides [401 BC] 1972. *History of the Peloponnesian War* (tr. Warner, R.) (rev. ed.). Harmondsworth, Gt. Lon., UK: Penguin.

Todd, O. 2000. "Introduction." In Camus, A. [1951], *The Rebel*. London: Penguin.

Tolman, E. C. 1922. "A New Formula for Behaviorism." *Psychological Review* 29: 44–53.

Tolman E. C. 1932. *Purposive Behavior in Animal and Men*. New York: Appleton-Century-Crofts.

Tolman, E. C. 1948. "Cognitive Map of Rats and Men." *Psychological Review* 55 (4): 189–208.

Touraine, A. [1973] 1977. *The Self-Production Society* (tr. Coltman, D.). Chicago, IL: University of Chicago Press.

Triandis, H. C. 1971. *Attitude and Attitude Change*. New York: Wiley.

Tsohatzidis, S. L. (ed.) 1994. *Foundations of Speech Act Theory: Philosophical and Linguistic Perspectives*. London: Routledge.

Tsoukas, H. 1998. "Forms of Knowledge and Forms of Life in Organized Contexts." In Chia, R. C. H. (ed.), *In the Realm of Organization: Essays for Robert Cooper*. London: Routledge.

Turiel, E. 1983. *The Development of Social Knowledge: Morality & Convention*. Cambridge: Cambridge University Press.

Turkle, S. 2007. "Introduction." In Turtle, S. (ed.), *Evocative Objects: Things We Think With*. Cambridge, MA: MIT Press.

Tversky, A. and Kahneman, D. 1973. "Availability: A Heuristic for Judging Frequency and Probability." *Cognitive Psychology* 3: 207–32.

Tversky, A. and Kahneman, D. 1974. "Judgement under Uncertainty: Heuristics and Biases." *Science* 185 (1): 124–31.

Tversky, A. and Kahneman, D. 1981. "The Framing of Decisions and the Psychology of Choice." *Science* 211: 453–58.

Tversky, A. and Kahneman, D. 1986. "Rational Choice and the Framing of Decisions." *Journal of Business* 19 (4): 251–78.

Udehn, L. 2001. *Methodological Individualism*. London: Routledge.

Unger, P. 1975. *Ignorance*. New York: Oxford University Press

Urmson, J. O. 1968. *The Emotive Theory of Ethics*. London: Hutchinson.

Urry, J., Dingwall, R., Gough, I., Omerod, P. Massey, D., Scott, J. and Thrift, N. 2007. "What is 'Social' about Social Science?" *Twenty-first Century Society* 2 (1): 95–119.

Uslaner, E. 2002. *The Moral Foundations of Trust*. Cambridge: Cambridge University Press.

Vallentyne, P. (ed.) 1991. *Contractarianism and Rational Choice*. Cambridge: Cambridge University Press.

Vallentyne, P. and Steiner, H. (eds.) 2000a. *Left Libertarianism and its Critics: The Contemporary Debate*. New York: Palgrave.

Vallentyne, P. and Steiner, H. (eds.) 2000b. *The Origins of Left Libertarianism: An Anthology of Historical Writings*. New York: Palgrave.

Vallentyne, P. 2001. "Introduction: Left-Libertarianism—A Primer." In Vallentyne, P., and Steiner, H. (eds.), *Left-Libertarianism and Its Critics: The Contemporary Debate*. New York: Palgrave MacMillan.

Vardey, P. and Grosch, P. 1999. *The Puzzle of Ethics* (rev. ed.). London: HarperCollins Religious.

Vardy, P. 2003a. *What is Truth*. Alresford, Essex, UK: John Hunt.

Vardy, P. 2003b. *Being Human*. London: Darton, Longman and Todd.

Vickers, G. 1983. *The Art of Judgement: A Study of Policymaking* (2nd ed.). London: Chapman and Hall.

Vickers, B. 2002. *'Counterfeiting' Shakespeare: Evidence, Authorship and John Ford's Funerall Elegye*. Cambridge: Cambridge University Press.

Vygotsky, L. 1962. *Thought and Language*. Cambridge, MA: Massachusetts Institute of Technology Press.

Vygotsky, L. 1978. *Mind in Society: The Development of Higher Psychological Processes*. Cambridge, MA: Harvard University Press.

Wahl, J. 1949. *A Short History of Existentialism*. Westport, CT: Greenwood.

Walker, L. J., Pitts, R. C., Hennig, K. H. and Matsuba, M. K. 1995. "Reasoning about Morality and Real-life Moral Problems." In Killen, M. and Hart, D. (eds.), *Morality in Everyday Life*. Cambridge: Cambridge University Press.

Walker, P. A. and Zacharias, G. W. (eds.) 2007. *The Complete Letters of Henry James, 1855–1872* (Vol. 1). Lincoln, NE: University of Nebraska Press.

Wallace, W. L. 1969. 'Preface.' In Wallace, W. L. (ed.), *Sociological Theory: An Introduction*. London: Heinemann.

Wallace, W. L. 1971. *The Logic of Science in Sociology*. Chicago, IL: Aldine Atherton.

Walsh, W. 1972. "Open and Closed Morality." In Parekh, B. and Berki, R. (eds.), *The Morality of Politics*. London: George Allen & Unwin.

Walter, M. 1983. *Spheres of Justice. A Defence of Pluralism and Equality*. Oxford: Martin Robinson.

Waltzer, M. 1992. "The Civil Society Argument." In Mouffe, C. (ed.), *Dimensions of Radical Democracy*. London: Verso.

Warburton, N. [1998] 2006. *Philosophy: The Classics* (3rd ed.). London: Routledge.

Warnock, G. J. 1962. "Introduction." In Berkeley, G. [1710]. *The Principles of Knowledge* (ed. Warnock, G. J.). London: Fontana Press.

Warnock, M. 1970. *Existentialism*. Oxford: Oxford University Press.

Warren, N. and Jahoda, M. 1966. *Attitudes*. Harmondsworth, Gt. Lon., UK: Penguin.

Watkins, J. W. N. 1952. "The Principles of Methodological Individualism." *The British Journal of the Philosophy of Science* 3: 186–9.

Watkins, J. W. N. 1957. "Historical Explanation in the Social Sciences." *The British Journal of the Philosophy of Science* 8: 104–17.

Watkins, J. W. N. 1968. "Methodological Individualism and Social Tendencies." In Brodbeck, M. (ed.), *Reading in the Philosophy of the Social Sciences*. New York: Macmillan.

Watson, J. B. [1924] 1930. *Behaviorism: A Textbook of Comparative Psychology* (rev. ed.). Chicago, IL: University of Chicago Press

Weber, M. [1903/1917] 1949. *The Methodology of the Social Sciences* (trs. Shils, S. N. and Finch, H.). New York: Free Press.

Weber, M. [1915] 1946. "The Social Psychology of the World Religions." In Gerth, H and Wright Mills, C. (eds. and trs.), *From Max Weber: Essays in Sociology*. New York: Oxford University Press.

Weber, M. [1921] 1968. *Economy and Society: An Outline of Interpretive Sociology* (tr. Fischoff, E., eds. Roth, G. and Wittich, C.). New York: Bedminster Press.

Weber, M. [1924] 1947. *The Theory of Social and Economic Organization* (tr. Henderson, A. M. and Parsons, T.). New York: Free Press. Available at http://www. emeraldinsight. com/Insight/manualDocumentRequest.do?hdAction=ref_document_request& r_contentId=0&r_atitle=&r_jtitle=The Theory of Social and Economic Organization&r_issn =&r_year=1947&r_volume=&r_issue=&r_startpage=&r_endpae=&r_publish er=The Fre- e Press&raut-hors=Weber, M.

Weber, M. 1962. *Basic Concepts in Sociology* (tr. Secher, H. P.). London: Peter Owen.

Wegner, D. N. 2003. *The Illusion of Conscious Will*. Cambridge MA: MIT Press.

Weick, K. E. 1979. *The Social Psychology of Organizing*. Reading, MA: Addison Wesley.

Weick, K. E. 1995. *Sensemaking in Organizations*. Newbury Park, CA: Sage.

Weiner, B. 1985. "'Spontaneous' Causal Thinking." *Psychological Bulletin* 97: 74–84.

Weinstein, E. A. and Deutschberger, P. 1963. "Some Dimensions of Altercasting." *Sociometry* 26 (4): 454–66.

Weissman, D. 2000. *A Social Ontology*. New Haven, CT and London: Yale University Press.

Welbourne, M. 2001. *Knowledge*. Stocksfield, Nthumb., UK: Acumen.

Wendt, A. E. 1999. *Social Theory of International Politics*. Cambridge: Cambridge University Press.

Wertheimer, M. 1945. *Productive Thinking*. New York: Harper and Row.

Wertheimer, M. 1961. "Some Problems in the Theory of Ethics." In Henle, M. (ed.), *Documents of Gestalt Psychology*. Berkeley and Los Angeles, CA: University of California Press.

White, A. R. 1970. *Truth*. Garden City, NY: Doubleday Anchor.

White, R. W. 1959. "Motivation Reconsidered: The Concept of Competence." *Psychological Review* 66 (5): 297–333.

White, S. 1991. "Narrow Content and Narrow InterpretationI." In White, S. (ed.), *The Unity of the Self*. Cambridge, MA: MIT Press.

Whitehead A. N. 1925. *Science and the Modern World*. New York: Macmillan.

Whitehead, A. N. and Russell, B. [1910–13] 1925–27. *Principia Mathematica* (3 vols.) (2nd ed.). Cambridge: Cambridge University Press.

Whorf, B. 1956. *Language, Thought & Reality: Selected Writings of Benjamin Lee Whorf* (ed. Carroll, J.). Cambridge, MA: MIT Press.

Wickland, R. and Brehm, J. 1976. *Perspectives on Cognitive Dissonance*. New York: Halsted Press.

Wicks, R. 2003. "Friedrich Nietzsche." In Zelta, E. N. (ed.) *The Stanford Encyclopedia of Philosophy*. Available at http://plato.stanford.edu/entries/nietzsche/

Wiggins, D. 1991. *Needs, Values and Truth*. Oxford: Blackwell.

Wildavsky, A. 1984. *The Nursing Father: Moses as a Political Leader*. Montgomery, AL: Alabama University Press.

Wildavsky, A. 1989. "A Cultural Theory of Leadership." In Jones, B. D. (eds.), *Leadership and Politics: New Perspectives in Political Science*. Lawrence, KA: University Press of Kansas.

Wildavsky, A. 1991d. *The Rise of Radical Egalitarianism*. Washington, DC: American University Press.

Williams, B. [1976] 1993. "Moral Luck." In Statman, D. (ed.), *Moral Luck*. Albany, NY: SUNY Press.

Williams, B. 1981. *Moral Luck*. Cambridge: Cambridge University Press.

Williams, B. 2006. *Ethics and the Limits of Philosophy*. London: Routledge.

Williams, B. 2006. *Descartes: The Project of Pure Enquiry*. London: Routledge.

Williams, C. C. and Windebank, J. 2003. *Poverty and the Third Way*. London: Routledge.

Williams. J. 2005. *Understanding Poststructuralism*. Stocksfield, Nthumb., UK: Acumen.

Williams, M. 1991. *Unnatural Doubts: Epistemological Realism and the Basis of Scepticism*. Oxford: Blackwell.

Williams, M. and May, T. 1996. *An Introduction to the Philosophy of Social Research*. London: UCL Press.

Williamson, O. E. 1985. *Economic Institutions of Capitalism*. New York: The Free Press.

Williamson, O. E 1994. "Transaction Cost Economics and Organizational Theory." In Smelzer, N. and Swedberg, R. (eds.), *The Handbook of Economic Sociology*. New York: Russell. Sage.

Wills, G. 1999. *Saint Augustine*. New York: Viking/Penguin.

Wills, T. A. 1981. "Downward Comparison Principles in Social Psychology." *Psychology Bulletin* 90: 245–71.

Wilson, B. 1979. *Rationality*. Oxford: Blackwell.

Wilson, C. [1956] 1957. *The Outsider* (2nd ed.). London: Pheonix.

Wilson, C. [1956/1967] 2001. *The Outsider* (Indigo ed.). London: Pheonix.

Wilson, E. 2007. *The Death of Socrates: Hero, Villain, Chatterbox. Saint.* London: Profile Books.

Wilson, E. O. 1976. *Sociobiology: The New Synthesis*. Cambridge, MA: Harvard University Press and Belknap.

Wilson, E. O. 1978. *On Human Nature*. Cambridge, MA: Harvard University Press.

Wilson, J. 1961. *Reason and Morals*, Cambridge: Cambridge University Press.

Wilson, R. A. 1995. *Cartesian Psychology and Physical Minds: Individualism and the Sciences of Mind.* New York: Cambridge University Press.

Winch, P. [1958] 1990. *The Idea of Social Science and its Relation to Philosophy* (2nd ed.). London: Routledge.

Winterfeldt, D. von and Edwards, W. 1986. *Decision Analysis and Behavioural Research*. Cambridge: Cambridge University Press.

Wittgenstein, L. [1922] 1961. *Tractatus Logico-Philosophicus* (trs. Peters, D. F. and McGuiness, B. F.). London: Routledge.

Wittgenstein, L. [1956] 1978. *Remarks on the Foundations of Mathematics* (eds. Wright, G. H. von, Rhees, R. and Anscombe, G. E. M., tr. Anscombe, G. E M) (rev. ed.). Oxford: Blackwell.

Wittgenstein, L. 1953. *Philosophical Investigations* (eds. Anscombe, G. E. M. and Rhees, R., tr. Anscombe, G. E. M.). Oxford: Blackwell.

Wittgenstein, L. 1969. *On Certainty* (eds. Anscombe, G. E. M. and Wright, G. H. von, tr. Anscombe, G. E. M. and Paul, D.). Oxford: Blackwell.

Wolf, E. S. 1988. *Treating the Self.* New York: Guildford.

Wolf, S. 1994. *Freedom within Reason*. Oxford: Oxford University Press.

Wolff, R. P. 1970. *In Defense of Anarchism*. New York: Harper & Row.

Wood, L. 1962. "Solipsism." In Runes, D. D. (ed.), *Dictionary of Philosophy*. Totowa, NJ: Littlefield, Adams.

Wood, S. 1996. "Christian Fundamentalism." In McLean, I. (ed.), *The Concise Oxford Dictionary of Politics*. Oxford: Oxford University Press.

Woodcock, G. 1986. *Anarchism: A History of Libertarian Ideas and Movements,* (2nd ed.). Harmondsworth, Gt. Lon., UK: Penguin.

Woodfield, A. 1976. *Teleology*. Cambridge: Cambridge University Press.

Wright, C. J. G. 1987. *Realism, Meaning and Truth*. Oxford: Blackwell.

Wright, C. 1989. "Wittgenstein's Later Philosophy of Mind: Sensation, Privacy, and Intention." *Journal of Philosophy* 86: 622–34.

Wright, C., Smith, B. and Macdonald, C. (eds.) 1998. *Knowing Our Own Minds*. Oxford: Clarendon Press.

Wright, G. H. von 1971. *Explanation and Understanding*. London: Routledge and Kegan Paul.

Wrong, D. 1994. *The Problem of Order: What Unites and Divides Society*. New York: Free Press.

Wundt, W. M. [1874/1902] 1904. *Principles of Physiological Psychology* (tr. Titchener, E. B.). Available at http://psychclassics.yorku.ca/Wundt/Physio/.

Wundt, W. M. [1896] 1897. *Outlines of Psychology* (tr. Judd, C. H.). Available at http://psychclassics.yorku.ca/Wundt/Outlines/.

Wuthnow, R., Hunter, J. D., Bergesen, A. and Kurtzweil, E. 1984. *Culture Analysis: The Works of Peter L Berger, Mary Douglas, Michel Foucault and Jügen Habermas*. London: Routledge & Kegan Paul.

Yamagishi, T. 1988. "The Provision of a Sanctioning System in the United States and Japan." *Psychology Quarterly* 51: 264–70.

Yamigishi, T. and Yamigishi, M. 1994. "Trust and Commitment in the United States and Japan." *Motivation and Emotion* 18: 129–66.

Young, J. 2005. *Schopenhauer*. New York: Routledge.

Young, K. 1979, "Values in the Policy Process." *Policy and Politics* 5: 1–22. Reprinted in Pollitt, C., Lewis, L., Negro, J. and Pattern, J. (eds.), *Public Policy in Theory and Practice*, Hodder and Stoughton and Open University Press, Sevenoaks, Kent, UK.

Young, R. 1986. *Autonomy: Beyond Negative and Positive Liberty*. New York: St. Martin's Press.

Zander, A. and Cohen, A. R. 1955. "Attributed Social Power and Group Acceptance: A Classroom Experimental Demonstration." *Journal of Abnormal and Social Psychology* 51: 490–2.

Zimbardo, P. 2006. *The Lucifer Effect: Understanding How Good People Turn Evil*. New York: Random House.

Zimmerman, M. J. 1988. *An Essay on Moral Responsibility*. Totowa, NJ: Rowman & Littlefield.

Zimmerman, M. J. 1996. *The Concept of Moral Obligation*. Cambridge: Cambridge University Press.

Zizek, S. 2006. *The Parallax View*. Cambridge, MA: MIT Press.

Znaniecki, F. [1940] 1968. *The Social Role of the Man of Knowledge*. New York: Harper and Row. Available at http://www.questia.com/PM.qst?a=o&d=77153330.

Zubiri, X. [1989] 2003. *Dynamic Structure of Reality* (tr. Orringer, N. R.). Champaign-Urbana IL: University of Illinois Press.

Zupančić, A. 2002. *The Shortest Shadow: Nietzsche's Philosophy of the Two*. Cambridge MA: MIT Press

Zuriff, G. E. 1985. *Behaviorism: A Conceptual Reconstruction*. New York: Columbia University Press.

About the Authors

John Dixon BEcon, MEcon, PhD, AcSS is the Distinguished Professor of Public Policy and Administration at the Kazakhstan Institute of Management, Economics and Strategic Research and Emeritus Professor of Public Policy and Management at University of Plymouth in the *United Kingdom*, prior to which he held senior academic positions in *Hong Kong* and *Australia*. He is an elected member of the British Academy of the Social Sciences (UK) and an honorary life member of Phi Beta Delta Honor Society for International Scholars (US). He has held visiting professorships at the Universities of Wisconsin (US), Rutgers University (US), the Research Centre of Economical, Technical and Social Development (China) and Wollongong (Australia). Overall, he has published 12 authored books, 17 edited books, eight journal symposia, and over 150 academic papers. Some of his research publications have been translated into Chinese, Spanish, Japanese and Hebrew. He has also been invited to present papers at academic and international forms in Australia, Belgium, Denmark, Canada, China, Fiji, France, Germany, Hong Kong, India, Iran, Italy, Malta, Norway, Spain, the United Kingdom and the United States.

Rhys Dogan BA Hons (Politics), MA (Politics) retired as Principal Lecturer in Public Policy and Management at the University of Plymouth in 2005. He has published papers in the *International Public Management Journal, Social Policy & Society, Community Development Journal, Review of Policy Research, Public Organization Review, Journal of Management Development, Corporate Governance: The International Journal of Business in Society,* and *Reason in Practice: the Journal of the Philosophy of Management.* He is currently living in Sydney, Australia.

Alan Sanderson BSc (Hons) (Community Work with Social Policy), Cert Community Work, PG Dip (Social Research), PG Cert (Learning and Teaching in

Higher Education), PhD is an Associate Lecturer in the School of Law and Social Science at the University of Plymouth and the Programme Leader of the Community Studies (Development and Youth Work) Degree at Truro College in the United Kingdom. He is a Member of the Chartered Management Institute, a Member of the Institute of Leadership and Management, a Member of the Institute of Learning and a Fellow of the Higher Education Academy. He has published papers in the *Community Development Journal* and in edited books in Belgium, Germany and the United Kingdom.

INDEX

A

abduction, 60
absolute idea, 65
abstract empricism, 51
absurdity, 50
accommodation, 14, 21
achievement, 18
Ackerman, 56
Ackermann, 57
acquisitions, 64
action frame of reference, the, 85
action theory, 15
  economics, 92
  in philosophy, 14
  in sociology, 1
action-theoretic mechanisms, 86
Adams, 108, 115, 162, 168, 196
adaptation, 17, 21
Adler, 21
adult, 81
Africa, 186
age, 52, 116
age of reason, the, 52
agency, 83, 94
  definition, 30
  intentional mental states
    individual authenticity, 84
  social actions grounded in
    rational self-interest, 92
  intentional mental states, 83
    individual self-rule, 83
  individualism, 86
  sociobiology, 90
  social actions grounded in
  the search for identity and authenticity, 93
  utilitarianism, 88
agent, 11, 28, 40, 50, 80, 82, 84, 86, 88, 92
agent-causation, 82, 87
agential intentions, 83
agentists
  free will
    compatibalists, 84
    incompatibalists, 84
agents, 12, 28, 40, 45, 86, 87, 92, 94
  corporate, 12
aggregates, 95
aggregation, 11, 12, 19
Ajzen, 89
Alabama, 187, 194
Alder, A., 15
alertness, 67
alienation, 93
allies, 12
Allport, 19, 25
alternative, 23, 61, 76, 77, 80
Althusser, 101
altruism, 31, 89
ambivalence, 101
amorphous, 29
Amsterdam, 146

analytical induction, 60
animals, 65
Animals, 131, 144
animism, 97
anomalous, 14
anomalous monism, 14
antagonistic, 98
antecedents, 90
anthropological, 99
anthropological structuralism, 99
anthropology, 19, 99
  psychological, 19
antirealism, 60, 76
antithesis, 102
anxiety, 69, 88, 103, 120, 141, 156
Appiah, 28
application, 31, 46, 58, 60, 69, 73, 97
archeology, 140
Archer, 18
archetypes, 14
argument, 42, 59, 72
Aristotelian thought, 43
Aristotle, 25, 97, 115, 118
Arizona, 161
articulation, 49
Asia, 176
Asian, 150
assemblage
  direct-contact. *See* also agents:corporate
assemblages
  direct-contact, 12
    rational-type, 12
    non-rational-type, 12
  indirect-contact, 12
  direct-contact
assignment, 17
assimilation, 21
assumptions, 4, 9, 24, 26, 27, 30, 41, 46, 51, 70, 72, 107
assumptive world, 20, 25
astrological determinism, 80
Athens, 118, 190
Atlantic, 127, 174
Atlas, 175
atomism, 74, 85, 86
  logical, 74
  social, 85
atomists, ancient Greek, 35
attitude, 25
  propositional, 14
attitudes, ix, 2, 4, 9, 14, 15, 16, 17, 23, 24, 25, 28, 96, 103, 105, 109, 110, 113
  actions, 15
  definition, 25
  formation, 26
  guided by cognitive systems, 28
  phenomenological, 70
  towards others, 25
attribution, 30, 105
attribution theory, 30
  causal attribution, 30
  causal schemata, 31
  covariation principle, 31
  fundamental attribution error, 31
audiences, 12
Australia, 199
authenticity, 5, 6, 84, 87, 88, 93, 111
authority, 40, 44, 87, 103, 109
authority figures, 103
autonomy, 5, 86, 87, 88, 101
awareness, 1, 9, 11, 13, 14, 17, 20, 26, 34, 55, 62, 67, 69, 70, 84, 88, 93
Ayer, 52, 54

B

Bacon, F., 25
bad faith, 66
bargaining, 10
barriers, 52
Beacon, 41
behavior, 1, 11, 12, 14, 15, 17, 18, 21, 25, 29, 30, 51, 75, 81, 86, 89, 90, 91, 92, 103, 104, 109, 110, 112, 142
  causation
    social learning theory, 15
  reason
    action theory, 15
    biological determinism, 15
    cognitivism, 15

Gestalt theory, 15
humanism, 15
planned behavior theory, 15
psychodynamism, 15
radical behaviorism, 15
reasoned action theory, 15
self ideals, 21
style-of-life, 21
behavioral control, perceived, 15
behavioral dispositions, 14
behavioral sciences, 27, 28
behavioral sciences, the, 27, 28
behaviorism, 14, 15, 129, 144, 186, 191, 193, 197
logical, 14
methodological, 28
radical, 15
being, 67, 68, 79, 93
being-for-itself, 67
being-for-others, 67
being-in-itself, 67
Belgium, 199, 200
belief systems, 62
beliefs, 1, 2, 4, 9, 11, 15, 19, 23, 24, 25, 29, 31, 34, 36, 38, 40, 44, 58, 59, 61, 77, 81, 85, 87, 90, 92, 99, 102, 104, 109, 110
benefits, 9, 10, 93
Bentham, 88, 89
Bergson, 40
Berkeley, 34, 41, 47, 48
Berkeleyan thought, 62
Berlin, 87
Bernard, 12
Bernoulli, 88, 89
Bhaskar, 96
bias, 31
Bible, 177
bifurcation, 107
binding, 99
biological naturalism, 13
biological processes, 90
biology, 99
blame, 80
blind spot, 20
blind spots, a person's, 20
blood, 52, 91
Bloomfield, L., 100
Blumer, 62
Boston, 121, 124, 126, 128, 145, 153, 159, 172, 176, 178, 184, 185, 186
boundary conditions, 24
bounded rationality, 92
bounds, 51
Bourne, 27
Bowne, B., 90
bracketing
phenomenological method of, 70, 71
Bradley, 48
brain, 4, 13, 14, 19, 34, 81, 91
Bretano, 59, 69
Brightman, E., 90
Britain, 148
Buber, M. , 16, 90
Buddhism, 150
buildings, 67
Burns, Robert, 20

C

calculus, 89
calibration, 17
Canada, 199
capitalism, 101, 102, 141, 176, 183, 195
capsule, 67
Carnap, 52, 53, 54, 127
Cartesian doubt, 31
Cartesian thought, 70
cast, 20
categorization, 17, 108
category a, 2
category b, 108
Catholic, 117
Cattell, 19
causa sui, 82
causal capacity, 27, 105
antecedently sufficient, 35
causal determinism, 28
causal inference, 60
causal powers, 18
causal relationship, 28, 35, 43, 50, 53, 55, 59

causality, 14, 45, 46, 59, 79, 82, 101, 104
  problem of, 59
causation, 3, 14, 27, 28, 35, 42, 48, 80, 81, 82, 87, 150
  adicity, 28
  agental, 82
  antecedenetly sufficient, 28
  causal determinism, 28
  conjunction, 50
  connection, 28
  deduction, 46
  direction, 28
  Hume, 42
  immanence, 27
  immanent, 82
  individuation, 27
  metaphysics of, 27
  selection, 28
cave, 26
celestial bodies, 80
Central Asia, 176
Central Intelligence Agency, 149
ceremonies, 75
Chaiken, 25
character, 88
charm, 35
Chesterton, G. K ., 29, 128
children, 81
chimera, 66
China, 199
choice, 88
  charactor creating, 88
  moral, 66
  rational, 92
  relationships, 27
  values and meaning, 67
Chomsky, 30
Christianity, 138, 166
citizens, 95
Civil Rights Act, 137
Clark, 11, 166
class conflict, 102
class consciousness, 98
class struggle, 102
classes, 98
classical, 3, 34, 63, 66, 79, 80, 82
classification, 107, 108
classification system, 107
Clerselier, 80
closure, 44
clusters, 57
codes, 4, 5
cognition, 11, 27
cognitions, 90
  definition, 23
cognitive ability, 16
cognitive biases, 85
cognitive consistency theory, 4, 23
cognitive development, 21
cognitive inconsistency, 108
cognitive map, 9, 20
cognitive perspective, 19
cognitive pluralism, 37
cognitive process, 15, 23, 24, 38, 58
cognitive relativism
  definition, 33
cognitive system, ix, 113
cognitivism, 15
coherence, 33, 36, 37, 43, 108
cohesion, 30
collective representations, 102
collective unconscious, 14, 154
Colombia, 144
colors, 47
Columbia University, 118, 155, 166, 168, 173, 183, 197
combustion, 90
common sense, 40, 58, 60, 70, *See* also inate cognition, *See* also inate cognition
communication, 30, 74, 93, 103, 105
Communism, 159
communisms, 101
Communist Party, 163
communities, 52
community, 46, 95
  organic, 95
compatibalism, 81
  classical, 82
compensation, 87
complex systems, 85

components, 29, 42, 85
composites, 95
compounds, 47
comprehension, 29
compulsion, 46, 81
Comte, 51, 96, 97
conatus, 89
conception, 18, 29, 31, 39, 97
conceptual semantics, 30
conceptualization, 69, 76, 81
concrete, 24, 31, 108
concreteness, 70, 108
conditioning, 80
Condorcet, 51, 97
confidence, 107, 109, 110, 111
configuration, 72, 108
conflict, 45, 102
Confucianism, 150
Confucius, 129, 138
confusion, 45, 74
conjecture, 57
connectedness, state of, 15, 16
conscious awareness, 13
conscious experiences, 24
conscious mental acts
    rational consciousness, 40
    universal mind, 40
conscious mental states, 1, 102
    action theory, 14
    existential isolation, 66
    experience of objects, 68
    group consciousness, 102
    layed consciousness, 70
    recollection, 71
    reproduction, 71
    retention, 71
    social dimensions, 64
    solus ipse, 34
    stream of consciousness, 73
    streams of consciousness, 71, 72
    structure of, 68
conscious perception, 59, 69
consciousness, 11, 13, 14, 15, 18, 23, 34, 40, 48, 62, 63, 64, 66, 67, 68, 69, 70, 71, 72, 98, 102, 148
    stream of, 71
consensus, 5, 27, 36, 37, 40, 60, 99, 110
constipation, 13
Constitution, 118, 143, 148, 182
constraints, 6, 7, 8, 9, 82, 83
construction, 15, 18, 25, 62, 64, 82
constructionism, 37
constructivism, 40
constructivist, 21
constructivist theory of knowing, 21
contextualization, 51, 61
contiguity, 42
continuity, 17, 20, 29, 98
contracts, 103
control, 4, 14, 15, 24, 28, 66, 80, 87, 89, 100, 105, 109
conventions, 105
conversation, 104, 117
    public, the, 105
conviction, 67
Cooley, 18
cooperation, 90
coping, 158
corporations, 12
correlation, 46, 49, 50, 94, 105
correlations, 50, 52, 53
costs, 9, 93
Cournot, 93, 130
creative self, 21
credibility, 61
Cressey, D., 60
crowds, 12
cues, 15
cultural artefacts, 73, 105
cultural artifacts, 73
cultural determinism, 81, 103
cultural practices, 104, 105
culture, 1, 18, 19, 26, 39, 63, 64, 70, 74, 76, 96, 99, 100, 101, 103
curiosity, 12

D

d'Ascoli, 80
danger, 54, 67, 108

Darwin, C., 90
Darwin's theory, 90
Darwinism, 132
Dasein, 67
death, 88, 93, 111
decision making, 15, 92
decisions, 3, 45, 57, 93
decoding, 56
deduction, 43, 60
deductive closure principle, 44
deductive reasoning, 37, 45, 58
deep grammar of a society, 104
defects, 44
defense, 55, 173
definition, 43, 46, 54, 58, 60, 75, 93
delusions, 66
demand characteristic, 23
Democritus, 35
denial, 46, 56, 66, 67
Denmark, 199
depersonalization, 90
Derrida, 100
Descartes, 13, 31, 43, 45, 46, 69
destiny, 21, 66, 88, 91, 93
destruction, 54
detachment, 16
determinism, 15, 27, 28, 47, 80, 91, 94, 101, 102, 104, 150, *See* also indeterminism
  and free will, 80
  causal, 28
  cultural, 81
  economic, 81, 101
  hard, 82
    astrological, 80
    divine, 80
    environment, 81
    environmental, 47
    fatalism, 80
    genetic, 81
    hereditarianism, 81
    neurobiological, 15, 81
    physical (physiological or neurobiological), 81
    psychological, 81
    psychological
      orectic, 81
      rational, 81
      situationalism, 81
    situational, 81
  linguistic, 81
  neurobiological, 91
  probablistic, 28
  social, 81, 102
  soft, 81
    economic, 98, 101
    linguistic, 100, 104
    structural, 94
  soft cultural, 103
dialectical logic, 102
dialectical monism, 14
dichotomy, 13, 14, 62
Dilthey, 53, 63, 64
direct realism, 44
disappointment, 89
disclosure, 154
discourse, 5, 6, 26, 37, 60, 79, 91, 100, 105, 109
Discovery, 143, 146, 164, 174
discrimination, 25
disposition, ix, 14, 25, 107, 108, 109, 110, 111, 113
  behavioral, 14
  cognitive, 14
  genetic, 103
  learned, 25
distribution, 10
divergence, 9
diversity, 61
divine determinism, 80
division, 37, 52
Dixon-Dogan social-reality dispositions framework, 108
Dostoevesky, 91
doubt
  Cartesian, 31
  definition, 35
dramaturgical analysis, 20
dual consciousness, 23
dualism, 13, 14, 46, 82, 99
  predicate, 14

substance, 4, 14, 82
duality, 63, 184
duration, 71, 89
Durkheim, 95, 96, 102
Durkheimian thought, 26
duties, 103

E

Eagly, 25
earth, 86
Eccles, 14
ecological, 30
economic determinism, 81, 101
economics, 3, 83
education, 124, 133, 141, 168, 200
Edwards, 89
Egalitarianism, 194
ego, 67, 70, 71, 72
of objectivication, 72
transcendental, 70
egoism, 31, 89, 90
eidetic reduction, 70
eidetic science, 71
eidos, 70
elaboration, 59
eliminativism, 4, 14
Elster, 85
embezzlement, 130
emission, 14
emotion, 12, 26, 69, 105, 153, 167
emotional, 2, 7, 19, 26, 30
emotional state, 26
emotions, 15, 18, 26, 30, 64, 99
definition, 26
mutual intelligibility, 64
empiricism, 39, 41, 45, 47, 49, 50, 51, 52, 58, 96, 153, 175
abstract, 51
extreme, 55
radical, 53
empowerment, 88
encounters, 1
energy, 69
engagement, 2, 5, 7, 13, 18, 19, 23, 63, 68, 87
Engel, 101
England, 52, 167
enlightenment, 116
entertainment, 103
environment, 2, 12, 13, 14, 15, 17, 18, 21, 24, 80, 91, 97, 101
environmental determinism, 47, 81
environmental factors, 91
environmental stimuli, 15, 81
Epictetus, 164
Epicurian thought, 89
epiphenomenalism, 91
epistemic relativism, 37, 62
epistemological, ix, 34, 36, 39, 41, 44, 45, 47, 50, 52, 53, 54, 56, 58, 67, 74, 75, 76, 77, 107, 108, 113
epistemological hermeneutics, 63
epistemological nihilism. See nihilism, epistemological
epistemological realism, 36, 44
epistemology, 27, 33, 39, 41, 49, 50, 51, 52, 53, 55, 56, 63, 64, 65, 66, 73, 74, 76, 107
and truth, 33
definition, 27, 33
empiricist, 50
feminist, 33
hermeneutic, 39, 53
hermeneutics. See hermeneutics
linguistic, 74
naturalised, 37
naturalism, 39, 107, See naturalism
naturalist, 41, 52, 55
nihilism, 34
skepticism, 34
solipsism, 34
equilibrium, 13, 37, 93, 99
esse est percipi, 48
essentialism, 49
fallacy of, 70
ethical principles, 25
ethics, 28, 132, 155
definition, 28
ethnomethodology, 62
Euclid, 43
Eureka, 3

Europe, 170, 190
European Community, 129
European Union, 162
evidentialism, 31
evocative objects, 2
evolution, 90
evolution, theory of, 90
evolutionary psychology, 91
exchange relationship, 11
exclusion, 26
execution, 87
exercise, 83, 94, 108
exist. *See* alos monism
existential isolation, 66, 67
existentialism, 65, 71, 88
expectancy-reinforcement value theory, 89
expected utility theory, 92, See also rational choice theory
explanation
  and theory, 51
  causal, 28, 35, 43, 48, 50, 52, 53, 54, 55, 57, 58
  constant conjunction, 50
  contingent, 50
  functional, 28
  reasons and motivational, 28
  truth, 35, 55
exploitation, 66, 87
exposure, 141
external environment, 11
extinction, 15
eyes, 18, 91
Eysenck, 103

F

façades, a person's, 20
face-to-face interaction, 12
facticity, 88, 94
failure, 55, 73
faith, 66, 160
fallacy of misplaced concreteness, 108
fallibilism, 56, 57
falsificationalism, 55
falsificationism, 55
  methodological, 58
family members, 11
Farr, R. M., 95
fatalism, 80
fate, 66, 93
fear, 59, 67, 88
fears, 24
feelings, 15, 18, 19, 20, 23, 26, 28, 29, 52, 59, 61, 64, 97, 110
feminist, 33, 40
feminist epistemology, 33
Fest, 138
fever, 91
Feyerabend, 76
Fiji, 199
Finch, 44
firms, 12
first-person experiences, 11, 13, 14
Fishbein, 89
flow, ix, 113
fluid, 12
focused interactions, 1, 12
focusing, 69
food, 103
forms of life, 64, 74
Forms, the Platonic Theory of, 40
Fort Worth, 136
Foucault, 18, 100, 139, 140, 196
Foucaultian thought, 26
framing, 29
France, 119, 126, 131, 199
Fraudian thought, 101
Fredericks, 60
free choice, 94
free will, 1, 80, 84, 94
  and agent-causation, 82
  and determinism, 80
    compatibility, 82
    incompatibalism, 82
  and immanent causation, 82
  and indeterminism, 82
    libertarian, 82
    libertarian incompatibalism, 82
  and reason attribution, 82, 94
  self-interest, 92

freedom, 66, 67, 80, 87, 88, 92, 93, 183
  classical, 66
  fate and destiny, 93
  genuine, 66
  libertarian, 66
  inescapable, 88
  metaphysical, 82
  negative, 87
  positive, 88
  reasoned social action, 80
freedom of will, 82
free-will. *See* also determinism and
  inderterminism
    libertarianism
      naturalistic, 82
      supernatural, 82
  and indeterminism
    event-causal libertarianism, 82
    simple indeterministic libertarianism, 82
Frege, 74
Freud, 14, 15, 19, 59, 70, 141, 178
Freudian thought, 70
Freudianism, 55
friendship, 89
fulfillment, 93
Fulton, 19
functionalism, 14, 28, 98
fundamental attribution error, 31
furniture, 49, 67
fusion, 58
Fuss, 49
futures, 13

G

Gadamer, 69
Galileo, 41
game theory, 93
games, 62, 103
Garfinkel, 62
geist
  collective, 40
geisteswissenschaften, 52
gender, 33
  and truth, 33
gene, 31, 41, 50, 54, 60
general equilibrium theory, 92
generalizations, 31, 41, 50, 54, 60
generation, 58, 60, 81
genes, 81, 90
genetic determinism, 81
genetic endowment, 30
genetics, 81
George Berkeley, 122
German philosophy, 52
Germany, 52, 104, 199, 200
Gestalt, 15, 24, 157, 194
Gestalt psychology, 24
Gestalt theory, 15
gestures, 30, 73
Ghost, 170
Giddens., 26
gifts, 94
Gillett, 105
glass, 18
Glasser, 60
goal attainment, 98
goals, 2, 4, 5, 7, 13, 14, 21, 24, 27, 30, 35, 64, 69, 83, 86, 88, 94, 107, 112
God, 40, 46, 62, 80, 91, 92, 97, 131, 138, 159, 173
Godwin, 86
Goffman, 1, 12, 20
google, 128, 140, 145, 160, 166, 168, 182
Gore, 144
Gorgias, 48
governance, 87, 89
government, 40, 88, 97, 154
grades, 12
gravity, 50
Great Britain, 135
Greece, 181
Gribbin, 50
grids, 14
Grote, J., 90
grounded theory, 60
group consciousness, 102
group integration, 103
grouping, 2, 95

groups, 1, 17, 26, 30, 37, 51, 62, 84, 86, 96, 105
guidance, 3, 9, 10, 27
guilt, 103

H

Habermas, 2
habit, 15, 42
habits, 19, 26, 42
hanging, 21
happiness, 69, 89
Harding, 59
harm, 20, 95
harmony, 20, 95, 168
Harré, 104, 105
Harvard, 117, 119, 120, 121, 123, 124, 129, 135, 136, 140, 141, 142, 143, 144, 149, 152, 153, 157, 159, 162, 171, 172, 175, 185, 189, 192, 195
Haselbach, 17
hate, 68, 126
Hayek, 86, 87
hearing, 49
heart, 56, 70
Hebrew, 177, 199
hedonic, 89
hedonism, 89
  evaluative, 89
  psychological, 89
  reflective, 89
Hegel, 52, 95, 104, 121, 186, 189
Hegelian idealism, 46
Hegelian thought, 40, 48, 102
Heidegger, 53, 67, 68, 69, 88, 100
Heider, 30
Heisenberg, 50, 127
Helix, 179
Helvétius, 47
Herder, 104
hereditarianism, 81
heredity, 14, 81
hermeneutics, 39
  epistemological hermeneutics, 63
  existentialism, 65
  linguistic epistemology, 74
  moderate subjectivism, 63
heterogeneity, 26
heuristic, 3
hierarchical motivation, 82
hip, 123
Hippocrates, 154
hips, 12
historical materialism, 97
historicism, 95
Hobbes, 44, 86, 92
Hobbesian thought, 87
Hobes, 86
holism, 27, 28, 94, 95
holistic, 24
Hollis, 49, 83
homeostatis, 86
homo economicus
  definition, 9
homo existentialis
  definition, 8
homo hierarchus
  definition, 8
homo sociologicus
  definition, 8
Hong Kong, 129, 199
horizon, 73
host, 2
hostility, 164
house, 132, 140, 147, 169, 175, 182, 197
human, 1, 2, 3, 4, 11, 14, 15, 20, 23, 24, 25, 28, 29, 30, 33, 35, 36, 37, 39, 40, 42, 44, 45, 47, 48, 49, 55, 56, 59, 60, 62, 63, 64, 65, 66, 67, 68, 69, 70, 76, 79, 81, 83, 84, 85, 86, 87, 88, 89, 90, 91, 92, 93, 94, 95, 97, 98, 99, 100, 102, 104, 133, 142
human actions, 1
human behavior, 1, 14, 15, 49, 86, 91, 92
human condition, 25, 66, 100
human development, 142
human experience, 70
human intentionality, 62
human interactions, 87
human nature, 25, 70, 81, 83, 88, 96, 99
  anxieties about

human condition unimprovable, the, 25
meaninglessness of life, 25
oppression justified, 25
personal responsibility unachievable, the, 25
definition, 25
not immutable or universal, 70
self-created, 88
human sciences, 60, 64, 133
humanism, 15
humanity, 46
humans, 20, 30, 87
Humboldt, 86
Hume, 20, 41, 42, 43, 50, 54, 92, 119
Humean thought, 35, 49, 81
husband, 103
Husserl, 2, 62, 68, 69, 70, 71
Huxley, 91
hypothesis, 16, 57, 60
hypothetico-deductivism, 51, 53, 57, 58
Hypothetico-deductivism verificationism, 51

I

Ibn Muhammad al-Ghazali, 80
idealism, 39, 48
absolute, 40
Hegelian, 46
metaphysical, 48, 65
subjective, 39, 40
theistic, 40
transcendental, 40
ideation, 61, 71
acts of, 71
identification, 2, 17, 19, 20, 40, 57
identities
plural, 17
identity, 1, 11, 14, 17, 19, 20, 24, 28, 62, 66, 71, 88, 102, 111
group consciousness, 102
personal, 18
search for authenticity, *93*
self, 18
self-identity, 88
social, 18
identity theory, 14
ideology, 163
idiographic method, 35
idiosyncratic, 2, 24
Illinois, 133, 165, 197
illusion, 19, 31, 81
illusions, 26, 29
images, 14, 26
imagination, 52, 91, 108
imitation, 15
immanent causation, 82
immanent realism, 94
impotence, 99
impression management, 20
inclusion, 26
incompatibalism, 82
libertarian, 82
independence, 3, 83, 84
indeterminacy, 60
indeterminism, 28, 82, *See* also determinism
indexicality, 61
India, 199
Indiana, 152, 172
individual, the
self-determining, 88
individualism, 28, 84, 85, 86, 88
existential, 88
libertarianism, 87
methodological, 85
ontological, 84
unqualified, 86
individuality, 63, 88
individuation, 27
indivuation, 24
induction, 42, 49, 51, 52, 53, 54, 58, 60
inductive-hypothetico-deductivism, 51
industrial, 52
inert, 67
inference to the best explanation, 60
inferences, 37
inferential realism, 49
infinite, 46
inheritance, 19, 84
inherited, 14, 81, 103
insight, 58, 101

inspiration, 52
instinct, 40
institutions, 26, 105
intangible, 15, 29
integration, 12, 36, 98
integrity, 59
intellect, 43, 45, 65, 99
intellectual development, 97
intelligence, 75
intentionality, 13, 15, 62, 68, 69
intentions, 1, 4, 14, 71, 82, 85, 87, 96
interaction, 12, 15, 17, 19, 25, 26, 30, 51, 62, 64, 73, 85, 91, 100, 109, 110, 111, 112
interactions, 1, 2, 3, 4, 5, 8, 9, 11, 16, 20, 25, 26, 63, 76, 86, 87, 90, 96, 99, 100, 109
interdependence, 16, 59, 99, 109
interface, 15, 24
interference, 66, 83, 87
internet, 119
interpersonal communication, 30
interpersonal relationships, 28, 90, 109
interrelationships, 30, 93, 95
intersubjectivity, 27, 30, 33, 57, 67, 68, 70, 72, 74
    definition, 27
intrinsic, 70, 84, 87
introspection, 13
introverts, 103
intuition, 40, 60
investigations, 195
Iran, 199
Ireland, 135
Islam, 175, 176, 180
Islamic, 137, 177
isolation, 66, 67, 90, 100
Israel, 151
Italy, 199

J

James, 13, 31, 36, 91
Japan, 196
Japanese, 121, 199
Jerusalem, 151, 178
Jews, 170
Johari window, the, 20
Johnson, 1, 24
Jordan, 154
judge, 34, 38, 50
judges, 24, 83
judgment, 36, 58, 70
Jung, 14, 15, 17, 19, 24, 153, 154
Jungian, 146
jurisdiction, 93
justice, 66
justification, 28, 31, 38, 46

K

Kant, 13, 37, 40, 48, 58, 62, 68, 72, 79, 86, 145, 155
Kantian thought, 50, 63
Kardiner, 19
Kazakhstan, 199
Kelley, 12
Kelly, G. A, 24
Keynes, 171
Kierkegaard, 65, 66, 67, 88, 108, 156
Kierkegaardian thought, 107
Kierkegaardt, 34
King, 60, 148, 156
King, G., 60
Kingdom of Spirit, 45
Knorr-Cetina, 59
knowledge
    a posteriori, 37, 41, 58
    a priori, 37, 41, 45, 58, 59
    analytic (a priori), 58
    as common sense, 40, 60
    as consensus, 40, 60
    as expert authority, 40
    as intuition, 40
    as reasoned deductions, 40
    as received wisdom, 40, 60
    as revealed wisdom, 40
    as sensory experience, 40
    as tesimony, 40, 60
    as traditions, 40
    embedded in lived existance, 66
    lived experience, 72

natural attitude, 73, 74
Platonic conception of, 31
scientific conception of, 31
self-knowledge, 64, 65, 67, 87
tacit, 26, 74
understood individualistically, 40
understood socially, 40
knowledge acquisition, 30, 66, 74
kulturwissenschaften, 52

L

La Forge, 80
La Mettrie, 91
labor, 12, 101
Lacan, 100, 101
language, 30, 35, 60, 62, 63, 64, 66, 69, 70, 72, 74, 75, 81, 84, 100, 104
a set of rules, 100
and constructuion of meaning, 101
and cultural practice, 105
as a prerequisite for subjective knowledge, 74
as objective communications mechamism, 74
private, 66
rules of, 63, 74, 75
system of, 100
language and reality
relationship, 74
language games, 62
law, 28, 95, 98, 103
laws, 1, 14, 28, 35, 39, 50, 51, 54, 81, 84, 95, 96, 97
Leach, 99
leadership, 12
learning, 15, 30, 31, 74, 104, 119
Leibniz, 28, 40, 42, 43, 46, 154, 159, 172
Leibnizian thought, 45
lens, ix, 4, 5, 7, 9, 27, 109, 110, 111, 112, 113
lenses, 4
Leucippus, 35
Levinas, 16, 68
Lévi-Strauss, 99, 103
Lewin, 24
libertarian, 87, 128, 196
libertarian incompatibalism, 82
libertarianism, 66, 87
event-causal, 82
left, 87
naturalistic, 82
right, 87
simple indeterministic, 82
supernatural, 82
liberty, 86
life space, 24
dimensions, 24
lifeworld, 2
limitations, 20, 50, 76
Lincoln, 145, 155, 192
linguistic, 2, 4, 30, 31, 33, 36, 43, 56, 60, 61, 74, 75, 81, 84, 96, 100, 104, 110
linguistic determinism, 81, 104
linguistic epistemology, 74
linguistic nativism, 30
linguistic rule, 30, 74
linguistic signs, 100
linguistic structuralism, 100
linguistically, 74
linguistics, 100
behavioral approach, 100
links, 30, 75
Locke, 41, 47, 52, 86, 87
Locus of Control, 123, 143, 159, 165, 170
logas, 92
logic
dialectical logic, 102
logical atomism, 74
logical behaviorism, 14
logical deduction, 45
logical empiricism. See logical positivism
logical fatalism, 80
logical positivism, 52, 53, 56, 57
Logical Structure of the World, 127
logical syntax, 75
Los Angeles, 116, 127, 135, 145, 149, 154, 161, 173, 174, 178, 181, 186, 194
losses, 10
Lossky, 45
Lotze, 90

Louisiana State University, 180
love, 68, 126
Lowell, 38
Luckmann, 2
Lukács, 98
lying, 91

M

M1, 140, 145, 160
Machiavelli, 44, 92
Machiavellianism, 172
machines, 90
Madison, 164
magnet, 65
mainstream, 24
maintenance, 90, 98
Malebranche, 80
malignant, 80
Malinowski, 98
Malta, 199
management, 20
Manderville, 92
Marcel, 11, 68
Maritain, J., 90
Markey, 1
Martin Heidegger, 174
Marx, 33, 97, 98, 101, 102, 116, 128, 136, 139, 159, 163
Marxism, 55, 101, 135
mask, 17
masks, 17
Massachusetts, 115, 192
Massachusetts Institute of Technology, 192
mastery, 67
material monism, 14
materialism, 39, 49
  historical, 97
mathematical logic, 75
mathematical methods, 97
mathematicians, 52
mathematics, 31, 53, 72, 75
matrix, 99
Maudsley, 91
May, 76, 93
McCloskey, 4
McTaggart, 46
Mead, 18, 19, 62
meaning
  picture theory of, 75
meaning system, 25
meanings, 7, 25, 27, 35, 63, 64, 67, 69, 70, 72, 73, 75, 77, 79
mediation, 50
membership, 12, 17, 94
memory, 15, 17, 23, 38, 40, 61, 71
men, 12, 25, 43, 47, 65, 84, 86, 97, 98, 102
Menger, 3, 86
mental acts, 69, *See* also cognitions
mental causation, 14, 82
mental image, 14
mental life, 64
mental processes, 23, 66, 69
mental representation, 20, 102
mental state, 13, 14, 15, 26, 29, 34, 49, 70, 80, 81, 82, 83, 85, 86, 91, 96, 99, 109
  conscious
    relational, 14
mental states, 13, 14, 15, 26, 29, 34, 49, 70, 80, 81, 82, 83, 85, 86, 91, 96
  anomalous monism, 14
  conscious
    biological naturalism, 13
    dual consciousness, 23
    intentionality, 62
    introspective, 13
    mysterianism, 13
    pure consciousness, 62, 71
  conscious acts of consciousness, 48
  conscious intentional, 13
  conscious intentionality, 15
  conscious phenomenal, 13
  consciousness
    streams of, 71
  eliminativism, 4, 14
  emotions, 26
  functionalism, 14
  identity theory, 14
  lack of consciousness, 13
  logical behaviorism, 14

mentalism, 14
physicalism, 4, 14
predicate dualism, 14
reductionism, 14
unconscious
collective unconscious, the, 14
unconscious, 101
uniting conscious and unconscious, 24
mental states conscious, 13
mentalism, 13
physicalism, 13
mental states unconscious
personal unconscious, the, 14
spiritual unconscious, the, 14
mentalism, 13, 14, 15
mentalism monism, 34
mentalist monism, 39
Merleau-Ponty, 68
messages, 26
meta-narratives, 26
metaphors, 20, 27, 35, 70, 71, 91
metaphysical freedom, 82
metaphysical holism, 95
metaphysical idealism, 48
metaphysical libertarianism, 92
metaphysical realism, 4, 44, 55
metaphysical solipsism, 34
metaphysics, 53
method of investigation
definition, 28
methodological
solipsism, 34
methodological individualism, 28, 85, 86
methodological relationalism, 28
methodological situationalism, 3
methodological solipsism, 34
methodology, 60
causal explanation, 28, 85, 109, 110, 111
definition, 27
functional explanation, 28
methodological
solipsism, 28
methodological holism, 28
methodological individualism, 28
methodological situationalism, 28
motivational explanation, 28
Miami, 130
micro-events, 3
Middle Ages, 68
Militant, 176
Mill, J. S., 51, 84, 86, 88, 89
Millennium, 145
Miller, 60
Mills, C. W., 51, 11, 166
Milman, 80
mind, the, 24, 34, 39, 42, 43, 46, 47, 60, 62, 70, 92, 104
Freudian metaphors, 70
social mind, 95
mind, the human, 2, 3, 4
Mind-Body, 165
Minnesota, 162, 175
Mirowski, 45
mirror, 118
misconception, 27
misleading, 68, 75
misunderstanding, 86
MIT, 119, 122, 127, 128, 129, 130, 132, 137, 139, 148, 151, 156, 157, 175, 177, 183, 185, 187, 191, 193, 194, 197
mobs, 12
modeling, 15
models, 25, 83, 100
models of man, 83
modernism, 4, 61
mold, 81
molecules, 90
monism
anomalous, 14
dialectical, 14
material, 14
mentalist, 34, 39
theistic, 80
monotheism, 97
moods, 69
moral agents, 11, 28
moral self-government, 88
morality, 98
Morgan, 12
morning, 4

motion, 80, 108
motivation, 82
motives, 15, 28, 82
motivetions, 15
Mournier, E., 90
movement, 11, 52, 67, 102
multiculturalation of meaning, 61
multiple interpretations, 100
multiplicity, 61, 71
Münchhausen, Baron, 92
Murphy, 38
muscles, 96
mutuality, 16
mysterians, 13
mythology, 103
myths, 75
  definition, 61

N

Nagel, 29
naïve realism, 44
narrative knowledge, 61
narratives, 1, 26, 61
  little, 61
  meta-, 61
narrow mental content, 87
Nash, 93, 168
Nash solution, the, 93
natura naturans, 65
natura naturata, 65
natural, 18, 28, 30, 39, 42, 47, 52, 54, 55, 56, 73, 74, 87, 90, 97
natural attitude, 73, See knowledge:natural attitude
natural instincts, 42
natural language, 30
natural laws, 39, 97
natural resources, 87
natural sciences, 52, 54
natural selection, 47, 90
natural selection,
  principles of, 90
natural social order, the, 96
naturalised epistemology, 37
naturalism, 41, 58, 59
  and knowledge, 41
  biological, 13
  epiricism, 47
  falsificationism, 55
  logical positivism. See
  positivism, 51
  verificationism, 51
Nebraska, 155, 192
Needham, 99
negotiating, 10
negotiation, 62
neopositivism, 51, See logical positivism
nerve, 92
nerves, 91, 96
nervous system, 13
network, 13, 36, 61
neural function, 91
neurobiological, 13, 14, 15, 81, 91
neurobiological determinism, 15, 81, 91
neurobiology, 26, 91
neurons, 13
New Science, 126
New World, 165
Newman, 90
Newton, 50, 55
Nietzsch, 100
Nietzsche, 18, 27, 31, 42, 44, 64, 67, 86, 88, 92, 100, 148, 152, 169, 181, 194
nihilism
  epistemological, 34
  Nietschean, 34
Nobel Prize, 155
nominalism, 84
nomothetic methods, 35
non-human, 67
nonrationality, 95
nonverbal, 24
norms, 1, 15, 30, 33, 40, 94, 95, 99, 100, 103, 105, 107, 109, 110
North Carolina, 120
Norway, 199
nothingness, 67, 88
Notre Dame, 115, 144, 149, 152, 165, 170, 178

noumena, 65
noumena, the Kantian concept of, 40, 48
novelty, 35
nuclei, 105

O

objectification, 20, 72
objective criteria, 37
objective reality, 74, 95
objectivism, 29, 39, 41, 62
objectivity, 37, 62, 67, 72
obligation, 7, 36, 103
obligations, 26, 75, 103
observable behavior, 51
observations, 30, 31, 41, 42, 49, 52, 53, 54, 57
observed behavior, 110, 111, 112
Occam's Razor, 108
occasionalism, 80
occupational, 12
Ohio, 162
oil, 91
omnibus, 31
online, 102, 142
ontological holism, 94
ontological individualism, 84
ontological security, 29
ontology
  agency, 83
  applied scientific, 79
  definition, 27, 79
  holism, 94
  pure philosophical, 79
  structuralism, 83, 94, See structuralism
opinions
  definition, 25
opportunism, 10
opposition, 29, 49
oppression, 25
optimization, 98
oral, 1
organ, 48, 91
organic, 52, 95, 97
organism, 99
orientation, 7
Orwell, G., 40
other, the, 16
  categorizing of, 2
  importance to self, 2
  labeling of, 2
  prototyping of, 2
  significant others, 2
  stereotyping of, 2
  subtying of, 2
Ouellette, 15
outliers, 94, 105
overweight, 3
ownership, 82, 87

P

Pacific, 126
pain, 89, 92
pan-European, 52
paradox, 66, 77
paradoxical, 66
Pareto, 171
Parker, 86, 95
Parkinson, 159, 171
Parliament, 167
Parsons, 85, 98
particulars, 84, 95
passive, 71
paternal, 87
paternalism, 87
pathos, 92
Peirce, 58, 59, 76
penalties, 103
Penn State University, 182
Pennsylvania, 168, 183
perception
  representative theory of, 47
perception, 13, 15, 23, 24, 25, 34, 38, 42, 45, 47, 48, 49, 56, 61, 71, 72, 93, 185
perceptions, 4, 15, 18, 20, 23, 46, 63, 66, 72
permit, 48, 94, 99
personal autonomy, 86, 87, 88
  authenticity, 87
personal benefit, 9
personal construct systems

core constructs, 24
loose constructs, 24
nonverbal constructs, 24
peripheral constructs, 24
preemptive constructs, 24
propositional constructs, 24
subordinate constructs, 24
superordinate constructs, 24
personal construct theory
definition, 24
personal goals, 88
personal identity, 17, 18
personal responsibility, 66, 88
personal unconscious, the, 14
personal values, 61
personalism, 90
personality, 90
personality, 3, 17, 19, 90
humanistic-existential perspective, 19
personalism, 90
psychoanalytic and neoanalytic perspective, 19
pure cognitive perspective, 19
traits perspective, 19
personality type, 19
personhood, 18
perspectivism, 61
pessimism, 57
Pettit, 80
phenomena
Kantian, 48, 65, 68
phenomenalism, 53
phenomenology, 68, 69, 70, 71, 72, 74
constitutive, 68
generative historicist, 69
genetic, 69
hermeneutic, 69
realistic, 68
Philadelphia, 131, 139, 157, 178, 183
philology, 63
philosophers, 52
philosophical, 19, 45, 50, 66, 74, 79, 90
philosophy, ix, 2, 14, 39, 40, 45, 52, 53, 62, 71, 75, 79, 96, 113
philosophy of the social sciences. *See* social sciences:philosophy of
physical (physiological or neurobiological) determinism, 81
physical determinism. *See* neurobiological determinism
physical environment, 67, 102
physical properties, 13
physical sciences, 12, 52, 55
physical world, 2, 41, 53
physicalism, 4, 13, 14, 15, 49, 86
neurobiological determinism, 15
radical behaviorism, 15
physics, 44
physiognomies, 75
physiological, 17, 26, 81, 84, 86, 90, 94
physiological determinism, 81
Piaget, 21
picture theory of meaning, the, 75
Pinker, R., 16, 25, 30
planned behavior, theory of, 15, 89
planning, 23
plastic, 96
Plato, 40, 43, 44, 66, 97, 174
Platonic thought, 31, 44
play, 17
pleasure, 70, 89
pleasure principle, 89
Plekhanov, 97
pluralism, 37
plurality, 26, 46, 98, 108
Poland, 13, 174, 188
political ideologies, 55
polytheism, 97
poor, 25
Popper, 3, 52, 55, 56, 57, 58, 76, 81, 86
Popperian thought, 58
positive regard, 18
positivism, 45, 51, 52, 53, 54, 55, 56, 57, 69, 86
logical, 52
neopositivism, 51
positivist, 52, 69, 96
post-modernism, 61
post-structuralism, 100

power, 3, 4, 5, 6, 10, 16, 33, 46, 55, 79, 80, 89, 92, 99, 101, 102, 111
  coercive, 102
  structures, 101
powers, 18, 47, 94
practice, 18, 33, 60, 77, 90
pragmatic, 36, 52, 59, 77
pragmatism, 36, 37, 38
praxis, 62
predicate, 14, 43
predicate dualism, 14
prediction, 50, 51, 53, 55, 76
preference, 8, 9
prejudice, 69
present value, 64
presynaptic, 14
primacy, 18, 65, 97
Primates, 133
Principle of Sufficient Reason, 28
Principle of Utility, 89
private, 30, 66, 87, 88, 104
private language, 66
probability, 14, 38, 41, 50, 92
probability theory, 38
probalitistic determinism, 28
problem-solving, 20
process character, 17
production, 97, 98, 101
profit, 102
property, 13, 33, 81
proposition, 14, 31, 34, 35, 36, 37, 41, 42, 43, 44, 46, 48, 49, 53, 54, 58, 62, 66, 69, 75, 80, 82, 84, 85, 89, 91, 95, 99, 101, 104, 109, 110, 111
propositional attitude, 14
proprium. *See* also self, the
prosocail transformation. *See* also communal relationships, exchange relationships, *See* also communal relationships, exchange relationships
Protagoras, 90
Proudhon, 86
psyche, 14, 67
psychoanalysis, 132, 141, 145, 157, 158, 178
psychological
  environment, 24
  field, 24
  hedonism, 89
psychological determinism, 81
Psychological Perspective, 165
psychological phenomena, 105
psychological utilitarianism, 89
psychology, 2, 3, 30, 67, 83, 86, 91, 99
  evolutionary, 47, 91
psychopathology, 67
pulse, 13
punishment, 15
punitive, 80
pupil, 69
Pyrrhonism, 34

Q

Quesnay, 97
questioning, 69, 75

R

Radcliffe-Brown, 98
radical behaviorism, 15
radical empiricism, 53
range, 13, 35, 63
Raspe, R. E., 92
ratio-empiricism, 58
rational choice theory, 92
Rational Emotive Behavior Therapy, 136
rational self-interst, 92
rationalism, 45, 46, 58, 108
  moderate, 45
  radical, 45
rationalist, 46
rationality, 3, 45, 86, 88, 92, *See* also rational choice theory
  bounded, 92
  cognitive-rational, 29
  communicative-rational, 29
  instrumental, 3, 92
reading, 4
realism

immanent, 94
realism, 36, 40, 44, 49, 55, 56, 58, 76, 94, 95
direct, 44
epistemological, 36
epistemological, 44
inferential, 49
metaphysical, 4, 44, 55
naïve, 44
scientific, 44
realist, 40, 55, 58
reality, vii, ix, 16, 23, 25, 27, 29, 30, 33, 34, 36, 39, 40, 42, 45, 48, 55, 58, 59, 60, 62, 67, 68, 71, 74, 76, 85, 90, 103, 104, 107, 108, 113
reality and truth
ontological perspective, 105
reason
cognition, 62
deductive logic, 45, 46
sufficent, 46
reasoned action theory, 15
reasoned action, theory of, 89
reasoning, 23, 25, 37, 38, 41, 43, 44, 45, 59, 60, 62, 65, 76
abduction, 60
cognition, 23, 38
deductive logic, 37, 39, 41, 43, 45, 46, 51, 53, 58, 109, 111
definition, 25
individal beliefs basis of, 65
inductive inference, 37, 39, 41, 50, 51, 52, 53, 56, 58, 60, 109, 111
intuition, 60
practical, 62
retroduction, 60
Scholastic method, 44
syllogistic, 43, 44
REBT, 131
received wisdom, 60
reciprocity, 16, 61, 72
recognition, 16, 55, 58, 59, 63, 64, 67, 72, 88
recollection, 71, 72
recreation, 23
reductionism, 14, 49, 85
redundancy, 33
reflection, 11, 15, 35, 47, 56, 60, 61, 65, 69, 71
reflexivity, 61
regular, 30, 49, 50
reification
danger of, 108
reinforcement, 15, 81, 89
rejection, 58
relationship, 1, 3, 5, 7, 9, 10, 12, 16, 28, 35, 47, 49, 53, 57, 61, 64, 68, 73, 74, 76, 95
relationships, 1, 5, 6, 7, 8, 9, 10, 11, 15, 19, 24, 27, 28, 43, 50, 52, 55, 59, 85, 90, 97, 100, 103, 109, 111, 112, 150
communal, 11
direct-contact, 12
exchange, 11
I-It, 16
indirect-contact, 12
I-though, 16
relativism, 37, 60, 76
epistemic, 62
pardox of, 77
social, 62
relevance, 59
reliability, 79
religion, 69
religions, 52
representative theory of perception, 47
reproduction, 71
reputation, 89
Research and Development, 190
resolution, 102
resources, 87
responsiveness, 17
retention, 71, 72
retroduction, 60
returns, 54
revealed wisdom, 40, 60, 107
revolutionary subjectivity, 98
rewards, 103
Reynolds, 125
Ricoeur, 64, 69
rituals, 75
Rogers, 16, 18
Rokeach, 25

role relationship, 5, 9
role-making, 20
role-playing, 20
role-taking, 62
Romanes, 91
romanticism, 52, 124, 176, 185
Romanticism, 63
Rosenberg, 19
Rotter, 89
Rousseau, 86
Rousseauian thought, 88
rule violation, 103
Rumi, Jalalu'ddin, 80
rumination, 60, 61
Russel, 49
Russell, 37, 44
Russia, 92
Russian, 45, 161

S

safety, 16
Saint-Exupéry, A. de, 25
sapience, 13
Sartre, 62, 67, 68, 86, 88
satisfaction, 89
Saussaure, 100
Saussure, 100
scepticism, 45
Schein, 30
Scheler, M. F., 90
Schelling, 52
Schlegel, 52
Schleiermacher, 52, 63, 64, 90
Schlick, 52
scholarship, 30
Scholastic method, the, 44
Scholasticism, 68
school, 52, 80, 87
Schopenhauer, 65, 81, 88
Schumpeter, 85
Schutz, 2, 68, 71, 73
scientific determinism, 28
scientific knowledge, 57
scientific method, 13
scientific realism, 44
scientific theory, 92
scores, 91
Scottish philosophical realism, 40
scripts, 91
Scruton, 30
search, 1, 38, 39, 45, 48, 56, 63, 66, 76, 88, 93, 140, 145, 160
searching, 68
security, 29
selecting, 29
self, 92, 95, 120, 121, 122, 125, 126, 127, 128, 130, 131, 132, 136, 137, 138, 139, 143, 147, 148, 150, 152, 154, 157, 158, 159, 162, 165, 166, 174, 178, 181, 182, 183, 184, 185, 187, 188, 189, 191, 194, 196
  bodily self, 20
  desired self, 20
  role-making, 20
  self-as-knower, 20
  self-as-rational-coper, 20
  self-esteem, 20
  self-extension, 20
  self-identity, 20
  self-image, 20
  self-objects, 20
  social image, 20
  social impressions, 20
  social self, 20
self awareness, 62
self ideals, 21
self identity, 18
self interest, 87, 89, 92, 93
self, the, 13, 18, 63, 65, 66, 67, 101
  concept of, 20
    behaviorist tradition, 19
    mentalist tradition, 19
    neuroscientific tradition, 19
  creative self, 21
  impression management, 20
  masks, 17
  me stage, the, 18
  solipsistical, 18
self-awareness, 11, 13, 93
self-concept, 19

self-conscious, 40, 89
self-consciousness, 18
self-control, 28, 83
self-delusions, 66
self-esteem, 20
self-evaluation, 2
self-government, 88
self-identification, 2
self-identity, 18, 19, 20, 24, 28, 66, 88, 111
  definition, 19
self-image, 15, 20
self-interest, 7, 9, 87, 89, 92, 112
selfish genes, 90
self-knowledge, 64, 65, 67, 87, 110
self-objects, 20
self-ownership, 87
self-reflection, 58, 69
self-relatedness, 93
self-worth, 18, 20
semantics, 30, 43
semiotics, 72, 100
sensation, 45, 47, 89
sensations, 47, 62, 90
sense organs, 42, 96
sense-datum theory, 34
sensory data, 48
sensory experience, 37, 40, 41, 47, 48, 49
sensory perception, 23, 34, 38, 41, 42, 48, 56, 61, 67, 109, 110, 111
sensory perceptions, 42, 53, 56, 67, 90
sentences, 75
sentience, 13
separateness, 16
separation, 44, 54, 70, 76
sex, 132
Shakespeare, W., 42
Shand, 40
shape, 6, 8, 12, 15, 24, 30, 66, 74, 81, 84, 90, 94, 96, 102, 105, 109
shaping, 81
sharing, 30, 61, 110
Shepherd, 59
shock, 16
short-term, 3, 70
Shweder, 27
sign, 72, 75, 99, 100
significant others, 2
signs, 30, 64, 75, 99, 100
Simmel, 1
sine, 73, 108
singular, 105
situational determinism, 81
situational logic
  egalitarian, 7
  egocentric, 7
  hierarchical, 7
  individualistic, 7
situational logics, 8, *See also* homo hierarchus, homo sociologicus, homo existentialis, homo economicus
situationalism
  in economics, 3
  in psychology, 3, 81
  in sociology, 3
  methodological, 3, 28
skepticism, 34
skills, 19, 56
Skinner, B. F. , 15, 19, 123, 186
Smith, A., 92
Smith, D, 24
social action
  definition, 1
Social Action Theory, 1
social actions, 14
  grounded in
    cultural partcipation, 103
    economic partcipation, 101
    linguistic participation, 104
    rational self-interest, 92
    social partcipation, 102
    the search for identity and authenticity, 93
social arena
  definition, 12
  individual constructs, 2
  material objects, 2
    evocative objects, 2
    social objects, 2
  social constructs, 2
social atomism, 85

social behavior, 7, 25, 30, 62, 104
social behaviorism, 62
social change, 85
social cohesion, 30
social construct, 36, 37, 110
social constructionism, 37
social constructivism, 36, 37
social context, 3, 11, 95
social control, 27
social determinism, 81, 102
social domain, 11, 77
social engagement setting
  definition, 13
social environment, 100, 103
social evaluation, 102
social factors, 109
social facts, 85, 97, 102, 103
social group, 17, 30, 95, 103
social identification, 19
social identity, 17, 18, 19
social identity theory, 17
social impressions, 20
social institutions, 85, 95, 96, 109
social interactions
  definition, 1
  focused, 1
  unfocused, 1
social knowledge, 15, 40, 73, 76
social learning, 15, 142
social learning reinforcement, 15
social learning theory, 15
social life, 26, 30, 37, 61, 64, 81, 85, 95
social mind, 95
social network, 1, 86, 96
social norms, 15, 105
social objects, 2
social order, 87, 97, 99, 109
social organization, 12
social origin of mind, theory of, 102
social parallax, 27
social participation, 102
social phenomena, 59, 85, 86, 96, 97, 100
  definition, 1
social reality, 16
social reality disposition
  hermeneutic agency, 110
  naturalist agency, 111
social relations, 1, 5, 6, 7, 8, 12, 19, 26, 73, 85, 97, 100, 102, 103, 111
  definition, 1
social relationships, 5, 6, 7, 8, 12, 19, 85, 100, 103, 111
social relativism, 62
social role, 2
social roles, 4, 5, 24, 109, 110
social rules, 103
social sciences, ix, 39, 54, 55, 64, 83, 113
  philosophy of, 39, 54, 113
social sciences, 27, 28, 55
social self, 20
social situationalism, 3
social stability, 99
social status, 2
social structure, 18, 62, 100
social systems, 98
social theory, 90
social wholes
  metaphysical holism, 95
  metaphysical individualism, 85, 111
  methodological individualism, 85
social world
  defintion, 1
socialism, 101
socialization, 19, 103
social-reality disposition
  hermeneutic agency, 108
  hermeneutic structuralism, 108
  naturalist agency, 108
social-reality disposition
  hermeneutic structuralism, 109
  naturalist structuralism, 108, 109
sociocultural, 2, 13, 33, 60, 61, 100, 101, 110
socioeconomic, 97
sociological, 3, 51
sociology, 3, 83
Socrates, 169, 195
soil, 52
solipsism
  definition, 34
  metaphysical, 34

soul, the, 66, 91
sounds, 30, 47
South Africa, 186
South Carolina, 171
sovereignty, 5, 6, 7, 8, 9
spacetime, 27
Spain, 199
spatial, 73
species, 56, 65
speculation, 39, 68
speech, 30, 35, 62, 66, 79, 105
speech-acts, 105
Spencer, 88
Spenser, 51
Spinoza, 43, 46, 80
spirits, 80
spiritual, 14, 46, 88
spirituality, 14
Spiro, 30
spontaneity, 89
stability, 99
standards, 28, 34, 38, 76, 77, 149
stars, 35, 80
stars, the celestial, 80
State of the Union, 170
statistical analysis, 51
Stegmüller, 76
stereotype, 2
stimulus, 15
Stirner, 86
stock, 26, 72, 73, 74
Stoic thought, 43
Stoics, 43
storage, 90
strategies, 90
Strauss, 60, 99
stream of consciousness, 71, 72, 73
streams, 13
strength, 31, 43
structural determinism, 94
structural dimension, 83
structural functionalism, 98
structural Marxism, 101
structuralism, ix, 94, 99, 100, 105, 108, 113
    anthropological structuralism, 99
    historical materialism, 97
    linguistic structuralism, 100
    natural laws and the natural social order, 96
    post-structuralism, 100
    social actions grounded in
        cultural participation, 103
        linguistic participation, 104
        economic partcipation, 101
        social participation, 102
    structural functionism, 98
structuralists, 94, 95, 101
style-of-life, 21
subconscious. *See* mental states:unconscious
subjective, 4, 8, 13, 14, 16, 19, 26, 28, 29, 37, 39, 40, 48, 52, 59, 60, 66, 68, 71, 72, 73, 74, 101, 107
subjective experience, 19, 72
subjective idealism, 39
subjectivism, 29, 39, 48, 59, 60, 62, 71, 95
subjectivity, 13, 37, 63, 66, 98
    revolutionary, 98
substance
    mental, the Cartesian concept of, 40
substance dualism, 4, 14, 46, 82
substance, God, the Spinozan concept of, 40
substitutes, 76
superego, 70
supernatural, 82
Supreme Substance, Sophia, 46
surprise, 9
survival, 90
symbolic, 62, 103
symbolic interactionalism, 62
symbolism, 75, 100
symbols, 1, 14, 18, 30, 44, 61, 75, 98
synapses, 13
syntax, 75
synthesis, 58, 72, 102

T

tabula rasa, 47, 102
Taine, 51
talent, 108
tangible, 15